# A Pride of Lions

## Joshua Chamberlain and Other Maine Civil War Heroes

William Lemke

COVERED BRIDGE PRESS

North Attleborough, Massachusetts

**A note about illustrations**

In addition to the fine photographs of Mainers from their collection, Maine State Archives also has reproduced maps, sketches and photographs from several sources whose citations are abbreviated with picture credits. These are J. W. Brown, *The Signal Corps USA in the War of Rebellion* (Boston: US Veteran Signal Corps Association, 1896); Joseph W. Morton, Jr., *Sparks from the Camp Fire* (Philadelphia: Keystone, 1890); *Atlas to Accompany the Official Records of the Union and Confederate Armies...* (Washington, DC: Government Printing Office, 1891–1895); John M. Gould, *A History of the 1-10-29th Maine Regiments* (Portland, ME: Stephen Berry, 1871); and Sewall Pettingill, *Memoirs of the Civil War* (Wayne Library Association, n.d.)

Cover illustration by Ken Hendricksen

Covered Bridge Press
7 Adamsdale Road
North Attleborough, MA 02760
(508) 761-7721

ISBN 0-924771-95-X


10  9  8  7  6  5  4  3  2

# Contents

**Contents**                                                      v

# Acknowledgements

A work like this requires the help of many individuals, and while space does not permit specifically crediting everyone, I would especially like to thank Sylvia Sherman of the Maine State Archives, Augusta, and her able staff: Jeff Brown, Arthur Dostie, and photographer Roy Wells. Earle Shettleworth of the Maine State Historic Preservation Commission rendered valuable aid and insights, as did Erik Jorgensen, Pejepscot Historical Society, Brunswick; Susan Radvin, Bowdoin College Special Collections; Brian Higgins, Brewer Historical Society; and Tom Gaffney, Portland Room Special Collections, Portland Public Library. Thanks also to Rep. Dick Campbell for a tour of Chamberlain-related sites in the Bangor/Brewer area, and Mae Billingslea of the Women's Christian Temperance Union for allowing me to view materials related to Neal Dow at the Neal Dow Memorial in Portland.

Special thanks goes to Maine artist Ken Hendricksen for allowing the use of his magnificent portrait of Colonel Joshua Chamberlain, and his enthusiasm for getting the faces of the Civil War era "right" on canvas. If I have done half as well in prose, I will be satisfied.

Words cannot adequately state my debt to typists Elaine Moesel and Eileen Morton; their hard work, patience, and professionalism made this book possible.

Finally, but most importantly, the support of my wife, Karen, my daughter, Larissa, and my mother, Lillian Lemke, sustained me in seeing this project through. Their love and the encouragement of family, friends and colleagues was my anchor.

# Preface

August 29, 1906, was a bright, beautiful day at the dawn of the twentieth century. The citizens of the picture-postcard town of Camden, Maine—nestled beneath green mountains and facing the broad, blue expanse of Penobscot Bay—were preparing to honor a native son hardly anyone remembered.

But the U.S. Government remembered, largely through the efforts of Captain John O. Johnson of the nearby village of Liberty. The warships that stood out to sea, beyond the island and ledges at the mouth of Camden harbor, were shining white symbols of American power. There were seven battleships of the North Atlantic Fleet, including the flagship, the new U.S.S. *Maine,* and five destroyers. Some of them would be part of the "Great White Fleet" President Theodore Roosevelt would send sailing around the globe, a spectacular display of America's emergence onto the international stage.

But in late August of 1906 they were off Camden to honor the memory of a sailor of the old Navy of wood and sail. William Conway was an ordinary salt whose obscure life was made extraordinary by an act of simple, understated patriotism. Conway, long forgotten, was a reminder of an earlier time, momentous in American history—the Civil War.

The Civil War (or "War of the Rebellion") was the Great Event of the previous generation, its ranks graying and thinning. A month earlier, Alden Miller, Jr., had passed away. Born in Warren, Miller had enlisted in the Twentieth Maine Volunteer Infantry Regiment in 1862. Rising to the rank of First Lieutenant, he was wounded in 1864, but remained in the Union Army until war's end in 1865. Moving to nearby Camden, he had been an active member of the community—selectman, town treasurer, postmaster, and, as the town historian wrote, "always an uncompromising Republican."

Like Miller, Maine was usually rock-ribbed in its Republican politics during the late nineteenth and early twentieth centuries. As William Pattangall, a Republican politician, wisecracked, there were only two subjects in Maine politics in those years: The Civil War and Prohibition. The latter was the legacy of a moralistic, reformist streak in Maine history, represented by the author of Prohibition, Neal Dow of Portland, who had been a Union general.

Governor William Cobb, who attended the Conway celebration, was a Republican who supported actually *enforcing* prohibition through a commission that prefigured the state police. That was sufficiently unpopular to allow Democratic gains; Camden was about to vote a Democratic majority. Cobb was from the busy seaport and lime-quarrying town of Rockland, just a few miles south of Camden. Rockland had provided the Union with warriors like Hiram Berry, Adelbert Ames, and Elijah Walker. Hiram, Adelbert, Elijah—Yankee names, and real lions in combat.

The *Maine* band entertained the townsfolk with a concert before the Bay View House on the evening of August 29. The warships provided even more striking entertainment by flashing their searchlights over the harbor and on the mountains behind Camden.

The day of the planned ceremonies, August 30, began engulfed in a heavy fog. By noon the gray mists had burned away, and each battleship landed a company of bluejackets to participate, along with public officials and a contingent of Civil War veterans. A festive crowd of 10,000, the biggest in the small town's history, gathered to view the event.

After the parade, marching to rousing patriotic music, wended its way through the streets to a park, speeches were made before the official unveiling of the monument to Conway. Like Conway, it was simple, a large boulder with an inscribed plaque. It had taken a team of sixty horses to pull the boulder to Camden.

The principal speaker was a man who personified Maine's role in the Civil War. No state had contributed more in soldiers and sailors per capita to the war effort. To many, no soldier had done more to win victory than the ramrod-straight old gentleman dressed in black, with a full head of white hair and a fierce white mustache, beneath a hawk's nose and blue eyes that still blazed—General Joshua L. Chamberlain.

When President Theodore Roosevelt had visited Maine a few summers before, in 1902, he had publicly saluted Chamberlain, who shared with him a flag-draped platform in Portland. The President had some experience of war, but not comparable to the hero of Little Round Top, who had won the Congressional Medal of Honor for gallantry in the greatest of all battles. A man renowned for his courage, eloquence, intelligence, and varied accomplishments, Joshua Chamberlain was destined to become an American legend.

William Conway, whom Chamberlain rose to honor this August day, was an ordinary man, belatedly remembered, soon to be largely forgotten again. But both were lions of a state that, in the nation's hour of need, produced a pride of lions.

This is their story.

---

*Joshua Lawrence Chamberlain c. 1904—Pejepscot Historical Society*

**Pride of Lions**

# William Conway

*"I will not do it, sir!"*

On January 10, 1861, a specially convened convention voted 62–7 that the independent "nation of Florida" withdraw from the Union, making Florida the third state to secede since Lincoln's election to the presidency. This action immediately put at risk Federal military installations in the state. Some of the key targets for seizure were at Pensacola, which contained several forts and a Navy Yard.

The commander of the tiny U.S. Army contingent of less than fifty men, Lieutenant Adam J. Slemmer, prudently withdrew his force to the largest and most defensible fort, Fort Pickens, on an island at the entrance to Pensacola Bay. His counterpart at the U.S. Navy Yard, Commandant Captain James Armstrong, was in a more difficult position. It was made worse by the influence of his pro-secessionist officers.

While the old man dithered, they schemed with the new order. When Florida commissioners showed up on January 12, with hundreds of state militia, demanding the Navy Yard's surrender, Armstrong gave up without a fight. He could have made one. Beside his handful of sailors and marines, there were gunboats standing offshore.

One of the traitorous Naval officers, a Lieutenant Renshaw, ordered an old salt doing duty as quartermaster at the Navy Yard to stand by the halyards of the yard's flag. William Conway obeyed.

Many years later, Admiral George Dewey, a young naval officer at the time, recalled Conway: "He was a typical Yankee man-of-war's man from Maine, tall, thin, with a nose like Wellington's, and, like all men-of-war's men from that section, very intelligent." Dewey added that Conway was "at all times most dutiful and subordinate."

The next order was to haul down the colors.

Conway was a long way from his native Camden, on the coast of Maine. Yet the story of his response would travel from one end of the fragmenting nation to the other.

"I will not do it, sir!" Conway was reported to have said. "That is the flag of my country under which I have sailed many years. I love it; and will not dishonor it by hauling it down now."

Lieutenant Henry Erben (who himself had engaged in fisticuffs with Renshaw's superior, Captain Ebenezer Farrand) recalled that Conway "took his life in his hands when he refused to haul down the American flag. He was surrounded by a crazed crowd. Conway was threatened to be cut down, but he still refused to haul down the flag he had served under for years in the Navy. Conway was a hero. When so many about him were disloyal, and when it required true courage to remain loyal, he knew his duty and was not afraid to perform it."

Renshaw hauled the flag down himself.

The two Naval vessels offshore hoisted all the colors they had in defiance. The soldiers at Fort Pickens, lacking a flagstaff, hung the stars and stripes over the wall.

Conway was arrested, put in irons, and briefly confined. Soon he and other loyal bluejackets—treason was restricted to officers, like Farrand and Renshaw—were sent off to Erben's ship, the U.S.S. *Supply*.

During the court martial of Captain Armstrong, the court publicly commended Conway for his action in the sorry affair at Pensacola. For a brief period, he was recognized as a hero of the Union. The old sailor was by then signal quartermaster on the steam frigate *Mississippi*. He was cheered by officers and crew when a commendatory letter from the Navy Department was read and a gold medal presented. One of the officers present later wrote, "Conway was very modest in speaking of the Pensacola incident, but he declared that if, when he refused to haul down the flag, there were any tears in his eyes, as the newspapers claimed, it was not because he was so affected by sentimentality, but because he was mad or had a cold."

After the ceremony on the *Mississippi*, George Dewey, the navigating officer, took Conway aside and asked him if he had "positively refused" the order to haul down the flag. "He said, in a modest, quiet way, with a touch of his cap, 'I didn't refuse, sir; I said, 'I can't haul down those colors, Mr. Renshaw,' and he excused me."

Maybe William Conway didn't have tears in his eyes that day, and probably his exact words were less eloquent, but his action was consistent with his character. It came three months before another American flag was forced down, at Fort Sumter, officially starting the Civil War.

A little over a year later, the *Mississippi* was part of Farragut's fleet steaming past the Confederate forts below New Orleans. Dewey, by then executive officer, noticed that other vessels were firing broadsides with Old Glory fluttering on each masthead. It was a night attack, and it had not occurred to him to have the flags hoisted.

Dewey turned to Conway, who had charge of the flags, and said, "Get our flags up quickly."

"They're up there, sir," was the response.

Conway had already hoisted the flags up in a ball, ready to be unfurled at a moment's notice.

---

*Governor Israel Washburn—Maine State Archives*

# Joshua Chamberlain

## *"Do it! That's how!"*

Israel Washburn, Jr., a man of many words, told a special session of the Maine Legislature on April 22, 1861, that the time for words was past. Short, stocky, a powerful orator with a wicked mastery of sarcasm, and possessed of a combination of capitalist and religious fervor spelled "Yankee," Washburn was nicknamed the "Little Giant" of Maine politics.

A member of Congress throughout the 1850s, Washburn had helped create the Republican Party in opposition to the 1854 Kansas-Nebraska Act promoted by Stephen Douglas of Illinois, the Democrats' "Little Giant." Washburn may well have been first to give the new party its name; in 1860 he was the victorious Republican candidate for Governor. At his January 3 inauguration in Augusta, he expressed confidence that Southern states "will not pass the brink of the precipice" and secede, sundering the Union.

They not only seceded and formed the Confederacy. They fired on Fort Sumter. Washburn convened Maine solons in Augusta in response to President Lincoln's call for the states to raise volunteer regiments to suppress the rebellion. The governor told them, "Gentlemen—this is no time for words—the hour for action has arrived—prompt, vigorous, decisive, patriotic action." The Legislature responded, voting to raise not the two regiments requested, but ten!

Across the Pine Tree State, many men and boys put aside their work or careers to answer the call. There was a rush of patriotism that would not be equalled.

But Joshua Lawrence Chamberlain was not one of those "boys of 1861." Indeed, the man who would become one of the Civil War's most celebrated soldiers would not enlist until midway through 1862.

Chamberlain, a professor at Bowdoin College, was fighting his own inner civil war during this period. A man of words and action, he remained a man of words at a time when he personally believed, like Washburn, that the time for words had passed.

Hardly prosperous on a college professor's salary, with a growing family and wife with expensive tastes, Chamberlain had recently, through the aid of a friendly local banker, purchased a house on Potter Street. It was just a short walk from the imposing, Gothic-style First Parish Congregational Church. There, in 1851, the wife of Professor Calvin Stowe, Harriet Beecher, experienced a vision which she transformed into *Uncle Tom's Cabin*.

Chamberlain, then a third-year man at Bowdoin, was choir director. He was much more interested in music than reform. Indeed, on that day and on most days he was more interested in the brown-eyed girl at the organ, Frances "Fannie" Adams, the adoptive daughter of the minister. While he attended discussions at Professor Stowe's house on Harriet's book in progress, Chamberlain later allowed that, like the author, he had not anticipated its great success. There is no evidence he shared the enthusiasm for Abolition that Stowe and some other professors exhibited. If he did, he kept it secret.

It is probable that his gruff but indulgent father, Joshua Chamberlain of Brewer, opposed the war. Conservative and a Democrat, the elder Chamberlain had named one of his sons after John C. Calhoun. The senior Chamberlain, a farmer and timber speculator, was not a man of words, but when he spoke he expected obedience from Joshua and his three brothers and sister. By all accounts, mother Sarah was more talkative, even witty, and certainly more responsive to the sensitivity of her firstborn son. But, deeply religious, she also discouraged the habit of reading anything not practical and perhaps immoral. The first novel Chamberlain read was as a class assignment at Bowdoin when he was nearly twenty—Nathaniel Hawthorne's *House of the Seven Gables*.

He was christened Lawrence Joshua Chamberlain, in honor of a naval hero of the War of 1812. He would always be "Lawrence" to friends and family. In college, however, he changed the order of his name to "Joshua Lawrence." Although his father had only seen militia service in the bloodless Aroostook War, there were soldier forebears on both sides of the family.

Joshua Senior sent his son to Whiting's Military Academy in Ellsworth for as long as he could afford to. He clearly wanted Lawrence to go to West Point. But the young Chamberlain had no interest in a career in the Army. The thought of it was too confining. He wanted someday to be something else—his own man.

Chamberlain's mother had her own plan for her eldest boy. She wanted him to be a minister. He joined the local Congregational church, but later wrote that he experienced no great sense of religious conversion; he particularly enjoyed the music recently introduced into church services. Lawrence allowed that if he were to be a clergyman, he would prefer to be a missionary. He could work to save the heathen in Africa or the South Seas. *Someplace far away.*

As he grew older, he would feel under increasing pressure to please his parents' conflicting plans for his future. Yet he managed to be a boy living a rather typical rural life.

He became an expert horseman riding a favorite mare. He learned to swim in the nearby river, and sailed on the broad Penobscot in a small skiff the family owned. The boy worked hard in the fields of the Chamberlains' hundred acre farm, and absorbed a basic New England sense of self-reliance.

One scene stuck out in his memory. He was haying with his father and the haywagon's bottom got stuck on some stumps. His father, across a stream, hollered for him to move the wagon. The seventeen-year-old, thinking he could not budge the wagon unassisted, said he couldn't see how it could be accomplished.

"Do it! That's how!" the father bellowed. That got Lawrence's adrenaline pumping. Lifting a wheel, he got the obstacle cleared. Recalling his father's exhortation, Chamberlain later wrote, "There was a maxim whose value exceeded the occasion. The solution of a thousand problems. An order of action for life, worth infinitely more than worn-out volumes of lifeless learning and years of thumbsucking irresolution."

*Do It.* But what do you do when, unlike the scene in a hayfield, there are conflicting choices? By his late teens, Chamberlain had secured his parents' blessing for a middle course, that at least deferred for the immediate future becoming a soldier or clergyman. He would attend Bowdoin College, and then the Bangor Theological Seminary. The balance seemed to tip in his mother's direction; one gets the sense, despite the father's authoritarianism, that that often happened.

With a definite goal, Lawrence set about with single-minded tenacity to achieve it. He spent a full year preparing for the heavily classical entrance examination at Bowdoin. For nine months he spent every day, from five in the morning until ten in the evening, studying in a garret room in the

Chamberlains' house. He also devoted time to physical exercise, which provided a release of tension. In the winter, he chopped wood.

"There is no muscle-making, man-building exercise in all the jockeying tricks and scientific gymnastics of modern 'scholarship' to compare with splitting wood, especially when this is yellow birch and rock maple," he wrote. In summer he practiced broadswordsmanship with his father, observing that "avoided head-splitting is as good experience as achieved wood-splitting."

The preparation was tested when a "green and pale-looking lad" of nineteen confronted several Bowdoin professors on the evening of his arrival at the Brunswick college. He had come down from Brewer with his Latin tutor in a sleigh, pulled by his faithful mare. As Chamberlain recalled in the third person, "He had expected juggernaut." Instead, he passed the entrance exams rather easily. The mare, his childhood companion, returned to the farm. Chamberlain knew somehow his childhood was gone with the horse. In some ways he had prolonged it beyond the length of the average Maine boy in 1848.

At Bowdoin, Chamberlain struggled not only to get good grades, but to make the grade socially. He desperately wanted friends and worked to dispel the image of a sober-sided "grind." He refused to drink, less from any prohibitionist mentality, than the fear the habit would get in the way of his studies. He was particularly happy to be called "Jack" by other students; he was to some degree one of the boys.

When a trip to the neighboring town of Lisbon to procure a tree to be planted on college grounds, a tradition at Bowdoin, degenerated into a drunken excursion, Chamberlain, who had not taken a drink, refused to "rat" on those who had. He ran the risk of expulsion, but believed he acted honorably. He told the college president, "I know well my father will be proud to see me coming home for this."

As it turned out, the other culprits confessed, and all got off with a reprimand. The incident illustrated Chamberlain's sense of honor as well as "male bonding." And his father's expected approval was crucial. By now he had assumed his father's name, Joshua.

Young Joshua Chamberlain was unable to avoid confronting another problem: his tendency to stammer. To avoid exposing his disability, the boy often kept quiet or used words without the dreaded letters "p," "b," and "t." This made him appear bashful at best, and stupid at worst. It most certainly contributed to an impression of a shy, non-assertive youth. At Bowdoin, where class recitations were a regular part of the educational regimen, Joshua Chamberlain was constantly devising strategies to avoid humiliation. He later admitted, "the sleepless anxiety on this score was a serious wear on the nervous system."

Typically, Chamberlain worked hard at a method of saying the dangerous letters without stuttering. It involved a manner of "singing" words that, along with speaking troublesome words quickly, conquered the disability. No wonder Joshua was, since childhood, attracted to singing. When he sang he could express himself free from fear. Eventually Chamberlain would come to be regarded as an orator with a musical voice, who spoke in swelling, musical cadences. Like so much about him, that did not just happen. He worked at it.

"Jack" Chamberlain involved himself heavily in church activities on and off campus. He was, apparently, preparing himself for the role his mother encouraged. Every Sunday afternoon he walked two miles down the Bath road to conduct a Sunday school. It seemed to be his main recreation.

All this striving to get good grades, to make the grade socially, to avoid stuttering, and to be morally good extracted a price. Halfway through college, at about the time of his twenty-first birthday, Chamberlain succumbed to a fever doctors could not treat. "The tension had been too great, the strain too unrelenting," he would later confess. He had suffered a breakdown. For nine long months it was "a fight for life" back home in Brewer.

Within a family cocoon, constantly under his mother's care, and also nurtured back to health by close proximity to the nature he loved, the young man recovered. He returned to Bowdoin, having missed a year's studies. Older than his classmates, he may have been wiser. But by 1851 there was another object for Chamberlain's pursuit—Fannie.

Fannie Adams was the daughter of Ashur and Amelia Adams of Boston. When the little girl was four she was sent to be raised by the Reverend George Adams and his wife, who were childless. She was aware of being "given away," and whatever the reasons, this awareness had to be traumatic. She would share the clergyman's home with her adoptive mother's "old maid" sister, Deborah Folsom, or "Cousin D," and another adoptive daughter, Anna Davis, the granddaughter of a Bowdoin faculty member.

George Adams was an active and innovative Congregationalist, working tirelessly to make his church less stodgy and more involved in the community. One of his many controversial acts was to support the building of a new, massive, Gothic-style church near the college, overlooking the town from its hill like a Yankee version of a medieval cathedral. There was considerable grumbling about its "popish" appearance, but the church was built. Adams brought more music into its sanctuary and, an ardent Abolitionist, he raised conservative eyebrows by inviting a black man to preach. He would introduce the first Christmas and Easter services. Clearly he was a most *involved* Christian.

But Fannie rebelled against fulfilling the "proper" role of a minister's daughter. Indeed, she adamantly refused to join George Adam's church. If he could challenge convention, so could she! Fannie loved to dress up—the fur trimmings on her winter coat set the town gossips tut-tutting. She reacted against discipline and conformity. On the one hand, Reverend Adams spoiled the temperamental Fannie by indulging her demands; on the other, he consistently treated her as a child. She responded by often acting the part, developing a reputation for being flighty and self-centered.

Although attractive, it seems Fannie was more vivacious than beautiful. She suffered from bad teeth and failing eyes, which caused pain and frustration. By the time Joshua Chamberlain became smitten with her, it was an open question if Fannie, two years his senior, was that interested in a permanent relationship with any man. She had decidedly unconventional and strong ideas about marriage and childbearing, which in Victorian America were automatically linked. Fannie thought making babies was a form of prostitution. She was more interested in making a career for herself in art or music.

It would outwardly seem that the serious, industrious, frugal farm boy from Brewer with religious inclinations had little in common with the likes of Fannie Adams. But appearances can be deceiving. They shared a passion for music, and probably both—in their own ways—were struggling to achieve some measure of their own identities. Chamberlain desperately sought acceptance while retaining his own individuality. Fannie, beneath her showy front, was probably crying out for attention, struggling against a sense of rejection.

Underneath his carefully constructed exterior of pluck and practicality, Chamberlain was a sensitive, high-strung sort himself. The boy who grew up on the forest's edge did not hunt; he saw no "sport" in killing wild animals. He briefly engaged in pursuing taxidermy as a boy and shot some birds for his collection. But he stopped that pastime for good. At age seventeen he remained careful, when haying on his family's farm, to avoid the nests of birds and bumble-bees with his scythe. He enjoyed the music of the wind in the trees and could distinguish what type of tree was singing which notes. He climbed Maine's highest mountain, Katahdin, and saw "boulders strewn as if hurled in the titan-sport of unearthly armies," a romantic metaphor he would apply to some contested hills in Pennsylvania. If Fannie sought to express her romanticism with brush on canvas, Joshua would set it forth in word pictures.

Joshua Chamberlain wanted badly to be accepted as "one of the boys," but, in many ways, he really wasn't one. And he knew it.

When he fell for the dark-eyed Fannie, he fell hard. There are fragments of evidence that Fannie, while enjoying his attentions and even fleeting intimacies, was not as fully in love with him. She worried about an obsessive, control-ling quality to his courtship, and shied away from a full commitment. When the subject of marriage came up, she avowed a preference for a Platonic relationship. A male friend, in whom Fannie confided, wrote that Chamberlain did not sound like the kind of man who could make her "feel that sort of love of which you have for years dreamed so wildly." That certainly did not sound Platonic.

For his part, Chamberlain constantly fretted that he could not afford to give Fannie the material things she en-joyed. He was a "poor boy." But it went deeper than that. Reverend Adams had doubts that Chamberlain, whom he liked, could make Fannie happy, and Chamberlain initially thought the clergyman to be an obstacle to gaining Fannie's hand. Adams's position was undercut when, soon after his wife's death, he married the sister of Fannie's Boston music instructor (who would write "The Battle Cry of Freedom"), only a few months older than Fannie!

In 1852, despite all this turmoil, Joshua and Fannie became engaged—and promptly parted for three years. Chamberlain went to Bangor to study at the theological seminary there, while Miss Adams went south to Milledgeville, Georgia, to be a music tutor with a prominent family.

Bowdoin's 1852 commencement, the school's fiftieth, should have been a moment of triumph for Joshua Chamberlain, who had won the honor of delivering the First Class Oration. It took place that September in the great Gothic church on the hill, the scene of so many key events in his life. For Chamberlain it became something akin to a Gothic horror story.

Confronted by an audience that included such famous Bowdoin alumni as Henry Wadsworth Longfellow, Nathaniel Hawthorne, and Franklin Pierce, soon to be elected President of the United States, the young orator panicked. And his old curse, so carefully repressed until it seemed conquered, returned. He stammered. He lost his train of thought.

Ironically his subject was "The Last Gladiatorial Show at Rome." Later, showing some appreciation of the humor of the situation, which he definitely didn't feel at the time, Chamberlain described the scene:

"Our gladiator was hit. For a moment all around him swum and swayed into a mist. But he only reeled, half-turned, and paced the stage, grasping some evidently extemporaneous and strangely far-fetched phrases, then suddenly whirling to the front, with more blood in his face than would have flowed from Caesar's 'morituri salutamus,' he delivered his conclusion straight out from the shoulder like those who are determined to die early. That public failure lessened the pang of parting. The crestfallen champion was glad to get out of town."

He gave serious thought to going to West Point—but he had promised his mother he would go to the seminary, and he went. Three years later, upon graduation, Chamberlain, who had also earned a master's degree at Bowdoin, accepted an invitation to return to the scene of his public humiliation and give the Master's Oration. This time the subject was "Law and Liberty," and Chamberlain delivered it flawlessly. He made such a favorable impression that he was offered a position at Bowdoin as an instructor of logic and natural theology.

He accepted. The salary was modest, but the job got him out of a predicament. While the distant Fannie had warmed to the idea of marriage, she had made it clear in her infrequent letters from Georgia that she was damned if she was going to marry a clergyman.

On December 7, 1855, Joshua and Fannie were married at the First Parish Church where he had sung in the choir, suffered public embarrassment and redemption. George Adams officiated at the ceremony. Fannie had changed her mind about more than marriage. In October of 1856, a child was born to the newlyweds. It took them six months to give the little girl a name, Grace Dupee. The name fit Chamberlain's liking. The girl, usually called "Daisy," was a living proof of God's grace, and Dupee was the Huguenot name of his mother's family.

All was not bliss in the rented house in Brunswick, however. Joshua discovered some love letters Fannie had imprudently kept. They were from before Chamberlain's time, but Fannie feared Joshua would sink into one of "those fearful, morbid states of feeling" he was prone to. She headed off to Boston after this episode blew over; it was to be a common routine of "getting away" that Fannie utilized to deal with such tensions.

Finances were also a problem, partly alleviated when Chamberlain's brother John, attending Bowdoin, boarded with Joshua and Fannie. Joshua Chamberlain Senior paid John's board, and helped out financially as he could. Brother Horace was also at Bowdoin; the brothers often socialized. In fact, they appear to have provided Chamberlain's only real social life.

In November of 1858, just before Thanksgiving, a baby boy was born, prematurely, and died within hours.

Chamberlain's academic career advanced as he became a professor of rhetoric and oratory (He saw the irony in this). Always gifted with languages, Joshua taught German and Spanish. By 1860 he was making, by Bowdoin's standards, a good salary of $1,100 a year. It was as much as older faculty members made. There was talk of making Chamberlain chair of modern languages and even granting him a two-year sabbatical to study in Europe.

Another son was born in the Indian summer of 1859, and named Harold Wyllys. The next year the growing family purchased a house on Potter Street, a short walk from the College and First Parish Church. It was a Cape in the Federal style, with an ell connecting it to a barn. There was a garden for the professor to potter about in, and the fact the young Longfellow and his new bride had roomed in the house when the bard was a professor at Bowdoin appealed to the Chamberlains.

Things seemed on the surface to be working out for the Chamberlains. And yet, underneath, tensions continued. Fannie, who had once viewed childbearing as male tyranny over a woman's body, was pregnant again. In the spring of

1860 Fannie, aged 35, gave birth to Emily. She was the picture of her mother. But she "departed with the flowers" in September of 1860.

That month, which was the month of Joshua Chamberlain's thirty-second birthday, was also election time in Maine. Foreshadowing the vote in other Northern states later that autumn, Maine voted for Abraham Lincoln. There was growing talk of sectional discord.

The period of Joshua Chamberlain's half dozen years of marriage had been a period of growing discord within the nation. By early 1861 it resulted in war. If Chamberlain had strong thoughts about the national crisis in this interval of his life, there is little surviving evidence of them. He was immersed in his work at Bowdoin. He tried to introduce some innovation in his teaching, but felt repressed by the general conservatism of the school. He graded 1,200 papers a year. He resisted being a pawn in the dreary academic politics of older faculty members. He was uneasy and bored, yet struggling to support his family. Fannie was often sick, unhappy. The death of little Emily hit both of them hard.

Yet, when the war came, Joshua Chamberlain did not rush to the colors. He was a thirty-two-year-old man, a college professor, with two young children, and a shaky marriage. It is not surprising that he was not one of the "Boys of 1861." For the first year and a half of the Civil War, Chamberlain was on the sidelines.

It was a time for other lions to roar, and Maine had them in abundance.

*Hiram Gregory Berry—Maine State Archives*

# Hiram Berry
*"Shall this flag ever trail in the dust?"*

Hiram Gregory Berry was a rising man in Rockland before it was Rockland. He was born in August of 1824 when it was East Thomaston, in the place called the Meadows. All told, he had four brothers and a sister, and grew up, a strapping farm boy, with an aptitude for math and athletics, and an abiding personal interest in military history. His grandfather fought in the Revolution, and his father was ready to fight in the War of 1812, but the opportunity never arose. "Hi" Berry was known as someone more than able to take care of himself in a fight, but more likely, if possible, to play the part of peacemaker.

Having attained a basic public education, Berry became a carpenter. He soon branched out to become a contractor and builder, establishing a lumberyard. By the 1850s he was one of the owners of a business turning out doors, sashes and blinds, and a year later one of the directors of the Limerock National Bank. His business prowess, related to his ability with numbers and willingness to work, was semi-legendary. It was no big deal for "Hi" Berry to carry on several conversations while moving lumber from a pile, and keep track in his head of every piece moved.

Berry was attracted to politics. Electoral contests may have provided an outlet for his military instincts. Certainly he was enthralled by tales of martial derring-do at an early age, and was upset when his mother vetoed a possible cadetship at West Point. In 1852 he ran for the state legislature from East Thomaston and was elected. By 1856 Rockland had been incorporated and Berry, a Democrat, ran for mayor.

No less than five candidates ran for the office, and predictably, none received the majority of votes cast required to be elected. Berry, who got the most, came in first in a field of three candidates in the next round—but still fell short of an absolute majority. In the third vote, where there were only two choices, Berry prevailed with a plurality of thirty votes. The local press noted that, despite the excitement generated by the three elections, "we recollect of hearing scarcely a word spoken derogatory to the personal character of the candidates."

*Fight hard, fight clean.*

A cannon placed in the field in front of Berry's imposing home banged away repeatedly upon his election until it burst; one of the metal fragments injured a passerby, Berry's first casualty. In this case, the wound was superficial.

Although Berry turned out to be a competent mayor, he was a Democrat at a time when the national party's antics made it difficult for Democrats at the local level. Berry was defeated for reelection by his previous opponent.

He redoubled his efforts at business and also immersed himself in playing soldier. Back in 1854 he had been the prime mover in the creation of a light infantry unit called the Rockland City Guards. They were mustered into Maine's Fourth Division of Militia, of which Berry already was Inspector. He was chosen Captain of the Guards.

They were a snappy-looking organization, with blue and gold uniforms and tall beaver-skin caps, complete with gold tassels. They were drilled by another Rocklander and West Point grad, Davis Tillson, who also headed up the spanking Rockland Brass Band. It was reputed to be the best in Maine.

The Guards, often accompanied by the brass band, showed their stuff in various parades and encampments. One of the latter was in Portland in 1856. Some of the Guards enjoyed themselves by dressing up in wolf skins and buffalo robes and interrupting the night's sleep of many citizen soldiers with their howls, cheers and catcalls as they paraded about under the moon.

One Colonel Bodfish, a veteran of the Mexican War, was unamused, and sallied forth from his tent armed with his sword and wearing his sash.

"By what authority are these troops paraded?" he demanded in a loud voice.

A lad named L. D. Carver thundered back, "By the same authority by which they have raised hell all night." General laughter resounding in his ears, Bodfish retreated to his tent. Carver would later become Lieutenant Colonel of the Fourth Maine Volunteer Infantry Regiment.

Hiram Berry was not involved in the Portland escapade. But he was front and center about the time of his birthday in August of 1858. Senator Jefferson Davis of Mississippi, formerly Secretary of War in the Pierce administration, was in Maine, and state and local officials fell over themselves vying to honor Davis, known as a hero of the Mexican War. He visited Rockland and was invited to attend a militia muster at Belfast.

The Rockland City Guards left for Belfast aboard the steamer *Daniel Webster*. The great Massachusetts statesman was dead, but his words, "The Union, now and forever," lived. The 1850s were a time when sectional loyalties competed with spread-eagle nationalism. Davis' association with the former were submerged in Maine by memories of his national fame. When Davis arrived by carriage in coastal Belfast, he was formally requested to review the assembled brigade, and responded "with that grace peculiar to the man" as Maine's adjutant general gushed. Berry's Guard, in blue and gold, to the thumping of Tillson's Brass Band, accompanied Davis to the reviewing stand. Davis proceeded to review the troops with "that air of ease and manliness which attaches to his every movement."

It was expected that Davis, as a hero and politician, would say a few words, which he did. The Mississippian concluded, "With such troops as are now before me, we may defy the combined forces of the world and shout the song of Freedom forever."

A few years later a goodly number of the men Davis addressed would be marching to defend the Union against the Southern Confederacy he headed. The Rockland City Guard would produce twenty-one commissioned officers for the Union, including a Major General named Berry.

The Guard was disbanded soon after Berry resigned to devote attention to his growing business interests. When, in April of 1861, Fort Sumter was fired upon, Berry immediately offered his services to Governor Washburn. Within a month he had recruited the Fourth Maine Volunteer Infantry Regiment from Rockland, Belfast, and other mid-coast communities. The regiment encamped at Tillson's Hill and Berry was elected Colonel, with fellow Rockland native Adelbert Ames chosen Lieutenant Colonel (although the Army had other ideas, so Ames, the recent West Point graduate, did not accept his volunteer commission).

Camp Knox was comfortable enough, with tent flooring of boards several inches from the ground, and subject to a parade of visitors, including Governor Washburn. When word came that the new soldiers should forget the original three-month term under which they were recruited and sign up for three years, most complied. The company from Winterport did not think this was right, and marched home, to be replaced by a new company from Brooks. By June 17 the grey-uniformed regiment marched through streets thronged with well-wishers to the wharf, where the same *Daniel Webster* which transported some of them to Belfast to escort Jeff Davis now awaited to begin the regiment on its journey to Washington—and to bloody war.

But this was the Spring of 1861. Boys heading off to put down the Rebellion were a novelty that thousands along the way turned out to cheer. Military display was, the *Boston Herald* observed, "the fashionable amusement of the time." On Boston Common, "whole troops of Maine girls" were prominent in the holiday-like crowd, and New Yorkers came out by the thousands to view the "strong and sturdy specimens of Maine's true nobility," reminiscent to a reporter of "the old northern warriors of Gustavus Adolphus."

In New York the Fourth Maine was presented with three flags and three long-winded speeches. Colonel Berry protested that his soldiers, foot-sore and drenched in perspiration after marching in the 95-degree heat wearing heavy knapsacks, were fatigued, but to no avail.

He said a few words himself. Grasping one of the flags, he held it aloft and shouted, "Shall this flag ever trail in the dust?"

"No, no!"

"Will you defend it so long as you have a right arm?"

"We will, we will!"

Baltimore was a different story. It was a Southern city with Southern sympathies, scene of an ugly incident between Massachusetts troops and an unruly crowd. Since then soldiers *en route* for Washington had quietly passed through, with only a drum tap, as they switched trains. Not Berry's Fourth Maine. They marched through Baltimore just like other cities with flags flying and the band playing. "We had no cheers to speak of, and no kind word spoken: men looked dark and sullen; did not know but we might have trouble," Berry wrote his wife. But none occurred.

Finally the Mainers reached Washington and encamped a couple of miles outside the capital at Meridian Hill. The Third Maine was already there, and pitched in to help set up the tents of the weary boys from Rockland. Not knowing any better, they chose a shady grove of oaks which seemed just dandy after long days exposed to the sun. Within a few days, however, Sol exited to make way for a rainstorm, which washed out most of the regiment's tents. The Fourth Maine would thereafter avoid the woods and seek open fields to camp in whenever possible.

This was just one of the adjustments to real soldiering that would be made in the next few weeks. Grey uniforms were exchanged for U.S. Army regulation blue. The national birthday was celebrated as the clamor in the press for an offensive against the Rebels continued unabated. Soon the orders came to move south, across the Potomac, into Virginia.

The Army was not ready. The generals knew it, the men sensed it, but the politicians wanted an offensive.

The boys of Berry's regiment, like 25,000 others in the Union Army, marched through a rolling green countryside, dotted with orchards and medium-sized plantations. " 'Tis sad indeed to see so fine a country in so bad a fix," Berry observed. The soldiers sang and bantered as they moved through forests of scrub pine and oak. The presence of the enemy was signalled by the increasing number of trees felled across roads. They formed minor impediments to the fifty axemen Berry assigned to clear the way. Maine boys were used to more challenging work than this. The speed and efficiency with which they did their work was the admiration of many officers from other states.

The Confederate Army, commanded by General Pierre Beauregard, was entrenched on a plateau of sorts surrounding a crossroads called Manassas. A sluggish little stream named Bull Run meandered through the area, and the battle that commenced on July 21 would be known in the North as the Battle of Bull Run.

Berry's regiment was part of Howard's brigade of Heintzelman's division. All morning as the fighting raged nearby, mainly for possession of some key hills, Howard's brigade was kept in reserve. Under a broiling sun, the troops waited. And waited. Noon passed, then one o'clock. As many a soldier would learn, the tension of awaiting battle played hell with one's nerves.

Two o'clock and finally the orders arrived: Advance at double-quick to the front and engage the enemy. What this meant was that the soldiers had to hustle for miles under a merciless July afternoon sun toward the sound of the guns. It was about three o'clock when the regiment arrived on the battlefield.

Howard's brigade was on the right of Heintzelman's division, which was trying to take a hill with a solitary house and thousands of Confederates on it. The seesaw battle here had shifted against the boys in blue about a half hour before the brigade arrived, due to the arrival of rebel reinforcements under General Joe Johnston. The way the tide was running became apparent when Berry's regiment, followed in line of battle by the Second Vermont, was ordered to march uphill to support a battery. Thrashing through troublesome thickets, the Fourth Maine found the guns had been overrun. Aligning with the Vermont regiment, the Mainers stood their ground on the brow of the hill.

"Our part," Berry said, "was to fight, and cover as far as possible the retreat."

For an hour, until ordered to fall back, Berry stood firm. "Strange as it may seem I was no more excited than when ordinarily in earnest. I did not believe I should be hit in any way, and I did not think of it at all. My mind was occupied by my command entirely," he wrote his wife.

Men about him were killed and wounded. The first casualty was Sergeant Major Stephen Chapman, who had approached Berry by the Regimental colors, smiling, to ask for orders. When the Colonel gave them, Chapman shook Berry's hand, cautioned him against unnecessarily exposing himself, and returned to his post. He was at once shot dead, a Minie ball through his heart. Sergeant Chapman had been the first man to enlist in the Fourth Maine. Now he was the first to die.

Others soon fell. P. Henry Tillson of Thomaston died almost instantly when a cannon ball sheared off both his legs. Berry's horse was shot from under him. When his color bearer was toppled, the Colonel seized the flag and carried it. Riddled by bullets and torn by cannon shot, it was no longer the beautiful linen presented to the regiment in New York.

But Berry did not allow it to trail in the dust.

In the heat of battle, the muskets of many of his men so overheated they were unfit for firing. Berry continued coolly to give orders and cheer his men. But tears streamed down his face.

The regiment lost twenty-three men killed, three officers and twenty-four men wounded, and three officers and thirty-three men missing at Bull Run. Unlike many other regiments, Berry's retreated in good order. To his wife he wrote "I never again, probably, shall be placed in such a position, should the war last for years, as that at Bull Run."

As panic set in, the retreat from the battlefield became a rout. James Shannon of the Fifth Maine, also in Howard's brigade, "concluded that alone I could not stem the tide setting so strong against us, and remembering that as a school boy I was taught that the shortest line between two points was the straightest and most direct one, I acted accordingly, and found hundreds of other boys engaged in demonstrating the same proposition."

Another Maine regiment in the battle was the Second Maine, raised in Bangor. Horatio Staples recalled it was the first time he had shot at other men and been shot back at. There was no time for sorting out sensations, like fear, when guns had to be fired and loaded repeatedly. As more and more of his comrades fell to the volleys of Rebels behind a fence, one emotion arose: "It was mad, clear, stark, swearing mad—a burning desire to get at the gray rats beyond that fence."

*Oliver Otis Howard—Thomas McDonald, Eustis, ME*

# Oliver Otis Howard

*"My religion consists in striving to do my duty."*

After assuming command of the Third Regiment, Oliver Otis Howard was discussing the volunteer army that had to be organized with James G. Blaine, the young Speaker of the Maine House of Representatives. "You, Howard, will be the first brigadier from Maine," Blaine said. At the time Howard considered Blaine's remark "visionary." The odds against such rapid advancement appeared long indeed.

But Blaine was right. Before Bull Run, Howard was promoted to brigadier general. The farm boy from Leeds, Maine, had traveled far. And it was only the beginning. Otis—as he was called from an early age—was hardly without ambition. He was, in 1861, also a devout Christian who did not believe in drinking or swearing in an army where many did. Furthermore, he was an Abolitionist. These attributes made O. O. Howard something of an oddity. Yet his beliefs and mannerisms, which often rubbed fellow officers and enlisted men the wrong way, did not prevent his steady advancement during the Civil War.

Howard endured considerable criticism, some of it deserved, but he also would write, in the early twentieth century, a long autobiography. It may have set the record straight, as Howard intended; it may also have told us more about the man than he meant.

He remembered his father, a farmer who was physically too frail for the demanding work a yeoman's existence required. Rowland Howard often seemed "stern and unbending," but enjoyed playing his flute and reading poetry. When Otis was about five, the sounds of fifes and drums signaled the local militia preparing to march north. They were off to confront the British in a border confrontation known then as the "Madawaska War," and later called the "Aroostook War." Hearing that his beloved father was drafted for service, the boy ran home sobbing until his mother told him that a substitute would go off to war in his sickly father's place. That was about the sum of his concern with anything martial in his youth.

When Otis was six, Pa Howard, back from a business trip to New York state, brought back with him a "little negro lad" named Edward Johnson. The black child lived with the Howard family for four years. Working and playing side by side with Eddie was, Otis felt, "a providential circumstance" which relieved him of any feelings of race prejudice. One day he would become the "Yankee Stepfather" to America's freed blacks.

From an early age, Otis had a religious bent. "There was no sign of religiousness in my first home," he recalled. Once, recounting a prayer meeting he had attended at a relative's home, the boy asked his father, seated in a high-backed chair, "Father, do you ever pray?"

Rowland Howard was silent for a few minutes. Then he said, "My son, would you like to have me pray?"

Otis said he would, and his father got out of his chair, knelt with his son, and recited the words of the Lord's Prayer. "This was the only time I heard my father thus offer a petition," Howard would write.

Not long afterward, on a Sunday when the west wind was howling, Otis was keeping watch over cattle in the field when his father called him to the house. He told the boy to get ready to go to the meeting house. His ailing father had helped rebuild it and had a hankering to see how his work looked. For some reason Otis begged off, and his parents and brother went without him. In church his father's lungs hemorrhaged suddenly "due undoubtedly to the strain of his morning call to me against the wind." By the end of April O. O. Howard had witnessed his first death scene.

*Our Father, who art in Heaven ...*

His mother remarried. John Gilmore was a widower with a farm on the other side of Leeds. He was a good man and Otis felt the new union was "a blessing to us all." He worked on his stepfather's farm and got advice from his namesake, Grandfather Oliver Otis, "Otis, always be kind to your employees." The boy did not exactly know what the old man meant then, but he would later when he held many men's lives in his hands.

After briefly attending public school in rural Wayne, he boarded with his Uncle John Otis in Hallowell, on the ancient Kennebec River. His uncle encouraged him to undertake preparatory studies at academies in Monmouth and North Yarmouth before entering Bowdoin College at age fifteen. If Otis did not know just what he wanted to be, he definitely knew it was not a farmer. In pompous schoolboy style, the freshman informed his mother, "my ambition is of a higher and more extended nature." Howard got good grades at Bowdoin, taught in country schools during the winter, and approached graduation with no clear idea of what he would do next.

His uncle, now in Congress, resolved the problem by offering to nominate him for a cadetship, his own son not gaining entrance to West Point. This seemed to Otis not only an opportunity to further his education, but the opening up of a career "which would relieve me from the anxiety of toiling too much for a support." It was a sober assessment; no visions of military glory danced in this lad's head. When he asked his mother's approval, she simply said, "My son, you have already made up your mind." This, Howard admitted, "was the nearest to an objection that she ever made." Not thrilled, but supportive.

By this time there was another woman in his life, a dark-eyed girl from Portland, Elizabeth Ann Waite. Lizzie was, if possible, more serious than Otis. They were engaged, but Otis' decision meant Miss Waite must wait a few more years to tie the knot.

West Point was, Howard discovered, the scene of "unpleasant feuds" among cadets. These usually had something to do with slavery. Otis was an Abolitionist, not in an outspoken way, but quietly. Nevertheless the word apparently got out and probably was at the root of an effort by a group of cadets to ostracize the introspective young man who wanted rather desperately to be liked. The situation made life miserable for Howard. One of the prime tormentors was the son of Colonel Robert E. Lee. When the commandant got wind of the cabal, he offered Howard some unofficial advice: "If I were in your place I would knock some man down."

Apparently the young cadet took this advice. For whatever reason, things straightened out during Howard's senior year. He even got elected president of West Point's only literary association, the Dialectic Society. In 1854 he graduated fourth in a class of forty-six. His former nemesis, Custis Lee, took first place in everything.

While Howard seemed little interested in politics, he made a friendship with an important rising politician while briefly stationed at the arsenal in Augusta. James G. Blaine, the Republican editor of the *Kennebec Journal,* was already a powerhouse in state politics. The earnest Howard knew the value of friends in high places.

He also finally married Lizzie Waite. The newlyweds settled down near Troy, New York, where the young lieutenant was stationed at another arsenal. A biographer would sum up Howard's comfortable existence: "He attended the socially respectable Episcopal church, smoked cigars after lunch, and avoided political controversy." And started a family as well.

But the Army at this point decided to send Howard to Florida, where it was still trying to defeat Seminole Indians fighting removal to the Indian Territory. Howard saw no action, but he was separated from his family and it was during this time that his attraction to religion accelerated. He was powerfully influenced by reading a biography of a British soldier who was an active Christian, Captain Hedley Vicars. Howard seemed certain of the date of his conversion: "It was the night of the last day of May, 1857, when I had the feeling of sudden relief from the depression that had been long upon me." From this point on religion was the overpowering force in Howard's life.

He was a math instructor at West Point for the next three years. Reunited with his wife and growing family, Howard devoted his spare time to religious study and teaching Sunday School. He advocated a paternal type of military leadership, where generals treated their men as fathers cared for children. This approach would win the love and obedience of soldiers, Howard claimed.

Absorbed in such concerns, Otis showed little interest in national politics. He seemed unaware of the seriousness of events. He pondered whether to take a six-month leave from the Army to study at the Bangor Theological Seminary. His brother Charlie was a student there, and the idea of becoming a minister would not leave his mind.

Until the Rebels fired upon Fort Sumter.

That got his attention. He wrote at once to Governor Washburn, offering his services. The governor reminded him that officers were elected by the men. Howard's friend

Blaine, now speaker of the Maine House of Representatives, was willing to fix that little problem. "Will you, if elected, accept the colonelcy of the Kennebec Regiment?" he wrote.

Howard, who had no real military experience in the field, wavered for a moment. Major meant more sense than colonel, didn't it? He went to the new commandant, Colonel John Reynolds, for his opinion.

"You'll accept, of course, Howard," Reynolds said.

And he did.

Oliver Otis Howard, through the influence of Blaine, was elected Colonel of the Third Maine, although nobody in the regiment had ever seen him. They saw him the next day, when he showed up at the camp by the State House with Blaine and Governor Washburn.

The governor had warned, "At first you will find 'the boys' a little rough," and Howard conceded that "I did not seem to those who casually met me to have the necessary toughness." But Washburn appeared confident in Howard. After the governor addressed the new regiment from atop a hogshead, and was heartily cheered, Washburn introduced the men's new colonel. The first impression was underwhelming. Howard noted that "the cheers called for were noticeably faint."

Abner Small of Waterville remembered the scene: "We saw a pale young man, taller than the governor, and slender, with earnest eyes, a high forehead, and a profusion of flowing moustache and beard. Howard talked down to us ('My men—') with the tone and manner of an itinerant preacher. He told us all about himself and his little family and the Ten Commandments."

The men's real choice was Isaac Tucker of Gardiner, a hale and hearty type under whom they could expect a good time. Now, as Howard lectured them against drinking and swearing (activities a good number were engaged in before Howard's arrival), the reaction was "Uh, oh."

Howard's own recollection: "I attempted an address, but had spoken only a few words when a remarkable silence hushed the entire assemblage; a new idea appeared to have entered their minds and become prominent: I pleaded *for work in preparation for war*, and not a few months of holiday entertainment, and hurrah boys to frighten and disperse a Southern rabble by bluster; after which to enjoy a quick return to our homes."

If Howard was not popular he was energetic in preparing the regiment to head south. Although Leeds was less than twenty miles distant from Augusta, Otis claimed he did not have time to visit his home town. Within a little over a week, the regiment boarded the cars of a train that chugged out of Augusta on a beautiful, cloudless day, June 5. All along the way, the Third was cheered.

In New York the Colonel sustained his first war-related injury. At an armory a beautiful flag was presented to the regiment. Howard stood on the limber of a gun carriage and made what Abner Small described as "a pious speech of acceptance," interrupted when the prop holding up the limber was accidentally knocked away. "The sudden shock caused me to lose my balance and spring to the floor," Howard wrote. "I alighted on my feet, but attached to my belt was my heavy saber, which fell, striking my left foot with great force. My great toenail was crushed and has troubled me ever since. This was my first wound in the war." Small noted Howard "almost swore."

Another incident was typical of Howard. A well-to-do merchant named Buck, originally from Bucksport, Maine, hosted a reception at the Astor House. At the meal's conclusion, Buck prepared to offer a patriotic toast. With wine glasses all poised, Howard grabbed a glass of water and made his own toast.

"Gentlemen, our country is in peril; I go at its call to do my duty. The true beverage of a soldier is cold water; in this I pledge you," he said.

"You should have seen how we all hustled around to get our glasses of water!" Buck recalled.

It was not, as Howard later admitted, "very gracious," but Howard was not about to drink in public!

In contrast to its reception in most cities along the way, the Third Maine arrived in Washington without any fanfare. A bowling alley and some nearby saloons provided hard floors to sleep on, and the Colonel, thinking this was a heck of a welcome, arranged for the whole regiment to have breakfast at Willard's Hotel the next day. Of course that added up to a hefty bill, which luckily for Howard, the state finally agreed to pay.

The Third Maine was moved to nearby Meridian Hill, near the site of the Second Maine's camp. Apparently one of the men accidentally discharged his musket, shooting the man ahead of him, as, in a downpour, they marched into camp. According to Small, "Colonel Howard then ordered all guns to be discharged into the air, and an indiscriminate firing followed, some of the balls flying into the tents of the Second Maine on the hill. In spite of the fusillade, the Second Maine boys took us in, dried our clothes, and gave us a warm supper."

The Third set up its own tents, and Howard set about drilling, disciplining, and preparing the boys for war. The boys were not happy, and were even more out of sorts when the Colonel stopped granting passes to visit Washington and its unholy attractions. A delegation assembled to protest, but to no avail. "Ours was not a holiday excursion," Howard wrote. He knew "there was considerable chafing," but when

General Irvin McDowell, hastily throwing together an army, ordered Howard to organize a brigade and march to Alexandria, he thought he was ready. His division commander, watching the Third march past, threw cold water in Howard's face by commenting, "Colonel, you have a fine regiment; they march well and give promise for the future, but you are not well drilled—poor officers, but good-looking men!"

The chastened colonel picked the Fourth and Fifth Maine Regiments, along with the Second Vermont, to join the Third Maine in his new brigade, which added up to about 3,000 men. Alexandria was not friendly. Howard's men, in turn, were not overly friendly to rebel property. "Soldiers at the best are like locusts: fences and trees are consumed, and private property generally is much infringed upon," he wrote his wife on July 7. It was a Sunday, and he hoped to get to church.

One of the locusts' victims was the stately home called "Clermont." Howard's troops hauled off bedding, silver plate, crockery, and cooking utensils; mirrors and marble-topped tables were broken, bookcases were toppled, and busts were decapitated. Cupids with broken wings were strewn about. Before war on actual Rebels, war on their property had commenced. "The defense is that it belongs to secessionists; this is true, but we do not allow people to steal even secession property," Howard noted. "I have had to fight this propensity to steal ever since I have been here. Nothing will be safe in Maine when we get home."

"Clermont" was converted into a brigade hospital. It would soon have broken men as well as furniture. The Union Army marched to Bull Run and fought Beauregard's force there on July 21. It was a Sunday. Howard did not like the idea, especially since the Federals had initiated the fighting that day. Some soldiers murmured, "It is Sunday! The attacking party on the Sabbath is sure of defeat!"

With scant sleep, the Union Army started moving in the dim morning hours, with Howard's brigade at the rear of the columns. All morning the brigade waited in oppressive heat, flags limp in the still air, listening to the rumble of battle nearby. The colonel fidgeted as he stood by his horse awaiting the order to go in, at one point succumbing to an anxiety attack. He was ashamed of himself and prayed for the strength to do his duty. Soon "the singular feeling left me and never returned."

When, finally, the order came, heat and fatigue dropped about half of Howard's men by the wayside before the battlefield was reached. Those who persevered threw away blankets, haversacks and canteens. One staff officer, spurring the brigade on, shouted, "You better hurry and get in if you want to have any fun."

By around three in the afternoon the "fun" began as Howard led two regiments, the Fourth Maine and Second Vermont, up the contested hill, returning in fifteen minutes to lead a second line composed of the Third and Fifth Maine. The smoke was so heavy that the enemy could not be seen; the noise was deafening. Abner Small of the Third Maine said, "We wavered, and rallied, and fired blindly; and men fell writhing, and others melted from sight." Amidst the din the order to retire was heard. Howard would insist his intent was only to pull back and reform, but men sensed the tide of battle was going against them, and walked away in increasingly disorganized groups.

There was no running at first. They were too tired for that. Howard vainly tried to halt the retreat of exhausted, confused, and angry boys baptized by fire, their faces streaked with dirt and sweat, mouths blackened by biting open powder cartridges. He was heard to say in a loud voice

---

that *he* would not run, better to be taken by the enemy than run. But his men were running now, as panic developed. General Heintzelman rode up, himself wounded, berating every officer in sight. He swore at Howard.

After the disaster, the brigades were broken up and Howard "with some disappointment" was sent back to his old regiment. The Third Maine was not delighted with him, either, and complaints made their way back to the home folks. A month after the battle Howard wrote a plaintive reply to one angry relative. "I have worked for my command early and late," he said. "I have been without proper food and sleep, and sometimes I am weary—weary; and then I am misrepresented and misunderstood." But, he added, "I have been unpopular before. My religion consists in striving to do my duty."

# Adelbert Ames

## *"I shall show them I am equal to the task."*

As Oliver Howard and Hiram Berry waited for the order to go in, another Maine officer, Adelbert Ames, had already seen plenty of action. Adelbert Ames was on his way out of the battle. Fresh out of West Point, Ames was a first lieutenant in Charles Griffin's Battery A of the Union artillery. These were some of the guns Howard and Berry heard booming in the distance.

*Battery similar to one Adelbert Ames served in at Bull Run*
—Sparks From The Camp Fire (1890)

The Union artillery were, as one participant later wrote, "the prime feature. The battle was not lost until they were lost." Griffin's battery advanced to within 1,000 yards of the Confederates on Henry House Hill, and knocked out the Rebel guns. For a while a Union victory seemed likely.

Ames was hit in the thigh by a Rebel bullet early in the fighting. Unable to ride a horse, he continued to help direct the battery's fire seated on a caisson. He refused to leave the field for medical attention. Whenever the guns were moved, so was Ames. In great pain and with blood oozing over the top of his boot, Ames felt himself fading.

So was the Union Army. As the Rebels gained reinforcements, they pressed back Federal infantry. Griffin's Battery A was separated from effective support when a regiment of infantry emerged from the woods to its right. Griffin, a no-nonsense Regular, at once prepared to give the approaching blue line a taste of canister when he was ordered to hold his fire by artillery chief Major Berry. Berry thought the blue men had to be a regiment sent forward by Sam Heintzelman to support Griffin's hard-pressed battery.

There was little uniformity of clothing at this point in the war, and unfortunately, the regiment was made up of Virginians. They poured a devastating fire into the Federal cannoneers, dropping almost every one of them. Many horses, necessary to haul the guns, also were casualties.

What was left of the battery retreated. Lieutenant Ames was not left on the field with the dead and dying. Plunked on an ammunition wagon, Ames endured the wild lurching of the vehicle as it was pulled across the broken ground to safety.

It was a long, agonizing journey back to Washington, but Adelbert Ames came from sturdy stock. The first Ames set foot in New England in 1634, and six generations later, Adelbert Ames was born on Halloween to Captain Jesse Ames and his wife Martha, in the rugged seaport of East Thomaston (soon to be Rockland). Mother Martha was related to the Perry line, which included such martial heroes as Oliver "We have met the enemy and they are ours" Perry of War of 1812 fame, and Matthew Perry, whose black ships "opened up Japan."

Jesse took young Del to sea on his schooner as a cabin boy; they sailed around the Horn, a rite of passage for any seafaring Mainer. Martha came along on some voyages, including one in 1846 taking corn to famine-ridden Ireland. On the voyage back to Rockland, family members took turns guarding the gold Captain Ames had received in payment.

Young Adelbert Ames picked up more than gold on his travels. He picked up a first-hand education in the real world to supplement the public-school education he had acquired in Maine. He saw slave markets in Southern ports, heard tales of the horror of slave ships, and shared the Ames family's disgust for the "peculiar institution." Relatives aided black fugitives from Dixie travelling the "Underground Railroad" in the antebellum years.

Yet it would be a mistake to think the boy was a fanatical opponent of slavery. Far from it. He was a tall, healthy lad, gifted with an analytical mind and a good-natured disposition—in some ways, a younger version of his Rockland contemporary "Hi" Berry. He had a special aptitude for math, liked to draw, and had a great love of music. His mother would later claim she kept Del home nights when he was an adolescent, away from the temptations and pitfalls of the waterfront, by the simple tactic of singing to her son. Adelbert Ames could never carry a tune himself—like Ulysses Grant, he would joke that he knew two tunes: one was "Yankee Doodle" and the other wasn't—but he appreciated music.

He also appreciated getting an education, and early set his sights on entering West Point. But he was twenty before, helped by an uncle with political pull, he secured appointment to the military academy. He took to it from the start and stood fifth in his class when the war clouds gathered. The Class of 1861 was rushed to graduation a month after Fort Sumter. Two months later Lieutenant Ames was fighting at Bull Run.

After being wounded, Ames spent a few weeks in a Washington hospital. Upon his release he was given command of a full battery of artillery. It was almost unprecedented for an officer of his limited experience to receive such a responsibility, he admitted, but "I shall show them I am equal to the task." His performance at Bull Run had not gone unnoticed (eventually he would receive the Congressional Medal of Honor for his gallantry there), and a proud Adelbert wrote home, "Ames' Battery will make a noise if I can have my way." But he was not to have his way until March of 1862, when he instructed gunners in the capital's defenses.

Then he was off to the Peninsula where, in May, he was sufficiently encouraged to write, "A successful battle here will soon terminate the war. I have no idea we shall be repulsed." Of course, he admitted, he had thought the same before Bull Run, but *this* time would be different.

It wasn't, but Adelbert Ames got a chance to make plenty of noise in the indecisive but bloody battles of the Army of the Potomac. At Malvern Hill, he fired 1,392 rounds into attacking Confederate infantry. It was going to be a long war. Command of a volunteer regiment, something he had not found attractive earlier, now seemed a more interesting possibility.

He would get command of the Twentieth Maine.

# Hiram Berry

*"It is conceded by all that my*
*brigade won the fight."*

It was Hiram Berry's biggest fault as a regimental commander, according to his old friend Elijah Walker. The big man
was simply "too tender-hearted." One example stuck in
Walker's memory. In camp one of the boys got "fighting
ugly." He positively refused to pipe down and go to his
quarters, so Walker, regimental officer of the day, tied his
wrists and left him, standing upright with no slack, tied to a
tree limb. When he promised to behave himself, Walker
would unstring the fellow. As soon as Walker had left the
spot, however, his victim screamed loudly enough to bring
Colonel Berry running out of his tent.

Berry took the suspended man in his arms, ordered
him cut loose, and bathed the man's wrists in his tent.
Walker got a scolding.

To Walker's thinking, this kind of soft-heartedness
made Berry an easy mark. It also made him a popular commander. Another story about him indicates he could impose
discipline, if in an unorthodox manner. After the Battle of
Bull Run, one of the privates made a great show of hobbling
about camp on a cane. Berry, going about the tents one
evening, discovered that the fellow's "principal disease was
black-leg." The allegedly lame private was playing cards.

"Hallo," said Colonel Berry, "how are you getting
along?"

"Oh, first-rate, Colonel," replied the limper. "I have won all this fellow's money, except what's on the board, and I think I'll take that." He flashed his hand to Berry. Clearly he was taking advantage of his unskilled prey.

Without another word, the Colonel grabbed the man's cane, broke it over his head, and ordered him on guard duty for the rest of the night. He got over his lameness soon thereafter.

Berry worked tirelessly at his military career. "I am here on stern duty," he wrote his wife in September, noting that his goal was to perform that duty "in a manner acceptable to my commander, myself, and those with whom I am immediately associated. I did not come here to make any political capital, nor do I again desire to hold a political position."

That month the Army of the Potomac got a new commander, the "Young Napoleon," George B. McClellan. Mac's policy of "masterly inactivity" meant months of monotonous camp life before the next campaign was launched in the Spring of 1862. This gave Berry plenty of time to build upon the reputation of the Fourth Maine, and incidentally, its commander. Vice President Hannibal Hamlin visited the camp, was mightily impressed, and would later tell the proud colonel that "my regiment is considered the very best in the Army of the Potomac." General Samuel Heintzelman, who had graduated from West Point in 1826, said the regiment "is the best he ever saw." By February of 1862 Berry wrote, "I have endeavored to study the art in which I am engaged, and so far have hit pretty near."

It was an opinion shared by his superiors. Berry was soon informed that he had been promoted to Brigadier General of Volunteers. "What pleased me most is that I was informed that I had earned my promotion by faithful duty, and good conduct at Bull Run," Berry told his wife. Vice

President Hamlin told Berry his appointment was not political, and Berry, a Democrat, was ready to believe that. He allowed that he had worked hard for his success, "more so than almost any man I know of."

He had help, and apparently none helped more than General Heintzelman, who himself had moved up to commander of the III Corps. He wanted Berry to serve under him. When Berry indicated he liked the looks of the Third Brigade of Hamilton's Division, the old warrior lobbied McClellan to award it to Berry. Mac was concerned that two of the brigades in the division were already headed by volunteer generals. The third brigade should have a regular army officer, he said, but Heintzelman pushed the issue until McClellan said, "Send General Berry to my quarters and let me look him over."

It was done, and within ten minutes Berry left McClellan's quarters with the order assigning him to command the Third Brigade in his pocket.

On March 25, 1862, Hiram Berry bade farewell to his old regiment "with much regret." He begged forgiveness if he had "in any way wounded the feelings of any," observing, "None are perfect and very few have more imperfections than myself." Command was handed over to Colonel Elijah Walker.

The Peninsula Campaign was soon underway. Instead of marching overland into Virginia, McClellan's Army of the Potomac was ferried to the tip of the James peninsula. From there it moved west up the narrow peninsula toward Richmond. Outside Yorktown, scene of American victory over the British in 1781, Berry reflected the widespread high hopes of the campaign when he wrote, "I think by July 1st the rebellion will be about played out." He was buoyed by news of Union victories in the West and confidence in McClellan. Yorktown was besieged when it was apparent that the Confederates meant to defend it, but Berry assumed it would ultimately be evacuated without a serious battle.

He was right, but when dawn of May 4 revealed abandoned Rebel positions, McClellan seemed at a loss. The methodical little general had planned to commence bombardment with heavy siege guns that had been laboriously brought up. When General Joseph Johnston, C.S.A., refused to hang around and be pulverized, Little Mac was without a plan. It was noon of May 4 before he set in motion some cavalry and two divisions to pursue the retreating Confederates. He did not personally accompany the pursuit because he was too involved in overseeing the organization of a Federal force that was supposed to land up the York River and try to cut off Johnston's army. That was Joe Johnston's biggest concern, and his main object was clearly to skedaddle up the peninsula before he could be flanked by water, and dig in outside Richmond.

The Battle of Williamsburg that ensued was an unplanned affair, intended by Johnston as only a rear-guard action to buy time for the bulk of his army to retreat. General James Longstreet, who always favored a good defensive position, was given one. In the area of Williamsburg, the peninsula narrows to only seven miles in width. A couple of streams, an earthen redoubt named Fort Magruder, and some smaller redoubts further narrowed the defensive perimeter to about three miles, and the slashing of a wide swath of timber before this line aided the defenders' field of fire. To add to the difficult situation, it started raining on the evening of May 4. It wouldn't stop raining for thirty hours.

Virginia mud was a key factor in the Civil War. It bogged down infantry and swallowed up artillery. "The mud in Virginia exceeds in depth and stickiness any I ever saw," Berry wrote. He thought he had seen mud in Rockland, but nothing like this. It "will fairly draw one's boots before giving way."

Now mud slowed the Federal pursuit, and the ineptitude of the senior Union officer, Edwin "Bull" Sumner, confused the situation. Hard-driving Joe Hooker, commanding one of Heintzelman's divisions, collided with the Confederates at dawn on May 5. For the next *nine hours* Hooker alone fought Longstreet's men. Hooker expected that Sumner, with 30,000 men of his II Corps in the immediate area, would support him. Instead, Sumner responded to Hooker's plea for help by directing Heintzelman to send in another division, which was located far from the battlefield.

The division called up included Berry's brigade of three Michigan regiments and one from New York. It had gained a new divisional commander, the fierce Phil Kearny. That Kearny was a warrior was immediately apparent from his missing left arm, lost at Churubusco in Mexico in 1847.

The colorful Kearny, who had inherited millions, preferred war to a career in business or law. He had fought with the elite French cavalry regiment, the *Chausseurs d'Afrique*, against the Berbers in North Africa. Combat there brought him "an indescribable pleasure."

With a commission in the U.S. Army procured with the aid of Winfield Scott himself, Kearny had fought Indians in the West; he was, after all, a nephew of the famed Stephen Kearny, commander of the crack First United States Dragoons.

On June 24, 1859, not content to be merely an American observer at the Battle of Solferino in Italy between French and Austrian armies, he entered the fray, leading a desperate French cavalry charge. For this fighting Phil was awarded his *second* Legion of Honor.

Berry's brigade was at the head of Kearny's column. When, by hard marching through the mud and rain, the brigade was seven miles from the battlefield, Berry could hear the guns. Another two miles, and his advance was blocked by Sumner's troops, clogging the road. While his orders appeared to require Berry to maintain his line of march, the new brigadier decided to depart from them, intent upon getting to the embattled Hooker. So he moved up along the side of the road, pushing aside Sumner's men. It was 10 a.m.

"Hearing heavy firing at the front and seeing that the troops that immediately preceded me moved very slowly—or at least it seemed slow to me—I resolved to push my brigade through to the front at all hazards," Berry later reported. Kearny, of course, encouraged him onward.

After about a mile and a half of this jostling progress, the brigadier sent his men, with artillery and ammunition train, down an alternate road. When this seemed to be leading them away from the battle, Berry had his men throw off their knapsacks and other cumbersome baggage. He led them toward the sound of the fighting through fields and forests, up and down ravines, and through marshes, until he came upon Hooker's battered, exhausted division.

Heintzelman was on the field. He had feared a defeat. Hooker had been pushed back and ammunition was running low. As one participant recalled, "the musketry fire sounded like the roll of a thousand drums, and the wet air was so laden with the battle smoke that foes could not be distinguished from friends fifty feet away." Old Sam Heintzelman saw the battle drifting away—until Berry's brigade emerged.

Almost tearful with joy, the Corps commander ordered the bands to play. Berry's men, answering with a cheer, moved double-quick to deploy in line of battle nearly a half mile long. The army hurrahed and Berry's men yelled, firing volley after volley at the rebels. It was 2:30 p.m.

General Kearny ordered an attack and Berry called "charge!" With a wild cheer, his brigade dashed forward with bayonets fixed. The ground was broken, visibility difficult, and the noise deafening. Enemy volleys left big gaps in the advancing Union line, but could not stop it.

By four o'clock, as the New York *Tribune* reported, the battle's "equilibrium" was restored. The other brigades of Kearny's division came up and joined the fighting.

Berry lost 299 officers and men at Williamsburg. After the battle, General Kearny wrote Maine's Governor Washburn, praising Berry's role. "General Berry charged with the left wing of our line of battle, evinced a courage that might have been expected from him (when as colonel of the Fourth Regiment of Maine Volunteers, he nearly saved the day at Bull Run) and also a genius for war, and a pertinacity in the fight that proved him fit for high command."

High praise indeed from a warrior like Phil Kearny.

Hiram Berry wrote on May 17, "It almost made my heart bleed to see so many of my men fall with each enemy volley. Still the object in view had to be accomplished, and by God's providence I was selected as the one to lead on the men, who saved our forces from defeat on that day."

"My clothes are somewhat torn with bullets; other than that I am all right," Berry confided to his wife. He had remained on horseback throughout the battle, while many officers and men were killed or wounded.

After the battle, McClellan had sent for him and, in Heintzelman's presence, the commanding general thanked and congratulated Berry. "It is conceded by him and by all that my brigade won the fight." This was important to hear, because in his first dispatches on the battle he never managed to arrive at, McClellan had given General Winfield Scott Hancock sole credit for the "victory."

Indeed, Hancock had, as one soldier would put it, "made a gallant little fight at a point distant from the main battlefield." If he had been supported, it might have been much more. Nobody really begrudged the gallant Hancock praise, but the press legend of "Hancock the Superb" overshadowed the effort of men who had marched and fought all day, and bore the bulk of casualties.

Those who were there knew Berry's record. It was a small battle, basically what Johnston had wanted: a well-fought delaying action. When the fighting ended that day, the lines were about where they were at dawn. The next morning Federal soldiers found the Confederate breastworks abandoned.

*Selden Connor served in the First Vermont and Seventh Maine before commanding the Nineteenth Maine—Maine State Archives*

# Selden Connor and Thomas Hyde

*" Boys aged very rapidly then."*

In September of 1860 Selden Connor cast his first presidential ballot, voting for the Republican ticket of Abraham Lincoln of Illinois and Hannibal Hamlin of Maine. The handsome, affable young man, born in the Martin Spring area of Fairfield in 1839, had graduated from Tufts College the previous year. He was bright, *Phi Beta Kappa,* and ambitious as well. In response to the urging of Tufts classmates, he moved to Vermont after the election to begin the study of law in the prestigious office of Washburn and March in Woodstock.

Connor heard the political rumbling from down South and, if he failed to detect in Woodstock "marked apprehension of an approaching cataclysm," he was sufficiently aroused to submit a poem, composed in fable form, to *Vanity Fair.* It described a vine hanging on an old oak tree, reading, in part,

One day the vine in anger said,
'My tendrils I'll untie,—
Alone, aloft I'll rear my head
And leave the oak to die.'

The winds were out, and strong they grew,
And hurtled through the air;
They whistled and blew the old oak through
And laid its branches bare.

The tempest ceased; its rage was o'er;
Gaily the sun did shine;
The sturdy oak stood as before,—
Low lay the lifeless vine.

The poem, really about South Carolina and the Union, was published in February, 1861. That month the Confederacy of Deep South states was organized as a provisional government. Yet Selden Connor would later say, in his characteristic facetious manner, that "the war cloud was not dark enough to cast any gloom on the cheerful pages of Blackstone, or to so darken the moon as to prevent sleighing, coasting and skating with the Vermont girls when opportunity offered itself." After Lincoln's inauguration in March, the young aspiring lawyer was primarily concerned with planning a summer vacation at Moosehead Lake. War seemed a remote possibility.

In April Fort Sumter was attacked and the administration called upon the states to raise 75,000 troops to suppress the Rebellion. Now, with boys surging up and down Woodstock's streets singing about hanging Jeff Davis from a sour apple tree, the study of law was comparably "dull music" for Selden Connor. "I try to read law, but fear that I do not fully apprehend the text as I turn the leaves over, for visions of 'bristling bayonets' and 'ensanguined fields' often blur the print," he conceded.

After quaintly writing home for his folks' permission, Connor enlisted in the "Woodstock Light Infantry." It was under the command of Captain Washburn, senior partner of Washburn and March. Connor would later analyze his reasons for signing up. Foremost was simple patriotism, a desire to avenge Fort Sumter and preserve the Union. He was no Abolitionist. He detested slavery but would not make civil war to end it. There was another impulse, secondary but powerful: Connor confessed he was eager to "vindicate the quality of Yankee manhood and courage," so long impugned by self-styled Southern sons of chivalry.

While Selden Connor never was tempted to participate in militia drill before 1861, he was strongly attracted to the "outdoor, Gypsy life of the soldier"; he felt he was "lining up" with the heroes of '76. And there was some curiosity, if not ardent longing, to "ascertain experimentally the sensation of facing death in battle." Lurking in his daydreams was a young man's longing for glory.

The little company of seventy-six men drilled frantically, aided by a cadet from the Vermont Military Academy. The next time Selden Connor would see the man was on July 1, 1863, at Gettysburg. But that was in a future unseen in the midst of preparation for a ninety-day war. Dan Stearns, a grocer from Skowhegan, Maine, a veteran of the Mexican War, said, "It makes me laugh to hear you boys talking of getting out after your three-months service. You'll find that when you have begun to follow the drum you will have to keep on just as long as the music holds out."

Following the drum, the company marched through the Green Mountains to Rutland, where it encamped with other units of the First Vermont Infantry Volunteer Regiment. Connor decided a morning dip in a nearby brook would get him in shape. Instead, he developed a severe cold that hung on for six months—twice the length of the First Vermont's existence. The steamer voyage to Fortress Monroe, Virginia, only made Connor sicker; the usually fragrant smells of tobacco smoke and coffee were transformed into "the vilest stenches imaginable." Sleeping arrangements were nonexistent and the boys were close to mutiny. Military life was not shaping up to be the romantic adventure Connor had daydreamed about.

Once ashore in Virginia, Connor quickly won popularity for his talents as barber and cook. In the latter capacity, he won praise for his brown bread and beanhole baked beans. "What do they think of us at Woodstock?" he wrote a friend there. "That we are a parcel of 'roughs' up to all manner of sin and ungodliness? I give you my private opinion that the members of the Co. on the whole act better *here* than they do *at home*. As for women, sins in that direction must be those of *contemplation* alone for man's counterpart is *wanting* to complete the sin."

In late May the First Vermont made a tentative reconnaissance and occupied Hampton. "The darkies were grinning as if they enjoyed the situation, and the white men looked very black and tried to put on an unconcerned air as if they did not see any Yankees." They did not have to see them long as, without any fighting, the Federals soon withdrew. A small version of a battle did occur on June 20 at Big Bethel, but Connor would recall more vividly a potshot by a Rebel officer on leave from a house the regiment passed. It perforated a sergeant's trousers. The Rebel got a kicking and his house was burned. When the First Vermont's three months were up, it had lost only five men. Mustered out at Brattleboro, over 500 of the "Boys of 1861" promptly reenlisted in other regiments.

Connor was one of them. A few weeks before being mustered out, he learned he had been chosen captain of a company being raised in Fairfield, Maine. He finished his hitch with the First Vermont, and learned he had been elected a major of the Seventh Maine. But so had Captain Tom Hyde of the company from Bath. The matter was resolved when Governor Washburn appointed Selden Connor Lieutenant Colonel of the regiment.

That was the way Connor recalled it. Hyde's recollection was a bit different. He was in camp at Augusta when he and other company officers were summoned to the Senate chamber in the State House. There, with the adjutant general presiding, they were called upon to elect their field officer. Tom Hyde proposed that they pick a colonel who was a regular officer, since "none of us knew much of the business." Somebody remembered seeing Captain Edwin Mason's name on a recruitment poster and he was chosen. A man from Kendall's Mills then piped up that Selden Connor was finishing his service with the First Vermont. He was promptly chosen Lieutenant Colonel. "We made no mistake there," Hyde recalled.

As for himself, Tom Hyde was elected Major of the Seventh Maine because he was the only person present with experience in drilling a company. Although thrilled, Hyde at first refused, until he was "almost forced" to assume a rank he knew he was not prepared for. "I did not know then that the principal duties of a major were to ride on the flank of the rear division, say nothing, look as well as possible, and long for promotion," Hyde wrote.

Thomas Hyde, scion of a wealthy and politically connected Bath family, was another young man who saw war as something of a lark in the summer of 1861. It is not surprising that he and Connor became close friends. But Hyde's perspective was that of someone close to events. In 1860 he left Bowdoin College for "the Western Wilds" of Chicago at the invitation of J. Young Scammon.

Scammon, a prominent lawyer and politician, wanted Tom Hyde to take his senior year with the new University of Chicago (so new and fledgling that his class would be made up of three students). It was at Scammon's house, where young Hyde stayed, that Abraham Lincoln first met his Vice President Hannibal Hamlin. Lincoln usually stopped there when in Chicago; after Hamlin departed, Hyde heard Lincoln comment, "Well, Hamlin isn't half so black as he is painted, is he, Scammon?" The swarthy Mainer was rumored to be a mulatto by Southern opponents of the "Black Republican" candidate.

In the weeks after Lincoln's election, Hyde saw a lot of Lincoln. Indeed, he helped sort through the president-elect's mail. Some boxes from nonadmirers contained black dolls and dead rattlesnakes. "Whenever a box looked particularly suspicious, we used to soak it in water, fearing some infernal machine," Hyde remembered.

Invited to join the Lincolns on their journey east to Washington, Hyde demurred in order to complete his studies. When news of war came back to Chicago, Tom Hyde joined the local unit of Zouaves. Hearing of the attack on Massachusetts troops marching through Baltimore, the excited youth crowed that he would give five years of his life if he could march a regiment through that city!

His wish would be fulfilled sooner than Hyde expected. "Events were hurrying swiftly, and boys aged very rapidly then," he recalled many years after the Civil War. Like Connor back east, Hyde burned to perform martial deeds in the tradition of his Revolutionary forebears. When he heard of the departure of many of his Bath friends to the front with the Third Maine, he could wait no longer. Receiving permission to get his degree early, he skipped commencement and hurried back to Maine.

The initial excitement seemed to have cooled in Maine; many people believed the war would soon be over. Thomas Hyde spent a few weeks at Bowdoin, teaching the elaborate Zouave drill. He "directed as skirmishers many future generals and colonels down Main Street to capture the Topsham bridge." One may have been a professor named Chamberlain.

A dejected Hyde went back to Bath, convinced martial glory had passed him by. He was moping around the family mansion when a neighbor shouted the news of the Union defeat at Bull Run.

Hyde was reinvigorated. The war would continue, more troops would be needed, and Hyde, with three friends, including the son of Senator William Fessenden, went to an attorney's office to be sworn into the nation's service. The next day Hyde was off to Augusta, where he obtained papers to set up recruitment of a company called the Harding Zouaves.

Although the office that Hyde and H. S. Hagar opened on Bath's busy Front Street had only one chair and a table, recruitment was brisk. Hyde was soon back at the capital with Company D of the Seventh Maine. He was elected major and, with Mason's colonelcy not accepted yet by the War Department and Connor finishing his hitch with the First Vermont, it was Hyde who led the Seventh to the front.

Hyde got his wish to parade a regiment through Baltimore. Unfortunately no ammunition had been issued to the Seventh, and the parade was made with only one revolver with cartridges. Bayonets proved unnecessary but the camp in a beer garden had predictable results. A drunken riot was put down by using the one loaded pistol, and the regiment marched back across town, the band tooting "Yankee Doodle," to a better site called Camp Patterson. Hyde and other young officers went out nightly to serenade Maryland's equally young girls. Strolling back after these interludes "by moonlight in the soft, flower-scented Southern air, it seemed as if soldiering was a very good business."

Hyde had plenty of time to enjoy himself. The arrival of Lieutenant Colonel Connor and Governor Washburn's choice to take the place of the unfortunate Mason, Colonel Thomas Marshall of Belfast, relieved Hyde of the anxieties and responsibilities of regimental command.

---

Hyde found Washington a "shambling, straggling, dirty, and forlorn place," one that seemed "hardly worth fighting for." In the Spring of 1862, however, the Seventh Maine was sent across the Potomac. On the picket line Hyde shot with his revolver—by now it was not the only weapon of the regiment with live rounds!—the only Virginians he claimed he killed during the war. He reported that the opossums, cooked in a kettle, tasted "fairly good."

"I enjoy this kind of life immensely," he wrote in March of 1862. "We expect to be in Richmond in a fortnight." Transported to the James Peninsula, his regiment's skirmishers were the first to make contact with Confederates at Yorktown. A Rebel shell whistled in and cut a soldier in two. The dismembered man used to work for Hyde's family in Bath. Now he was the first man Major Hyde saw killed in action. Burying Joe Pepper's remains that night, Hyde pulled the dead man's wife's picture from a bloody pocket. For a moment the horror struck him so forcefully that he thought he would give anything to get out of the Army.

After this small baptism of fire, Hyde received a more intense exposure to combat at Williamsburg. The Seventh Maine was part of General Hancock's command on the Union right in that incredibly uncoordinated action. Lying flat on the ground at the crest of a hill, the Mainers watched rebels chase Federal troops across a plowed field. Hancock rode up and ordered the Seventh to charge. Selden Connor wrote that the Maine boys made "a terrible yell" as they jumped up and loosed a volley into the enemy, followed by a steady fire. "It was an ecstasy of excitement for a moment," Thomas Hyde remembered.

The Confederates were tired from running across rough ground. Under the impact of the diagonal fire they "seemed to dissolve all at once into a quivering and disintegrating mass and to scatter in all directions," Hyde wrote. The Confederates, Connor said, fell like tenpins in a row.

At day's end, Major Hyde walked over the ground littered with disfigured and bloating corpses. He was trying to develop a tough skin. It took some learning at this early stage of the war. He and Connor sat on cracker boxes in the mud, huddled in rubber blankets against the rain, talking, unable to sleep. Connor spun stories and recited poetry. The boy-men talked through the night. The faces of the dead glowed phosphorescent in the flickering reflection of watchfires, adding a weird backdrop to their conversation.

It was not always so bad. On a later moonlit Virginia night, as the Army of the Potomac encamped after another day's creeping advance toward Richmond, Connor and Hyde spied a distant mansion from the picket line. The sight of that stately building gripped the young bucks with a "spirit of adventure," and they slipped out of camp and galloped several miles to the mansion. They were, of course, within Rebel territory, but counted on the enemy being asleep.

Riding up a long avenue overarched by elms, Connor and Hyde left their horses at the veranda with an orderly. They proceeded to explore the mansion. The half-packed trunks scattered about testified to the haste in which the occupants had fled.

"We lighted candles and explored the grand old rooms, looking at ourselves in the ancient pier glasses, and made acquaintance, in its sadness and desolation, of a Virginia homestead of the olden time when the county families vied with the nobility of the England from whence they came," Hyde mused. Trembling, a black butler materialized to serve the Union officers Madiera from "quaint decanters."

A snoring sound led them to the third floor, expecting to capture a slumbering Rebel general. Instead they rousted a Federal signal officer who had gotten lost, and had decided to spend the night at the deserted mansion.

Connor and Hyde loaded their horses with bottles of Madiera and other mementos. While perusing some books in the library, they were alerted by black servants, acting as sentinels, that the enemy approached. They galloped back to their lines. As Hyde put it, "Such little episodes sweetened the usual grind of campaigning."

Then it was back to war. Four miles from Richmond, the Seventh Maine came under heavy fire. Colonel Mason, who had finally replaced the sickly Marshall, tumbled into some bushes, along with his horse, when a Rebel artillery round landed beside him. The pale colonel told Hyde to assume command in Connor's absence, which he did until the lieutenant colonel arrived on the scene. A cannon ball grazed Hyde, knocking him over. By the time he regained his footing, the Rebels were scurrying away. General McClellan rode up and called the little fight a "dashing affair."

"I suppose people think one goes into a fight as the picture books have it," Hyde wrote his family. "I was blacked with smoke, my trousers were all caked with mud, my sword rusty, and I wet to the skin."

And this, Tom Hyde realized, was only the prelude to the *real* fighting to come. War was an odd juxtaposition of romance and the macabre, the scales constantly shifting back and forth. The ambivalence of mood exhibited by young soldiers like Connor and Hyde was reflected in the experience of thousands of others.

On the Peninsula in the Spring of 1862 there were soldiers whose "hearts were not then so eaten out by the fear of death long delayed. The best and the bravest who were to fall on so many fields were then with us," wrote Hyde.

# Neal Dow

*"I have long since knocked my
broad-brim into a cocked hat."*

When the Civil War began, Neal Dow of Portland was the
most famous person from Maine to command a regiment.
He was also perhaps the most inexperienced. He defined the
term "political general" when, without any combat experience, he was promoted to brigadier general.

*Neal Dow's Army sash, hat, gloves and epaulets on desk where he wrote
the "Maine Law"—Neal Dow Memorial, photograph by author*

But, with enlistments lagging in the fall of 1861, Governor Washburn made it clear to Dow in a State House meeting that he was counting on the "Napoleon of Temperance" to draw teetotalers to the colors. He could have the command of the Thirteenth Maine if he wanted it.

And Neal Dow wanted it. By 1861, he was a most controversial fellow looking for a way to refurbish his reputation. With curly brown hair going gray, penetrating eyes, a sharp nose, and thin, tightly compressed lips, Neal Dow looked like the moralistic reform zealot he was. A tireless and abrasive advocate of prohibition, Dow was the driving force behind the enactment of the "Maine Law" outlawing the sale of liquor in 1851. In 1855, as the "Cold Water Mayor" of Portland, Dow made himself more unpopular than usual by his heavy-handed use of force to quell a riot. Three years later, he managed to get elected to the State Legislature, and was preparing to run for Governor when his business dealings with a State Treasurer caught defrauding the state muddied Dow and lost him his political base. When war came Dow, an Abolitionist and Republican, was ready to leave Maine's political wars for warfare—and the opportunity of military glory—down South.

Neal Dow was 57 in 1861, long in the tooth to play soldier, but he vetoed his eldest son Fred's desire to enlist. With the death of the family patriarch, Josiah, at the ripe old age of 94, Fred's place was to manage the business ledgers of the highly profitable tannery Josiah had established. Neal Dow, who was a bank director, as well as the director of a railroad company and president of a gaslight business, used his considerable connections with Portland bankers to raise a $250,000 loan to the state to aid in raising volunteer regiments.

Aside from the honorary title of Colonel bestowed during the Aroostook War period, and ordering city militia to fire on rioters in 1855, Dow's only military knowledge came from books. He made sure the field officers of the Thirteenth Maine were men from Maine regiments with real experience of war. Dow's fame as a teetotaling crusader quickly attracted a regiment that would gain an instant reputation for its sobriety. Recruits in other regiments encamped near the capitol in Augusta would, when arrested for drunkenness, loudly proclaim they belonged to the Thirteenth Maine and any fool knew no soldier of "Neal Dow's regiment" would ever get drunk!

The Thirteenth Maine set up its tents on the grounds of the U.S. Arsenal in two feet of snow in December, 1862, and drilled on the frozen Kennebec River. Before departing Augusta in February, the regiment actually repelled a cavalry "charge." The boys were lined up before the capitol steps listening to a flag presentation when Colonel John Goddard's First Maine Cavalry Regiment started parading between the Thirteenth Maine and the presentation speaker. This struck Dow as rather rude behavior and he motioned for the cavalry troop to halt. When it refused, the feisty little man ordered the Thirteenth Maine to fix bayonets and block the horse soldiers' passage. Colonel Goddard swore blue thunder, but the horses shied away from contact with the bayonets. Later, in better humor, Goddard, a lumberman from Cape Elizabeth, told Neal Dow that was the *only* time enemy bayonets had broken a "charge" of his unit.

The Thirteenth Maine was ordered to report to the command of General Ben Butler, a Massachusetts politician who had gained more military experience than Dow during the war's early months. Butler had been commissioned to lead Army forces in an expedition with the Navy to seize New Orleans. Enroute to Boston, Colonel Dow, astride his favorite horse "Billy," decked out in blue uniform and brass buttons, was actually cheered at Portland's City Hall, where a few years earlier he had ordered nervous militiamen to shoot rioters. Along with a fancy dress sword, he was awarded a handsome pair of revolvers.

As he handed the big guns to the little colonel, Reverend Henry Moore said, "It is a striking commentary on the times that I, a minister of the gospel of peace, should present to you, the son of a Quaker, these weapons of carnal warfare."

"I have long since knocked my broad-brim into a cocked hat," Dow replied. That was an understatement. He had long ago been shunned by the Society of Friends.

Outwardly confident, the colonel privately pleaded for political strings to be pulled in order to transfer his command from Butler's expedition to the Army of the Potomac. Dow knew Butler's reputation as a partisan Democrat who had supported the proslavery Democrat John C. Breckinridge for president in 1860. Despite Butler's subsequent Union activity, Dow suspected they would never get along.

Their first meeting confirmed Dow's fear. Four companies of the Thirteenth Maine were crammed aboard the steamer *Mississippi* with the entire Thirty-First Massachusetts at Boston. The ship, with about 1,600 men aboard, packed in tiers of bunks like sardines, set sail for Fortress Monroe, Virginia, where General Butler awaited. The *Mississippi* arrived on a fine May morning, greeted by a cool breeze and fluttering seabirds. The pleasant scene evaporated as soon as Butler and his staff clambered aboard. The general, Dow wrote his wife, was "in a very bad temper, and made a fool of himself." Dow was the subject of Butler's verbal ugliness. Squat and cockeyed, with stringy hair hardly covering a prominent bald head, and a fat cigar habitually protruding out from under a curved mustache, Butler was bound to look repulsive to the clean-shaven, physically fit Dow.

---

Dow had, according to the Thirteenth Maine's surgeon Seth Gordon, "an eye to the creature comforts at sea, as well as on shore," and the colonel had made use of Butler's stateroom. Finding Dow's pants decorating the room irritated Butler mightily, and he snapped, "Orderly, tell Colonel Dow to report to me."

Dow "tiptoed" up to Butler and saluted. "General Butler, I have the honor to report," he said.

"I understand you have been occupying my stateroom from Boston," the general snarled, as only Butler could snarl. "Get your things out of there damned quick and then apologize."

The chaplain, Reverend Moore (who had presented Dow his "carnal weapons" in Portland), cowered nearby with the surgeon, exclaiming, "Doctor, he is an awful man." It was a sentiment Dow shared; he considered resigning.

The *Mississippi* had not been out to sea long when a real storm overshadowed the personal one brewing between the two political soldiers. A howling wind blew up a gale and enormous waves smashed against the vessel, surging over the deck and spilling into the crowded hold. The hatches were unsecured to allow some ventilation for the men suffocating below. Now the water posed a threat to the furnaces. To increase the confusion, shot and shell packed aboard smashed loose and rolled about, collapsing the teetering bunks of many soldiers. Most of the men were landlubbers who were, as Reverend Moore wrote, "in momentary expectation of going to the bottom."

The fear was justified as the ship steadily took on water. Dow, no mariner himself, had men in the Thirteenth Maine who were old salts. He volunteered their services, and Butler immediately gave his profane blessing. The Maine boys moved easily, even cheerfully, about the pitching deck closing the hatches and rigging up a windsail by one hatch to allow minimal air for the scared, seasick, angry men below. Then the Thirteenth Mainers set up a bucket crew to bail out the waterlogged *Mississippi*. After hours of slipping and sliding on slick decks through the roaring night, they gained an upper hand on the rising water. The storm was weathered and the bucket crew more than earned the three lusty cheers it got for its work.

A day later another disaster threatened. In broad daylight, off Cape Fear light, with buoys clearly marking the channel, the *Mississippi* nevertheless set a course straight for the deadly (and well-known) Frying Pan Shoal. The captain would later argue that so many rifles stowed on the ship had disoriented the compass. Since the ship was no less than 100 miles off course and in clear view of the landmarks mentioned, this explanation did not hold much water. Indeed, one of the Thirteenth Mainers scrambled to the pilothouse to warn the officer that the shoal was dead ahead.

"You will be on there in half an hour on this course," the man said. "If you don't believe me, go and see how the propeller is stirring up the sand." He was told to mind his business. The *Mississippi* then proceeded to run aground.

Any apprentice sailor knew it would be stupid to drop anchor at this time, but that was done. Predictably the anchor stove a gaping hole in the ship's bow. Once again, water poured into the hapless vessel, as men scurried to plug the hole.

If any kind of wind or heavy sea developed, the stranded ship would be smashed to pieces. To lighten her enough to get loose, the four companies of the Thirteenth Maine were transferred to the gunboat *Mount Vernon,* which prudently stood off a mile from Frying Pan Shoal. When Reverend Moore tried to join the boats of soldiers setting off for the gunboat, Butler bellowed, "Here, you long-haired chaplain, come back, if we are going down we want you to pray for us." After awhile, the general relented. Once the rattled clergyman was aboard the *Mount Vernon*, he promptly wrote out his resignation from military duty. The Thirteenth Maine had to make do without a chaplain for a few months.

Dow remained on the *Mississippi* until it was dislodged. Its forward compartment flooded, the vessel briefly anchored off Cape Fear. Rebel soldiers in a mud fort scurried about in anticipation of trouble. They need not have worried. As Dow noted, "we were in no condition to fight even a fishing smack armed with a rifled twelve pounder." There were no appropriate shells for the one cannon aboard the *Mississippi*. At Port Royal, South Carolina, his troops rejoined Dow aboard the steamer. The remainder of the voyage to the Gulf of Mexico was uneventful.

On March 20, 1862, Dow and his regiment reached Ship Island. Ten miles offshore from the Confederate state of Mississippi and sixty-five miles due east from New Orleans, it was a sandbar seven miles long and averaging a quarter mile in width. At high tide, half of the island was submerged. This was the rendezvous point and staging area for the planned assault on New Orleans.

The Fourteenth Maine was one of the other regiments on Ship Island, and Algernon Miller of the Fourteenth described the island as "a miserable place. There was no drinking water, except what we got by digging holes in the sand and letting the sea filter through. It was awful to drink." The sand fleas attacked with a vengeance. "You would itch and burn and never see a thing, they were such tiny things," Miller lamented.

It was quite a change for Maine soldiers who had left Augusta with the temperature stuck at zero to be plunked under the broiling Gulf sun, with spoiled rations and with sanitary conditions aptly described as "most lamentable."

Epidemics of typhoid and diphtheria threatened. In such an unhealthy and monotonous place "the utmost exertions were required to prevent universal despondency and discontent." Suicides mounted.

Neal Dow could have made use of a chaplain at this point. He passed the time drilling his troops and writing letters to newspapers about how the war would emancipate the slaves. When Butler went off to join Farragut in taking New Orleans, Colonel Dow was left on Ship Island. It was a deliberate slight as far as he was concerned. He continued his own war on slavery by encouraging slaves to flee to his island domain.

When slaveholders complained, Dow was unmoved. "Doubtless some of our friends will hold me heartless because I do not shed tears of sympathy for those who have lost such a valuable piece of property," he wrote home, "and say I am wrong not to issue orders which would be more agreeable to the 'massa' than to the slave." Well before emancipation was the policy of the Lincoln administration, Dow, on his own initiative, was pushing Abolitionism and gaining a Southern reputation as a "nigger thief." He considered it a compliment.

He also continued to pursue temperance, now with military power to enforce his will. "How I wish I had the Maine Rumsellers out here, driving their trade," he exulted. "Wouldn't I fix them nicely and properly!" For decades Neal Dow had relied on his power of persuasion. He enjoyed the ability to rely upon power alone.

# Oliver Otis Howard

*"I was surprised to find the
heavy burden was gone."*

A more sympathetic picture of Oliver Otis Howard comes
from the diary of a nurse, Amy Morris Bradley. The plain
but pious Miss Bradley, from Vassalborough, Maine, was
impressed with the Colonel from the first time she met him.
It was in his tent with the brigade surgeon and some other
nurses, and the little group had lunch. When Howard
"meekly bowed his head and asked our Father's blessing
upon the food before us," Miss Bradley thought this was
hardly the rough camp life she had expected. "And, I said,
'No, this reminds me of a camp meeting only more quiet.' "

About this time Howard learned that a sutler was
selling booze, and within five minutes he had booted the
wretch out of camp. Miss Bradley noted, "He may make enemies by being so strict, but in the end the moral courage
which he manifests will be appreciated."

Maybe, but when Howard got the coveted commission
of a brigadier general, the regiment was probably as glad to
see him go as he was to leave. He fired off a farewell address
which acknowledged the Third Regiment was owed much
for his own "worldly notice and position." His critic,
Sergeant Small, conceded Howard "had set us a brave example in battle and otherwise had led us ably enough, but
his vanity and cold piety had wearied and repelled us."

Howard gave Amy Bradley a lock of hair, a Victorian token of friendship. The thick ash-brown lock had threads of silver.

His new command was a brigade made up of regiments from New York, Pennsylvania, New Hampshire and Rhode Island. It was part of Richardson's division in Sumner's II Corps. Howard had a knack for befriending superior officers, if not enlisted men. He was sympathetic to General McClellan, but experienced "considerable impatience" with Mac's ponderous siege of Yorktown. He broke up the monotony of April 1862 with visits to hospitals, where he prayed, read the Bible, and loaned religious tracts to patients.

His brigade arrived upon the battlefield after the vicious fight at Williamsburg was over. Walking amongst the dead and dying, he came upon the covered corpse of a Federal soldier, resting in apparent peace beside the uncared-for body of a Confederate. The general wished the boy in gray had also been covered, and thought, "May God hasten us to the close of such a war!"

But the Civil War was moving toward greater ferocity. When the Army of the Potomac finally reached the outskirts of Richmond, the woodsy terrain was bisected by the Chickahominy. Normally not much more than a creek, steady rainfall had transformed it into a swollen river. Johnston saw an opportunity to pounce on part of the Union force south of the river, and did so on May 31, starting a battle known as either Seven Pines (Confederate name) or Fair Oaks (Union). Either way, like many Civil War battles, it was fought in and around woods.

General Sumner had foreseen such a possibility and had detailed some of his men previously to build bridges across the rising Chickahominy. To hasten the work, "Bull" gave the workers a barrel of whisky. Predictably, Howard objected; it was not good for the men's health. "Yes, general, you are right," Sumner replied, "but it is like pitch on fire which gets speed out of an engine though it blows out the boiler."

When the Confederates pounced on May 31, the rickety bridges were vital. The Federal forces were badly pummeled. Even the timely arrival of Kearny's division with Berry's brigade again in the lead could not reprise their success at Williamsburg. Sumner's Corps, finally ordered across the Chickahominy, helped stabilize what had been a potential Union defeat into stalemate by sunset.

The next day, June 1, was a Sunday. Again Howard would have to make war on the Sabbath. Skirmishing began at five o'clock in the morning, and, through the day, fighting broke out in violent spasms at different points along the front.

When the Rebels appeared on the verge of punching a hole through an area held by Richardson's division, Howard's brigade was called up to stem the Virginians. A heavy roll of musketry pelted Howard's force as it started to advance through the trees, hitting Howard's brown horse. He dismounted, awaited another, and yelled at his inexperienced men to "Lie down!"

As soon as another horse, a big gray, was brought up, Howard swung into the saddle, and ordered his men up and "Forward!"

About the time Howard reached the embattled Union line, a Confederate ball wounded his right forearm. His brother Charles, his aide, was riding a "zebra" horse Howard was very fond of; it was also shot dead. Charlie ran up to him and bound his arm with a handkerchief. Unfazed, General Howard continued to press the attack.

Moving over uneven ground, the brigade came upon a bunch of abandoned Union tents at the Seven Pines crossroads. The retreating Confederates had stopped to use the tents for shelter, halting Howard's men with volleys fired at a distance of 35 yards.

At 10:30 a.m. Howard's new horse's left foreleg was broken; apparently simultaneously Howard was wounded again in the same right arm. This time his elbow was shattered. In the excitement of combat, he was not aware that he had been hit again until a lieutenant from one of his New York regiments ran up to him. "General, you shall not be killed," the man exclaimed as he pulled Howard from his crippled horse. A moment later the lieutenant fell dead himself.

Slipping in and out of consciousness, Howard asked Colonel Francis Barlow to assume command. The Rebels soon fell back, but not before mounting a serious flank attack blunted by Howard's old regiment, the Third Maine.

Luckily for Howard, Surgeon Gabriel Grant was working on wounded men near a large stump, oblivious to bullets whizzing about like upset hornets. Grant bound Howard's arm. He bound it so tightly the tourniquet caused great discomfort, but staunched the flow of blood.

Charlie Howard, who had been missing, showed up, shot in the thigh, limping along with his empty scabbard making do for a cane. A fox skin that had been on his saddle was now draped over his free arm. No getting around it: Charles Howard cut a ludicrous figure.

Oliver Otis Howard could not help asking, "Why weary yourself, Charlie, with that robe?"

"To cover me up if I should have to stop," he replied.

Howard thought that was O.K.

The surgeon dressed Charlie's wound, and had him placed in a stretcher, to be hustled off the battlefield.

Howard preferred to walk. Another wounded soldier helped the general along, and about 11:00 p.m. they reached a house a half mile north of Fair Oaks Station. Here another surgeon looked at Howard's arm, ascertained that it was broken, and had Howard placed on a double bed squeezed into the hut of a black couple. The aged blacks were terrified, apparently afraid "some of us might discover and seize hidden treasure which was in that bed."

Howard's brigade surgeon arrived. The arm had to be amputated, Dr. Palmer said.

"All right, go ahead. Happy to lose only my arm," Howard said.

"Not before 5:00 a.m., general."

"Why not?"

"Reaction must set in."

Thus Howard waited another *six* hours before the surgeon returned with four soldiers who again plunked him on a stretcher. They transported him to "a place a little grewsome withal from arms, legs, and hands not yet carried off, and poor fellows with anxious eyes waiting their turn."

Dr. Grant, back from his battlefield labors for which he would be awarded the Medal of Honor, loosened Howard's tourniquet. Gas and chloroform were administered, and Howard drifted into unconsciousness.

When he awoke, he was "surprised to find the heavy burden was gone," Dr. Palmer having removed his arm above the elbow.

The next day Howard and his brother were preparing to depart in an ambulance when General Phil Kearny and his staff trotted up. Kearny, his left arm lost in Mexico, grasped Howard's left hand with his right.

"General, I am sorry for you," he said, "but you must not mind it; the ladies will not think the less of you."

Showing humor not usually detected, Howard replied, "There is one thing that we can do, general, we can buy our gloves together."

# Joshua Chamberlain
## *"I feel now like laying aside words for deeds."*

In August of 1861 Professor Chamberlain, appointed to teach Modern Languages, was granted a two-year paid leave to study in Europe. It was similar to the sabbatical Longfellow had once been awarded. But Chamberlain delayed his acceptance of this academic plum. He would travel, but not to Europe.

1861 was a hard year for the nation; it was hell for Joshua Chamberlain. Still trying to come to terms with the loss of little Emily, Chamberlain saw his brother Horace sicken and die. Horace was closest to him of his brothers, both in age and personality. Horace was his great confidante, a brilliant, sensitive young man with a promising legal career and young wife. But he was stricken with tuberculosis; Chamberlain was at his brother's side the final three weeks. The death of Horace was crushing. Joshua wrote his sister Sae (who would take Horace's place as the sibling to whom Joshua poured out his feelings) that "one of the greatest sources of pleasure in this world was sealed up."

Horace died on Joshua and Fannie's sixth wedding anniversary. Fannie was in poor shape. The only surviving letter from Chamberlain in 1861 in Bowdoin's collection today is addressed to youngest brother Tom. Unlike his other brothers, Tom did not follow him to Bowdoin; he was a storekeeper. Joshua wrote Tom requesting a keg of "Portsmouth" ale for his ailing wife. Fannie was afflicted with terrible headaches and had lost much weight. Joshua explained his request. He wanted to "see if I can't put a little flesh onto Fanny's cheeks, she is thin as a shadow." More than ale was needed to aid the depressed woman. Chamberlain spent a lot of time at his on-campus study.

But it was difficult to concentrate on grading mindless themes, preparing lectures, and fighting dreary academic political battles when real battles raged down South. In September of 1861 he turned 33. Chamberlain's hair was turning gray. He watched the student drills of the Bowdoin Guards and the Bowdoin Zouaves, saw former and present students enter the ranks, corresponded with boys once in his classrooms now at the front.

And then he walked back to the less than happy home on Potter Street.

The winter of 1861–1862 was a turning point in Chamberlain's life. Nerved-up, depressed, frustrated, he uncharacteristically complained about his aches and pains. Joshua badly needed an outlet for his pent-up emotions. Whatever the state of his union, he would act to help save the Union.

He was giving speeches urging others to action. The fragmentary notes for these exhortations that survive tell much about his own state of mind. Admitting he was a man of words, the professor said, "I feel now like laying aside words for deeds."

It no longer mattered what people thought about the origins or conduct of the war. It did not matter what one's opinion was of the Lincoln administration. The war was a reality and could only be ended by "a swift and strong hand. Gentlemen may cry peace, peace, but there is no peace." We are fighting, Chamberlain said, for our country and our flag, "fighting to settle the question whether we are a nation, or only *a basket of chips*."

"Come out from your shady retreats," Chamberlain entreated. Clearly he was mentally ready to leave his.

He accepted the leave to study abroad. Intending to use the time to go elsewhere, he then telegraphed Governor Washburn: "I have a leave of absence for two years to visit Europe, but wish to know whether I have a country. Can you make any use for me?"

Washburn shot off a reply. "Come and see me. I am organizing a regiment."

It was the Twentieth Maine.

The professor had also written the governor. On July 14, 1862, he stated, somewhat pompously: "Perhaps it is not quite necessary to inform your Excellency who I am. I believe you will be satisfied with my antecedents. I am a son of Joshua Chamberlain of Brewer. For seven years past I have been Professor in Bowdoin College. I have always been interested in military matters, and what I do not know in that line *I know how to learn.*"

"Nearly a hundred of those who have been my pupils, are now officers in our army. I do not want to be the last in the field, if it can possibly be helped," Chamberlain wrote. In another letter, he claimed he could raise a thousand men in short order.

All of this maneuvering Chamberlain performed without telling his wife, family, or the College. The secret, however, was out in the press even before Chamberlain was formally tendered a commission by Washburn. In a July 22 letter to Washburn, Chamberlain insisted he had only discussed his plans with General Howard as he stopped in Brunswick en route back to the front.

There is no record of his wife and family's reaction, although it can easily be imagined. There is evidence of the reaction of the College. Professor William Smythe told Chamberlain point-blank the only glory that awaited the professor in the Army was the possibility of being killed or so "shattered" he would be of no further use to Bowdoin.

**Pride of Lions**

Smythe and other faculty protested against Chamberlain's commission to the governor. And Attorney General Drummond wrote Washburn, "Have you app'td Chamberlain Col. of 20th? His old classmates here say you have been deceived; that C. is *nothing* at all; that is the universal expression of those who know him."

Chamberlain would later describe the source of the faculty's opposition. To professors like Smythe, he said, he was viewed as a pawn in the conservatives' campaign to keep out potential Unitarians from department chairs. That Smythe's stated reason was sincere he did not concede. At the time, in yet another missive to Washburn, he simply stated, "I regret that I am obliged to act against the wishes of my colleagues, but I feel that I can make no other decision."

Washburn was not influenced by Chamberlain's critics. He sent the professor his commission as Lieutenant Colonel of the Twentieth Maine Volunteer Infantry Regiment. He had offered him the colonelcy, but Chamberlain demurred. He preferred to be Lieutenant Colonel and learn the trade of war.

The College accepted his *fait accompli.*

He was to have a first-rate teacher. Lieutenant Adelbert Ames of the Regular Army was commissioned Colonel.

On September 1, 1862, the citizens of what Chamberlain privately called "this slow town" of Brunswick presented him with a token of their esteem: a magnificent gray stallion, dappled white, known as "the Staples horse." He christened the stead "Prince." Chamberlain was on his way to glory.

And a shattering wound.

*Adelbert Ames—Maine State Archives*

# Adelbert Ames

## *"This is a hell of a Regiment!"*

The Twentieth Maine was made up of the "leftovers" from
the Sixteenth, Seventeenth, Eighteenth and Nineteenth
Maine Regiments. So many Mainers had answered the government's call for 300,000 more volunteers in 1862, that there
was a spillover, which was pulled together to constitute
Maine's last three-year regiment organized that year. All
told, there were 979 men, a trifle short of Chamberlain's
promised 1,000. They came from ten of Maine's counties.
Farmers, fishermen, lumbermen, mechanics and laborers,
most did not come from the state's larger towns and cities.
There was a decidedly rural, "native-stock" predominance,
even more than usual for a Maine regiment.

By mid-August they had assembled at Camp Mason,
near Portland, the biggest city most of them had seen. Four
companies came from coastal towns, another four were fresh
from the farmlands of south-central and western Maine.
Two, Companies B and H, hailed from the tall-tree environs
of Piscataquis and Aroostook Counties.

Major Charles Gilmore greeted them. He had commanded a company of the Seventh Maine, which made the
Bangor man unique among the officers. He had fought on
the Peninsula in Virginia, and had actual knowledge of what
war was. He set about instilling some sense of order in a decidedly disorderly camp. His independent-minded charges
had no sense of military discipline, not even from militia
musters, which had declined drastically since the time of the

bloodless Aroostook War affair. Captain Ellis Spear, recently a schoolmaster in Wiscasset, admitted he "scarcely knew a line of battle from a rail fence."

The Company G captain was typical. Other officers included such neophytes as Adjutant John M. Brown, a Portland lawyer, Bowdoin Class of '60, and Quartermaster Sergeant Tom Chamberlain, hardly a scholar, whose main experience was in running, sort of, a country store.

Lieutenant Colonel Joshua Chamberlain had a first-rate, but fearsome, instructor. On August 21 Lieutenant Adelbert Ames got leave from the Regulars to accept command of the regiment. His initial reaction when he arrived at Camp Mason: "This is a hell of a Regiment!" Except for Gilmore, *nobody* seemed to have the foggiest idea of what they were getting into.

And there was precious little time even to try to get the green boys into shape. The Twentieth Maine was officially mustered in on August 29, the day Lee set about whipping the Union again at Second Bull Run. The Twentieth was ordered south at once.

On September 1, Fannie showed up at camp, with the Rev. Adams, to see Joshua and his regiment off. They spent a rainy, windswept night in Chamberlain's tent. Chamberlain's own father was not there. Always a staunch supporter of states rights, the elder Chamberlain, whatever his feelings on slavery, did not believe a bloody war to keep the Southern states in the Union was justified. He wrote his soldier son, "This is not *our war.*"

But Joshua senior added, "Come home with honor, as I know you will if that lucky star of yours will serve you in *this war*. Take care of Tom until he gets seasoned to the trenches. Good luck to you."

Adelbert Ames was pleasantly impressed with the Lieutenant Colonel. The man was bright and eager to learn.

He began his tutorial work with the professor on the trip south. The Twentieth Maine left Portland without fanfare. There was no colorful send-off for a regiment associated with no particular county or city, just Maine.

On September 7 the orphan regiment arrived in Washington, a city shaken by the disaster at Bull Run, oblivious to a few Maine hayseeds. That night the regiment slept in an empty lot near the U. S. Arsenal on, as Captain Spear put it, "a downy bed of cats, bricks, and broken bottles." They marched, or attempted to, across the Potomac to Arlington Heights, after being issued Enfield rifles and other paraphernalia. They made such a sorry sight that Ames exploded, "If you can't do any better than you have tonight, you better all desert and go home."

It was all so hurried the Twentieth lacked the usual niceties. On September 10, Corporal Holman Melcher wrote his brother in Maine, "We have been three nights without tents but we have our rubber blankets so it was not so bad." The regiment was soon heading into Maryland, as McClellan sought to close with Lee. From bivouac in a Maryland field Melcher wrote, "Dead horses lie in every direction, causing an unpleasant stench and beef-cattle partly devoured, the secesh not having a chance to savor their beef-steak! We shall probably have a chance at the business before tomorrow night as the roar of the artillery about 15 miles off is incessant, jarring the air."

The noise was the fighting at South Mountain. It was over by the time the regiment came upon the scene. At Turner's Gap, Chamberlain dismounted from Prince to have a closer look at one of the many bodies strewn about. A Rebel sat under a tree, wide-eyed and staring, his shirt caked with blood. He appeared to be about sixteen. "This was my enemy—this boy," Chamberlain wrote. "He was dead, the boy, my enemy; but I shall see him forever."

The battle of Antietam was fought without the participation of the Twentieth Maine, part of V Corps, over 20,000 strong, which McClellan withheld from committing. Chamberlain and several officers and men of the regiment scrambled up a hill and watched as Hooker's I Corps moved into a cornfield, to be cut down as if by a great scythe.

On September 21, encamped near the battlefield, Corporal Melcher wrote his brother Nathaniel that the Twentieth Maine was still without tents, still relying on rubber blankets. "Dead men (mostly rebels) and horses lying here and there, broken wagons and levelled fences, destroyed cornfields and gathered orchards. How badly we should feel if this were in our own state! May it be spared."

And then he added, "I get along well as I expected, but by all means don't you enlist. If you are drafted, well, but do not enlist."

A few days after the battle, as Lee retreated, the Twentieth Maine started to ford the Potomac, running low, at Shephardstown. A rear guard of Rebs began spraying them with minie balls; most splashed in the water but some found their mark. One corporal, appropriately enough named Waterhouse, got his toes knocked back by a bullet. Chamberlain, astride a borrowed horse rather than risk his white stallion, remained at midpoint in the river, initially to warn soldiers fording the river of a deep spot and then to direct their retreat. Three men were slightly wounded, but the Lieutenant Colonel kept his exposed position until his boys were out of harm's way. The horse was not so lucky. It was the first of many shot carrying Joshua Chamberlain in battle.

The regiment did a little picket duty and a lot of drilling after this, particularly at the site of an iron works near the Antietam battlefield. On October 10, Adelbert Ames wrote his parents, "I have to say officers think we were in (a little at least) but I do not think we were in enough to speak of it." He allowed that, at Shephardstown, "there was quite a little fight." Ames did not expect there would be any more fighting for awhile. "At least my regiment will be disciplined when we do," he said.

Adelbert Ames was a pistol. He was absolutely determined to break in the wet-behind-the-ears boys of the Twentieth. They were damned lucky they were not put into the battle at Antietam, but they would be ready next time. Irritated with one Downeast soldier's absolute lack of military posture, Ames bellowed, "For God's sake, draw up your bowels!"

This approach did not endear Ames to his regiment. He could not have cared less. Tom Chamberlain wrote to sister Sae of the prevalent feeling among the boys toward Ames: "I swear they will shoot him the first battle we are in." In a later letter in this vein, Tom wrote that Ames was hated "beyond all description" and "will take the men out to drill and he will damn them up hill and down." He wished the colonel was either put in the state prison or promoted to brigadier general. "I tell you, he is about as savage a man you ever saw."

If Tom Chamberlain would be glad to see Ames get another star, so would Adelbert. "General Berry still urges (or pretends to) my advancement," Ames informed his parents. "Whatever may be his motives, he still aids me by word, by praise at least. I shall aid him all I can in my position."

"I am well aware that his appointment to a higher position at this time may be considered hurried and premature by some," Hiram Berry wrote Vice President Hamlin, "still in the present emergency of our country such consideration should not avail." Berry thought Ames should be made a brigadier general. Noting his bravery and intelligence, Berry added Ames "is also an excellent disciplinarian." General Hooker, also championing Ames' promotion, noted "I know of no officer of more promise."

In his grudging way, Tom Chamberlain admitted Ames was shaping the regiment up. "I drill the company every day and do it like an old soldier," he wrote. "I tell you we have to do it well or get a damning." Corporal Melcher wrote his brother on October 23, apologizing that he had not written for weeks, but, he explained, with so much drill and dress parade, little time was left for anything else.

The horror of Fredericksburg was a couple of weeks away in the Twentieth Maine's future. Thanks to the "savage" Ames, it would be ready.

*Thomas Hyde—Maine State Archives*

# Thomas Hyde

## *"I wished I dared to disobey orders."*

Major Thomas Hyde's Seventh Maine did not see action at Fair Oaks. After that battle, the Army of the Potomac retreated, hammered by Lee's Confederates. Hyde was frustrated that the boys in blue were not allowed to counterattack. He was not alone in this sentiment. Hyde would look on with pride when, after a scrape at White Oak Swamp, Lieutenant Colonel Connor led the Seventh across a plain swept by heavy Rebel fire. The Seventh took its time, apparently in no hurry, as onlookers wondered why the Maine regiment did not double-time it. Connor would not give the Johnnies the satisfaction.

After federal gunners had massacred assaulting Confederate infantry at Malvern Hill, Hyde hoped the high command would give the Army of the Potomac the order to seek its rations in Richmond. It would have been greeted with a cheer from the rank and file. They were "there for business then," Hyde wrote. But instead the Army of the Potomac fell back in the drizzle to Harrison's Landing, "the hottest place we had yet discovered," to be attacked by a "plague of flies." In this malarial setting, men dropped like flies themselves; about half of the Seventh was shipped north to presumably more sanitary hospitals. The thinning ranks of the Maine regiment were eventually transported back to the Washington area; McClellan was sacked and replaced by General John Pope. A loud-mouthed Westerner, Pope would show the damned Eastern sissies how to fight.

When Pope collided with Lee on the old Bull Run battlefield, Hyde watched the long lines of battle smoke representing the two armies. Changes in position of the smoke indicated which side was winning. As the day passed, "it became painfully obvious which side it was, as our line contracted toward us, and the hills and fields became dotted with the stragglers and the wounded."

The Seventh Maine was given orders to set up a skirmish line, to repel any enemy attempt to intercept the retreating Federals. After spending some hours standing on a big stump, looking for an attack that never came, Hyde and his men bivouacked on the hilly outskirts of Centerville. There were a couple of farmhouses in the area. Hyde did not realize that, in one of them, his friend and Bowdoin classmate Sam Fessenden, who had signed up with him in Attorney Fred Sewall's office in Bath, lay dying.

About 11:00 p.m., the Seventh's tired men were required to head out into the night and stem the tide of stragglers tramping by. By dawn they had corralled over 2,000 men.

There was little glory in such affairs. After Second Bull Run a pall hung over the Army, which was only lifted by the return to command of McClellan. "Confidence seemed to cling about this man. Why was it? He proved no Napoleon, but we all believed in him," Major Hyde remembered.

With Connor under the weather and Mason absent, Hyde commanded the remnant of the Seventh Maine, part of the army that now marched into Maryland. Lee was on the move, following up his Virginia victories with invasion of Union-held territory. For a change, Hyde noted, the girls mostly cheered the boys in blue. Maryland was more hospitable ground. As they moved deeper into Maryland, "the happier we became." What was left of them.

Although he constantly counted and recounted his men, Hyde could not come up with more than 225. He knew each man by name, and was proud of his veterans. He believed they could, man for man, stand up to the best.

After a violent brush with Lee's army at South Mountain by a few thousand troops on both sides, the Seventh camped along the summit. Hyde, on night picket, was stricken by a throbbing toothache. It required immediate attention. Come morning, the Major rode off in search of a doctor. He located one, a diminutive fellow. Try as the little doctor might, he could not extract the painful molar with his crowbar-like device. A passing teamster did the job. After "a refreshing night in a half-filled hay-cart," Hyde rejoined his little regiment on its dusty march.

Nobody in the ranks knew where they were headed, except it was toward the growing noise of the guns. It was September 17, 1862. The bloodiest day in American history had begun shortly after dawn when Hooker's First Corps attacked the right of Lee's line strung out before Sharpsburg, near Antietam Creek.

To bolster the size of his regiment, Hyde armed his drummers and fife players with guns picked up from the roadside, dropped by some of the growing legion of wounded. The Seventy-Seventh New York, whose dust the Maine boys had been eating, kicked up more as they double-timed toward some woods ahead. These were the East Woods and the Maine boys soon passed what was left of the Tenth Maine.

The Tenth had seen heavy fighting, reflected in the fact it was no bigger than a squad. Part of Crawford's Brigade of XII Corps, the regiment had spent the previous night trying to sleep in a field next to where their new corps commander, Brigadier General Joseph Mansfield, caught a few winks under a blanket on the grass. Mansfield made a good impression. The old (fifty eight seemed old to troops in their teens or early twenties) Regular Army soldier was an unpretentious, fatherly sort. As the Tenth marched toward the sound of battle the next day, "we all saw General Mansfield riding about the field in his new, untarnished uniform, with his long, silvery hair flowing out behind and we loved him."

However likeable, Mansfield had minimal control of events. As his troops moved up, Fighting Joe Hooker rode up to the Tenth Maine, and ordered it to aid his pummeled I Corps. "You must hold those woods!" he yelled, and so the Tenth and other regiments of Crawford's Brigade veered toward the East Woods. Marching *en masse,* they were "almost as good a target as a barn" for Rebel skirmishers. Without bothering to consult General Mansfield, Colonel George Beal put his men in a line and ordered them to get up to the woods double quick. There they tangled with Confederates firing from the cover of trees, and a ragged fight, often at close range, developed. Watching from a distance, the corps commander thought the Maine men were shooting at other Federal troops, and gestured frantically for them to cease fire. He was, understandably, ignored by the few who saw him; Mansfield then rode up to some companies not in the woods, hollering above the racket of musketry, to stop firing.

"You are shooting your friends. There are no Rebs so far advanced," he cried.

Some men pointed at gray forms in the trees immediately ahead, taking aim. Mansfield peered into the woods and admitted his error—just as two Confederate regiments belched lead from the tree line facing the general. The war was over for the fatherly but confused general. The boys, fighting for their lives, had neither a general or their immediate officers.

Even before the deadly volley that ripped a hole in Mansfield's chest, a sniper had sent a bullet tearing through Colonel Beal's horse's head. At the same moment, another ball passed through both of the wounded animal's rider's legs. Beal fell off the frenzied beast, which came upon Lieutenant Colonel James Fillebrown and kicked him in the stomach and chest. As one soldier put it, "that worthless, broken down, and dying plug sent him flying end over end."

The violent game continued for about an hour, as the Tenth Maine and a Pennsylvania regiment gradually pushed back several Confederate regiments. The Rebels darted from tree to tree, shooting lead and curses. "Give it to the damn Yankee sons of bitches!" they screamed. It was, Major Gould wrote, an order "one would think they had learned in infancy, by the ease and frequency of their giving it." Adding to the noise was the steady barking of the regiment's mascot, an old dog named "Major," who snapped at bullets that whizzed by.

Eventually only seventy men and the dog remained in the woods, others either dead, wounded, or having left in twos and threes carrying the wounded out. But the East Woods were cleared of rebels. It was about 8:40 a.m.

It was high noon when Colonel William Irwin's Brigade of VI Corps arrived on the scene. The brigade was made of four New York regiments and the Seventh Maine. Major Hyde asked the whereabouts of two acquaintances in the Tenth Maine, Colonel Beal and Lieutenant Colonel Fillebrown. Informed they were both casualties, Hyde pushed through the woods and into the plowed field of the Mumma farm. He had no time to ponder his friends' fate. Squarely ahead, beyond the farm, were the West Woods, framing a small white Dunker Church. Although Tom Hyde could not know it, it was the center of the Confederate line. A breakthrough here and Lee's Army of Northern Virginia, its back to the Potomac, could be smashed.

Ordered to support the German-American Twentieth New York, Hyde detoured briefly to drive off a cluster of North Carolinians around some barns on his left flank. Within a few minutes Hyde's charge sent the Rebs flying. His ranks depleted by a dozen men, Hyde's boys wheeled back over rows of Confederate corpses in Mumma's corn-field to support the Twentieth New York and the rest of the brigade before the Dunker Church. The Mainers took cover behind boulders as Confederates poured fire out of the West Woods.

The hot, horrible afternoon saw the Confederates pushed back to the left of where the Seventh Maine hun-kered down, at a sunken road thereafter known as Bloody Lane. A Yankee bridgehead across the Antietam had been effected—finally. But McClellan refused to commit his re-serves and Lee contested every inch tenaciously.

The stalemate in the Dunker Church vicinity dragged on; one of Hyde's crack shots, Private Knox, crawled off and, perched in some boulders at the west end of Bloody Lane, proceeded to spend the afternoon picking off members of a Confederate battery near the Piper Farm. When a stray fragment of a Rebel shell broke the breech of his rifle, Knox crawled back to the Seventh, collected several weapons dis-carded by wounded soldiers, and went back to work. Some skirmishers were also sent to the Bloody Lane to drive back Knox's counterparts around the Piper Farm.

That was not enough for Colonel Billy Irwin. Although Hyde did not know it at the time, Irwin was indulging his love of the bottle on September 17. Irwin ordered Hyde's Seventh Maine to drive the snipers around Piper's out. Hyde, who thought at least a brigade of Confederates lurked in the trees around the swale, considered the order preposterous. He asked Irwin to repeat his command.

When the colonel did so, Major Hyde said "I have seen a large force of rebels go in there, I should think two brigades."

Irwin exploded as he repeated his command a third time. "Are you afraid to go, sir? Those are your orders sir." The colonel added a string of oaths for good measure.

Many years later, Hyde would write, "I wished I had been old enough, or distinguished enough, to have dared to disobey orders."

But, at 4:45 p.m. on the bloodiest day in American history, the twenty-four-year-old Hyde could not. Instead, he said, "Give the order so the regiment can hear it, and we are ready, sir."

For the fourth time Colonel Irwin screamed the order.

Crossing over the mangled heaps of Rebels killed earlier in the day in Bloody Lane, the little regiment headed for Piper's barns. Major Hyde, riding his Virginia thoroughbred along the right wing, had his boys rush through the cornfield, bayonets glinting in the dimming light. Twice they stopped to fire a volley. Confederates around the barns and haystacks dropped their flag as they fled.

Hyde, riding slightly ahead of his onrushing soldiers, was about to grab the fallen standard when shots rang out from several directions. About two thirds of the Seventh was hit in the crossfire. Realizing they outnumbered the Maine regiment, the Confederates countercharged.

To escape the deadly fusillade, Hyde ordered his regiment to move left, over and through a rail fence enclosing Piper's cow yard. While this was easily accomplished by infantry, Hyde's thoroughbred was pinned against the fence. As Sergeant Benson knocked away the rails, canister perforated his haversack, blowing hardtack in every direction.

Despite the danger, Hyde and Benson could not help laughing as they raced for a nearby apple orchard.

Halfway up the hillside leading to the apple trees, the Major's horse reared back in agony. As his regiment re-grouped in the orchard, Hyde inspected his horse's wounds. Finding they were not fatal, he had barely remounted when his color bearer went down. Trying to recover the flag, Hyde found himself cut off from his men. The Rebels were so close he could read in the gathering darkness the word "Manassas" on one of their battle flags.

Weaving his way through the low trees of the orchard, Hyde reached another section of fence, which his men were clambering over. Once again his horse was pushed up against the rails. A dozen rebels closed in on Hyde when, shouting "Rally, boys, to save the major," blue soldiers shoved their guns through the fence slats and blasted the approaching Confederates.

Sergeant Hill hacked an opening in the picket fence with his saber bayonet. Hyde rode through and reformed what was left of his regiment—three officers and sixty-five enlisted men—under fire from Confederate muskets and Yankee artillery, intended as support. The flag had been saved but over a hundred men littered Piper's swale.

The Seventh Maine returned to the Union line, retiring, the Confederate General James Longstreet said, "like a me-teor that loses its own fire." It was a gallant charge but, un-supported, it was doomed.

When the bruised remnant of the Seventh returned to Bloody Lane, a Vermont brigade cheered. But Major Thomas Hyde curled up under a blanket with some other officers of the regiment as total darkness descended. They cried them-selves to sleep.

When the regiment had set out on its charge, a Ver-mont general, watching, turned to his colonels, who begged to be sent in too, and said, "You will never see that regiment again." Hyde came to the conclusion that, had his regiment been joined by the Vermonters, they could have sliced through the Confederates to the Potomac. And with a few more brigades, they would have "ended the business, as at that moment Lee's much-enduring army was fought out."

Maybe. As it was, Hyde had "the consolation of knowing that we had gone farther into the Rebel lines than any Union regiment that day, that we had fought three or four times our numbers, and inflicted more damage than we received."

But it was never consolation enough, especially when he learned the attack was not made resulting from any plan from McClellan's headquarters. Just from "an inspiration of John Barleycorn" in Colonel Irwin's head. He would always wish he had been insubordinate.

There were 12,401 Union casualties at Antietam. Confederate losses totalled 10,318.

# Joshua Chamberlain
## *"The living and dead were alike to me."*

"I wish you could hear Lawrence give off a command and see him ride along the battalion on his white horse," Tom Chamberlain wrote home.

Disease was taking a heavy toll within the regiment; there were more than 300 men on the sick list by the end of October. But the Chamberlain brothers were fit. Tom actually gained twelve pounds eating maggot-infested hardtack or, as he put it, "living on worms." His brother, thirteen years older, felt better than he had in years.

That he felt liberated was clear. "I have my cares and vexations too," he wrote his wife on October 10, "but let me say no danger and no hardship ever makes me wish to get back to that college life again." He couldn't *breathe* when he thought of the last two years. "Why, I would spend my whole life in campaigning rather than endure that again," he told Fannie.

He could hardly be more emphatic: "One thing though *I won't* endure it again. My experience here and the habit of command will make me less complaisant—will break the notion that certain persons are the natural authorities over me."

Later that month, he returned to the same theme: "I feel that it *is* a sacrifice for me to be here in one sense of the word; but I do not wish myself back by any means. I feel I am where duty called me." The warning he received before departing from Brunswick from Smythe—and quite possibly from others, including Fannie—was on his mind:

"The *'glory'* Prof. Smythe so *honestly* pictured for me I do not much dread. If I do return 'shattered' and 'good-for-nothing,' I think there *are* those who will hold me in some degree of favor better than that which he predicted. Most likely I shall be hit somewhere at sometime, but all 'my times are in His hands,' and I cannot die without His appointing."

Chamberlain assured his "dear little wife" that the few women soldiers saw seldom exceeded "the requirements for *sweepers* in College," supposedly selected for their ugliness to preclude sexual advances. He longed to see "somebody who is the constant center of his every dream and the soul of his every thought!" He hoped to meet Fannie somewhere more suitable than the field to fulfill his erotic longings. "My rubber blanket is not quite big enough to accommodate ever so sweet and welcome a guest," he teased.

In the immediate circumstances, what Chamberlain longed for were more letters from Fannie. On November 4, after again complaining on that score, the lieutenant colonel said that he delighted to hear about the children. Yet "the little particulars" his wife shared also made him sad.

"You must not let them dwell too much on me, and keep me too vividly in their affections. If I return they will soon relearn to love me, and if not, so much is spared them." And to his wife, these words: "I want you to be cheerful and occupy your mind with pleasant things, so as not to have any time to grow melancholy. You must not think of me much."

What Fannie thought comes through in a letter she wrote, describing Thanksgiving at the Adams parsonage: "You cannot imagine how lonely I am this Thanksgiving night, when you ought to be at your own home, with all

---

those who long to see you so." She wondered pointedly where *he* had spent the holiday.

But Chamberlain had told her where he was: "You can find the place on the map I used to look so longingly at." Anyway, it was more than a question of geography. "I am in the right place," he summed up.

He was a student again, and learning fast. He asked Fannie to send his copy of Jomini's *The Art of War*, so that he and Ames could peruse it together. Jomini was a renowned military authority, but his maxims were from an era made obsolete by the rifled smooth-bore musket. The best texts Chamberlain had were Ames himself and the actual experience of war.

By December the Army of the Potomac was on the move again. Its latest commander, General Ambrose Burnside, planned to cross the Rappahannock and give battle to Lee somewhere between Fredericksburg and Richmond. But the pontoons were not ready for some reason, and Burnside waited opposite Fredericksburg until they were brought up. And Lee had time to establish the Army of Northern Virginia in strong defensive positions just beyond the town, with batteries able to rake any troops crossing the river.

On December 11 Union batteries bombarded Confederates in the city as a preliminary to crossing the river with the now-available pontoons. Chamberlain, watching, "I should think almost within pistol range," thought the spectacle "was grand beyond anything I have ever witnessed, or expect to witness."

The city was enveloped in smoke and fire, with Federal artillery sending shells screaming at Rebel sharpshooters, scattering them as they burst. Ambulances could be seen carrying off the wounded. The work of assembling the bridges was interrupted as a pontoon would, from time to time, break loose and float against the shore like a stranded whale.

Behind Chamberlain the Union forces glittered as the sun bounced off thousands of muskets. "Antietam was not anywhere equal to it," he observed, "because more extended; this is gathered into one focus."

Corporal Melcher did not see as much. He could "see nothing of what was going on, on account of the smoke." The next day was the same until a stiff wind blew enough smoke away in the afternoon to reveal Union troops crossing the swaying pontoons into the city. Melcher scanned the Confederate batteries through a glass. "I could see in a moment what must be the sacrifice of life to take them," he wrote.

The following day, December 13, Burnside started throwing troops against the Rebel entrenchments beyond Fredericksburg. Below Marye's Heights a stone wall was manned. Chamberlain and others watched from across the river as blue lines worked their way across a plain and uphill toward the stone wall. Brigade after brigade went in and was mowed down. "I see tears in the eyes of many a brave man looking on that sorrowful sight, yet all of us are eager to dash to the rescue," he wrote.

This time, after being kept in reserve for long, nerve-wracking hours, V Corps was committed. General Hooker, in command, protested Burnside's order, but was overruled. Griffin's Division, which included the Third brigade the Twentieth Maine was in, was set in motion crossing the river. After the First Brigade was put in, Griffin snapped, "There goes one of my brigades to hell, and the other two will soon follow."

Finally, it was the Third's turn. "Griffin gave us a searching, wistful look, not trusting his lips and we not needing more," Chamberlain recalled.

---

It was about three o'clock when the brigade entered the battered town. Bodies blown to pieces by artillery were bloody fragments everywhere. Two new Reb batteries opened up on the blue brigade. To Chamberlain "it seemed as if the ground were bursting under foot, and the very sky were crashing down upon us; the bullets hissed like a seething sea." The "hellish din" was pierced by a bugle calling the Third Brigade.

Chamberlain was standing beside Colonel Ames, in front of the Twentieth Maine's colors. Ames, a veteran artilleryman, took one look at the Rebel batteries, including one swinging into position to the brigade's right, and said, "God help us now!"

"Take care of the right wing!" he said to Chamberlain. For some reason the New York regiments that were supposed to be there were not moving up. Ames, twenty paces ahead of his line, sword drawn, shouted, "Forward, the Twentieth!"

"I held my breath and set my teeth together, determined not to show fear if I could, by will, keep it down," Adjutant Brown would recall. Beside the dead and dying, "I remember that the sun was setting, nothing else except that I was running up and down the line urging the men on."

Fences and other obstacles meant the officers had to walk, leaving their horses (and blankets) behind. With Brown, Chamberlain worked to keep order on the regiment's right, hit not only by fire from the Rebs ahead but raked on its flank by a battery.

After splashing on the double quick through a ditch filled with icy water, the regiment came up to a board fence. For a moment, the men hesitated. Chamberlain started ripping off boards, yelling, "Do you want me to do it?" They did it.

It was a brief lapse. Colonel Robert Carter, a Regular further up the slope with another regiment, looked over his shoulder. He saw the smoke lift and the Twentieth Maine, new flag fluttering, come across the corpse-littered field as if on parade. "It was a grand sight, and a striking example of what discipline will do for *such* men in *such* a battle," he said.

They passed over four lines of survivors of earlier attacks, hugging the cold earth. The prone soldiers called out warnings to the Mainers: "It's no use, boys; we've tried that. Nothing living can stand there; it's only for the dead!"

They reached a small crest, below the murderous wall, "almost within speaking distance" of the entrenched Rebs, Company H's Theodore Gerrish recalled. This was the most advanced Union position in the sector. Ames walked coolly over piles of bodies, and asked, "Who commands this regiment?" When its colonel responded, Ames quietly said, "I will move over your line and relieve your men."

"The utter impossibility of taking the Rebel position was manifested to every man in the regiment," Gerrish wrote, "but we blazed away at the enemy, and they at us." Only darkness stilled the exchange of volleys.

If possible, that night on the wind-swept plain was even more gruesome. Chamberlain and Brown walked about in the darkness, looking for a blanket or overcoat they could borrow from the dead. But others were ahead of them. Finally, they sought sleep, or attempted to, with those eternally asleep. Soon after the battle, Chamberlain wrote, "I did sleep though, strange as you may think it, in the very midst of a heap of dead close beside one dead man, touching him possibly—the living and dead were alike to me." Much later, Chamberlain wrote: "Necessity compels strange uses." The lieutenant colonel claimed he had not only lain between two bodies, but used a third for a pillow. He pulled the flap of the corpse's coat "over my face to fend off the chilling winds, and, still more chilling, the deep, many-voiced moan that overspread the field."

The cries of the wounded that frigid night aroused Chamberlain to again walk the field before returning in his macabre bed. The noise of a shutter banging on a brick house sounded to him like the constant refrain *never-forever; forever-never!* straight out of Edgar Allan Poe. And Chamberlain also recalled a vampirish moment when another soldier, possibly also looking for covering, "lifted the dead man's coat-flap from my face, and a wild, ghoul-like gaze sought to read whether it was of the unresisting."

Gerrish remembered mixed thoughts that sleepless night: "We were wishing the hours away, and yet dreaded to have the darkness disappear." And Holman Melcher wrote his brother that he had managed to get some sleep "but I must acknowledge it was far from being sweet."

Dawn finally came. It was impossible for the living Union soldiers to raise their heads without inviting a shot from a Rebel sharpshooter. Numb with cold, mud-covered, their hungry stomachs growling, the men of the Twentieth Maine embraced the ground, waiting for darkness again. Corpses were used for cover; minie balls making dull thuds as they hit the human barricades. "Thus passed away the Christian Sabbath and what a way to spend this holy day!" Melcher wrote. That evening, after thirty-six hours on the ground near the awful wall, the regiment retired to Fredericksburg.

Ames walked about among the men bivouacked in the streets. He praised them for their good showing. The Twentieth had come through its baptism of fire.

But they were not quite done with Fredericksburg. The evening of the following day the Twentieth Maine was sent up with other regiments of the Third Brigade near its earlier position. The lines were so close Chamberlain wandered in the blackness up to a Rebel digging a rifle-pit. To elude detection, the professor of languages adopted a Southern inflection and moved quickly back to safety.

Exactly what was the brigade's mission Chamberlain and others could only guess. In his low-voiced, even way, Ames told Chamberlain, in charge of the regiment while the colonel supervised the line, to hold the position "to the last."

"A strange query crossed our minds: Last of what? No dictionary held that definition. As a general term, this reached the infinite!" wrote Chamberlain.

Some time, around midnight, he got an idea of what was transpiring when a staff officer materialized and in an excited, loud voice said, "Get yourselves out of this as quick as God will let you! The whole army is across the river!"

*So that was it.* They were on the field to screen the Union Army's retreat. But Chamberlain could not afford to let the officer's outburst alert the nearby Rebs to their vulnerability. For the benefit of the Confederate pickets he said in a ringing voice, "Steady in your places, my men. Arrest this stampeder! This is a ruse of the enemy! We'll give it to them in the morning."

Then Chamberlain and Ames started sending men in small groups, a hundred or so yards at a time, back downslope to the nearly deserted streets of Fredericksburg. By daybreak of December 17, the Twentieth Maine was the last regiment to recross the Rappahannock.

General Hooker came upon Lieutenant Colonel Chamberlain sitting beneath a tree, exhausted and dejected. From where he sat he could look across the river at the green slopes behind Fredericksburg blue with Union dead. He was surprised to see Hooker. He had not seen the general for several days; he "had no business to be where we were." He should be running his command somewhere.

Hooker, trying to cheer Chamberlain up, said: "You've had a hard chance, Colonel; I am glad to see you out of it!"

"It was chance, General," Chamberlain replied sharply, "not much intelligent design there!"

"God knows I did not put you in!" Hooker crisply retorted.

But Chamberlain would not let it go, rank be damned. "That was the trouble, General," he said. "We were handed in piecemeal, on toasting-forks."

It was plain-speaking, but Hooker did not reprove him. He rode off, and Chamberlain rejoined his regiment. He was lucky to find it largely intact. The Twentieth Maine suffered only four killed and thirty-two wounded at Fredericksburg. Total Union losses were almost 13,000. Two-thirds came from the frontal assaults against the stone wall.

# Oliver Otis Howard

*"I sought death everywhere I could find an excuse to go on the field."*

Back in Maine to recuperate, Otis Howard found there were advantages to being a one-armed soldier. The disadvantages were more obvious. On the Fourth of July, 1862, appropriately enough, the general slipped and fell down a flight of steps. Instinctively trying to break his fall with a hand that no longer existed, he only succeeded in driving his stump against the ground. It was an excruciatingly painful experience but, Howard thought, it was nothing compared to the pain that the Union Army was enduring in Virginia. Anxious to do his part, Howard spent much of his time giving speeches encouraging recruitment. His empty sleeve was a dramatic testimony to his sacrifice for the Union. And Howard made use of it. Speaking before a big crowd in Brunswick, sprinkled with Bowdoin students and former professors, the general called upon his men to enlist to go back with him to win back the ground where his right arm was buried. It had a powerful effect.

He spoke briefly with Professor Chamberlain, who was then securing his commission with the Twentieth Maine. Howard encouraged his junior classmate at Bowdoin.

By the end of August, Howard was back in the war zone. The Army had not expected him back, at least not so soon, and his brigade had been entrusted with another. "Bull" Sumner promptly gave him another brigade, in General John Sedgwick's division. II Corps was kept out of the disaster at Second Bull Run, but Howard got the dismal assignment of commanding the rear guard of the retreating army.

"Who will forget the straggling, the mud, the rain, the terrible panic and loss of life from random firing, and the hopeless feeling—almost despair—of that dreadful night march!"

Although he could not know it, Howard was to experience a lot more of panic and despair on another night at Chancellorsville. But that was in the future; during the intervening months Howard continued to climb up the military ladder of command. At Antietam "Uncle John" Sedgwick was wounded, and Sumner gave Howard command of his division. Rifle balls hissed and whizzed about him in the West Woods but, whenever Howard appeared overly nervous, brother Charlie, back as his aide, quietly said, "Aren't you a little excited?" That was sufficient to calm the general down. He came out of the war's bloodiest day without a scratch. Later, at Fredericksburg, one look at the landscape to be contested made Howard "unusually sad," but he led the first Federal division into the town and came out of the ensuing butchery with his reputation intact.

The revolving door at the top brought "Fighting Joe" Hooker in as commander of the Army of the Potomac. And Howard got command of a division. It was not unsolicited. When Hooker gave General Dan Sickles III Corps, Howard protested that, as Sickles' senior in rank, he was due a corps command. Hooker accommodated Howard by placing him in command of XI Corps.

This was the beginning of Howard's trouble. The corps had a large number of German immigrants in its ranks. The corps had been commanded by a fellow *Deutschlander*, Franz Sigel; "We fights mit Sigel" was a phrase associated with the

"Dutchmen" of XI Corps. When Sigel resigned in a snit over rank, it was expected that he would be replaced by another German-American, Carl Schurz. That is what Schurz expected, and when Hooker picked Howard, the division leader sought transfer to another corps.

He did not get it, and later would maintain that he was not really that upset. Schurz was bright, well-read, and articulate, but he owed his position in the Army to his reputation as a German-American politician, not to any military experience. He therefore expected—or so he claimed—a Regular Army man to be appointed, and welcomed the Mainer "with sincere contentment." Maybe, but his first impression of Howard was less than flattering: "He did not impress me as an intellectually strong man. Certain looseness of mental operations, a marked uncertainty in forming definite conclusions became evident in his conversation." Schurz hoped Howard's actions would prove more reassuring than his talk.

The dissatisfaction spread down into the ranks. The reaction to "Old Prayerbrook" was cold; not a cheer could be elicited when the new commander rode along the front. "And," Schurz wrote, "I do not know whether he liked the men he commanded better than they liked him."

Howard realized that the Germans were unhappy, but hoped to gain their support, if not affection, over time. He did not, he suspected, help the situation by bringing in new Yankee brigadiers like Francis Barlow and Adelbert Ames. Yet he felt such men were needed to shape up a corps which needed shaping up. In fact, a majority of the command were "Americans" (as Howard called his non-immigrant soldiers). Nativist hostility to "foreigners" had mushroomed in the prewar years and the pious, teetotaling, Bible-quoting Howard was exactly the type of Yankee many of the Germans had learned to be wary of. Schurz was right. Howard wanted a corps, and he had got one, but it seems doubtful he would have chosen this one.

On April 27, 1863, Hooker set the Army of the Potomac in motion by crossing the Rhappahannock above Fredericksburg to flank Lee's forces at that town. Sedgwick's VI Corps was left facing Lee across the river, prepared to attack when, as anticipated, the Confederates were pulled off to face Hooker coming at them from the west. "Bobby" Lee would be caught in a vice and smashed. On paper, it was a great plan.

On the first day of the campaign, Howard failed to reduce his supply trains to the minimum required. Hooker, riding by with his staff, twitted the self-conscious Howard. "General Meade has done better than you," he said. This, Howard recalled, was "my first mortification" of a campaign that would be one big mortification.

Hooker did not help matters when, once across the river and almost out of the forested area called the Wilderness, he decided to fall back to a defensive position at Chancellorsville. His order surprised Howard. Indeed, it has puzzled military historians ever since. Hooker's priority should have been to get out of the tangled mess of scrub trees, thick underbrush, and nettlesome vines as quickly as possible. That would become apparent. What was clear at once was that the usually aggressive Hooker had surrendered the initiative to Lee. The withdrawal "gave to our whole army the impression of a check, a failure, a defeat," Howard wrote.

Hooker set up a defensive line in the midst of the Wilderness, stretching from his left on the river to his extreme right along a turnpike that meandered off to the west. XI Corps was plunked on the far right, in open patches surrounded by apparently impenetrable woods. To Hooker it probably appeared the safest place to put his weakest corps.

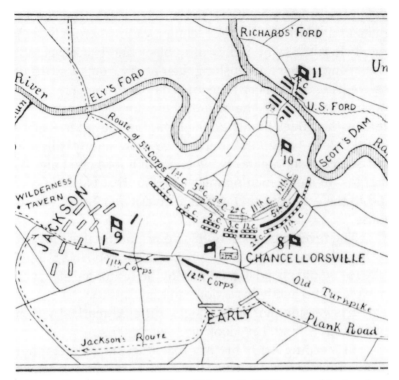

*Chancellorsville: Note position of Howard's XI Corps and Jackson's flanking movement—U.S. Army Signal Corps map*

Howard established his headquarters at Dowdall's Tavern, located near a crossroad of the turnpike and a plank road. Most of his divisions were strung out to the west, facing south, the direction the rebels were expected to come from. At the tavern and a farmhouse down the turnpike, Howard and his staff peered into the green wall and waited.

Howard would later use a metaphor from childhood to explain his sensations as the battle approached:

"In my youth my brother and I had a favorite spot in an upper field of my father's farm from which we were accustomed, after the first symptoms of a coming storm, to

---

watch the operations of the contending winds; the sudden gusts and whirlwinds; the sideling swallow excitedly seeking shelter; the swift and swifter, black and blacker clouds, ever rising higher and pushing their angry fronts toward us. As we listened we heard the low rumbling from afar; as the storm came nearer the woods bent forward and shook fiercely their thick branches; the lightning zagged in flashes, and the deep-bassed thunder echoed more loudly, till there was scarcely an interval between its ominous crashing discharges. In some such manner came on that battle of May 2nd to the watchers at Dowdall's Tavern and Talley's farmhouse."

The revealing aspect of this description is that Howard portrays himself, unintentionally but accurately, in a passive role. He would spend a good part of the rest of his life trying to explain and justify his actions on May 2, 1863.

His version, not surprisingly, differed markedly from that of Carl Schurz. Let's look at Howard's first.

In keeping with his approaching storm metaphor, Howard wrote that the first sign came at evening of May 1. He heard intermittent skirmishing along his line. In retrospect he concluded this was a Confederate "rolling reconnaissance," probing for the Union flank. They found it and, as Howard should have known at the time, he was "in the air."

Sunrise of May 2 brought the sound of men cheering. It was not a sound Howard was familiar with, but its recipient, General Hooker, was used to it. He was a dashing, handsome figure on horseback as he inspected Howard's lines, accompanied by a retinue of staff officers. Viewing the IX Corps barricades, Howard would remember Hooker repeatedly saying, "How strong!"

He also remembered Colonel Comstock, of Hooker's staff, riding up to him and saying, quietly, that there were gaps in Howard's defenses. "General, do close in those spaces!"

Howard responded, "The woods are thick and entangled; will anybody come through there?"

"Oh, they may!"

Howard would insist Comstock's words were heeded. But his prime attention that morning turned to activity to his left. Dan Sickles, whose III Corps was stationed there, saw Confederate troops moving through a gap in the green wall on his front and, with Hooker's blessing, moved his corps to make contact with the Rebs. This left Howard's line disconnected from the rest of the Union Army.

When the noise of small arms and artillery mounted from Sickles' direction, Howard cautioned his division commanders to be ready. At about this time, well into the afternoon, Howard was ordered to detach Barlow's Brigade, his reserve, to assist Sickles. Reports were also coming in of enemy movements in the woods near Howard's positions. He sent out scouts, who reported enemy troops were in motion a few miles from XI Corps. Schurz "was anxious" and was allowed to rearrange a couple of regiments to face westward to receive a possible attack. Howard also sent out some of the limited cavalry available to see if any assault seemed to be coming.

Charlie Howard came back from Sickles to report that that general was about to mount a major attack on his front. Since one of his brigades was involved, Howard decided he should see what was transpiring and galloped off with Charlie and one of his division commanders, Von Steinweher, to do just that.

Finding not much activity with Sickles, he returned to his headquarters. How he could leave his own corps for about an hour, given the signs of *something* happening beyond the screen of trees, was—and remains—incomprehensible. But, as Howard admitted, "I did not think General Lee would be likely to move around our right." That would involve splitting his smaller army in the face of the much larger Union force. The affair with Sickles encouraged Howard to believe, as Hooker did, that it was a brush with Lee's retreating army. After all, Hooker had more sources of information, and if *he* thought Lee was on the run, he *must* be.

Howard's state of mind around five o'clock, as he prepared for supper at Dowdall's, was reflected in a comment to a battery of gunners nearby. "Unharness those horses, boys, give them a good feed of oats," he said. "We'll be off for Richmond at daylight."

He had not dismounted long when he again heard the sound of skirmishing, off to his right. Before he resaddled, "there arose the ceaseless roar of a terrible storm."

The roar was Stonewall Jackson with 26,000 men, screaming the Rebel yell, and shooting, as they came out of the woods from the west and rapidly crumpled Howard's line facing south and eating supper.

Carl Schurz would later write that, when Howard said he was anxious that day, he should have added he was also *right*. If Howard had been more anxious, perhaps the disaster would not have been quite as bad as it was.

Soon after Hooker's morning inspection, Schurz, responding to reports of enemy movement, took a look for himself. Through gaps in the treeline he observed gray infantry, wagons, and artillery moving parallel to XI Corps' front. He hurried to Howard with the information. He had a flash of intuition that what he glimpsed was the famous master of flank attack, Stonewall Jackson, preparing to move around the corps and attack from the west. A line of battle should be set up at a right angle with the turnpike. Howard shook his head. He and Hooker believed Lee was retreating.

"Did it make any sense for a retreating army to be marching along our front," Schurz countered, "instead of away from it?" Howard ended the discussion by noting that Hooker had inspected the XI Corps' position and pronounced it good.

That was true, but Hooker had experienced second thoughts. Later in the morning he sent Howard a dispatch, warning that no defenses "worth naming" had been erected and too few troops had been posted on Howard's right. "We have good reason to suppose that the enemy is moving to our right," Hooker's headquarters said.

Howard insisted he never received this dispatch. Nevertheless he sent a message to Hooker at 10:50 that morning, assuring Hooker that he was "taking measures to resist an attack from the west."

On the issue of the warning from headquarters, Schurz would flatly contradict Howard when the general explained his version of events long after the war. Howard did get the dispatch, Schurz wrote. He should know; he was at Dowdall's receiving dispatches while Howard took a nap. When Hooker's message arrived, he took it to Howard and read it to the awakened general. After handing the document to Howard, they had "another animated discussion," interrupted by a courier bringing a similar dispatch.

The meeting left Schurz in a desperate and heartsick mood. When he persisted in raising his concern about the impact of an attack on the extreme right, Howard simply said the men would have to fight if attacked. That was that.

Later in the afternoon, tenacious if nothing else, Schurz was back at it at Dowdall's Tavern. Howard informed the agitated German that he had just been ordered to send the corps' reserve to support Sickles. This proved that no flank attack on XI Corps was really expected, Howard said.

---

Soon after Howard returned from "a mere wild-goose-chase," Stonewall Jackson fulfilled Schurz's fears. Long after the battle, the controversy about it would continue. Howard would maintain he had done all he could. Hooker would accuse him of criminal negligence. Of course Hooker had done plenty to set the stage for disaster. Yet it seems clear Howard was too passive that day. He watched the signs of the storm coming, but apparently did little to mitigate its effects. In Howard's eyes the storm was blowing away.

The surprise was so complete that the only warning the troops of XI Corps had was the sudden appearance of wildlife and birds bursting out of the nearby brush. They were scared by thousands of men pushing through the supposedly impenetrable woods. In moments, men emulated animals, leaving meals untouched and guns stacked. It was worse than Bull Run.

Howard would never forget the onslaught: "It was a terrible gale! The rush, the rattle, the quick lightning from a hundred points at once, the roar, redoubled by echoes through the forest, the panic, the dead and dying in sight and the wounded straggling along; the frantic efforts of the brave and patriotic to stay the storm!"

Riding toward the storm, Howard's horse reared straight up, spooked by the gunfire. The general was thrown to the ground. Remounting, he rode up to the disorganized mass of running, shouting soldiers. Clutching a battle flag with his stump, the bare-headed Howard pleaded with the fleeing men to stop and stand with him. Most ignored him. A Pennsylvanian of the Eighth Pennsylvania Cavalry came upon the general, maimed but courageous. Thinking this was a man to stand by, he unhooked his sabre and, with a few officers, tried to stem the tide. He soon concluded that it was as hopeless as the Pharaoh and his chariots trying to hold back the Red Sea, and resumed his own race to the rear.

Due to a phenomenon called an acoustic shadow, Hooker was unaware of the collapse of his right flank. There was no sound to interrupt casual chatter on the porch of his headquarters, the Chancellor House. Then one of his staff saw the human wreckage approaching and shouted, "Here they come!" It was later claimed that, in anger and exasperation, staff officers and privates shot at the "Dutchmen" streaming by.

Further down the turnpike, Howard's men made scattered resistance at several points. These desperate actions delayed for vital minutes Jackson's advance. Confusion among the advancing Reb units in the dimming light also slowed the juggernaut. As darkness gathered and Hooker scrambled to set up a defensive line, every minute counted.

An unsympathetic soldier, running past the "rattled" Howard, claimed the general was screaming, "Halt! Halt! I'm ruined, I'm ruined. I'll shoot you if you don't stop. I'm ruined, I'm ruined."

But a member of Howard's staff remembered urging the general to fire some reserve artillery into the fleeing horde, to stop them and slow the rebels immediately beyond. "No, Colonel," Howard said, "I will never fire at my own men."

More than killing others, at this point, for the only time in his life, *Howard wanted to die.* "That night I did all in my power to remedy the mistake," he later conceded, "and I sought death everywhere I could find an excuse to go on the field."

# Hiram Berry

*"I shall seek no more exposed places."*

In his moment of supreme need, the crisis of the Army of the Potomac (and of his career), General Joseph Hooker turned for aid to Major General Hiram Berry.

Berry commanded a division of III Corps, Hooker's old division, that had been held in reserve near Chancellor House. Hooker rode over to Berry and screamed, "General, throw your men into the breach—receive the enemy on your bayonets—don't fire a shot—they can't see you!"

It was dark now, dark as Joe Hooker's greatest fear, dark as Oliver Howard's worst nightmare. Hiram Berry's hour had arrived, and if ever a man was ready for it, Berry was that man. His star had steadily ascended in the Army of the Potomac as a lion of a commander. At Fair Oaks he had repeated his performance at Williamsburg, where he rescued a beleaguered Hooker. His brigade spearheading Kearny's division, he knocked back the advancing Rebs so far he was in danger of being surrounded and cut off. At Fredericksburg his brigade, in particular the new addition from his home state, the Seventeenth Maine, performed so well under terrific fire that Confederate General A. P. Hill sent his personal compliments.

Berry and Hooker got along famously. They were both natural-born fighters. When word filtered out that McClellan intended to retreat after Fair Oaks, Berry joined Hooker, Kearny, and Hentzelman to argue with Mac against such a course. And when, in the late summer of 1862, Hannibal

Hamlin came to Hooker seeking a recommendation for Berry's promotion to Major General, Hooker was more than willing. He told the War Department he classed the man from Maine "among the promising officers who have grown up during the Rebellion, and from whom I have learned to expect great deeds before it is ended." Berry had no superior, if any equal. That Fighting Joe was employing more than hyperbole to please Hamlin, an ally in his own search for advancement, was evidenced by Hooker's desire for Berry to command his old division. That was not something "Fighting Joe" took lightly.

Berry owed his advancement to major general to political allies as well as a spotless battlefield record. But it was a well-known fact that Hiram Berry was idolized by the common soldier in a way few generals were. That was because they not only knew he would take any risk they did, but they believed he really cared for their welfare. "Lay down, men! Lay down! I am here to take care of you, and I'll do it if you will let me and will obey my orders," he told the raw Seventeenth Maine boys at Fredericksburg. Or, in another version, the general, waving his sword, bellowed, "Keep those heads down or I'll cut them off." Either way, the enlisted men responded.

"All the soldiers loved him," a major in the Thirty-seventh New York wrote. "I remember saying often that the men never waited for orders to cheer Kearny, Sickles or Berry. Their applause came from their hearts involuntarily." Berry could get the kind of whole-hearted support Howard so desperately craved, but lacked the personality to achieve. Private John Haley of the Seventeenth, who usually grumbled about his regiment's officers, recalled: "When I say that General Berry was loved I use no idle phrase."

By any measure a success in the military, Berry was, in ways physical and otherwise, not the man who paraded off to war in 1861. Without an overcoat, food, or sleep for thirty-six hours at Williamsburg in the rain and tension of battle, Berry "got pretty used up." In letters home during the warfare on the Peninsula, he portrayed himself as hale and hearty. "I am tanned so that I look almost as black as a mulatto," he wrote. "I wear a blouse and black wide-brimmed hat, an old leather belt, cavalry sword, and large pistols." He had a new horse that allowed him to jump any fence or ditch like Dick Turpin of literature. But, he added, he had ridden so much his legs were almost useless. In a later letter, Berry finally admitted he had been laid so low by sickness he could not sit up for days. "My system was completely poisoned by the malaria," he said. On July 28 he wrote: "My flesh is all gone. I don't think I was ever so thin. I see no end to this war."

He wanted to be home that summer, at least by August for his daughter's sixteenth birthday. He felt "at peace with all mankind," thanked Providence for sparing his life, and promised, "I shall seek no more exposed places." Some of his Michigan soldiers wanted him to move to their state, but he wanted to live in his Rockland on the Penobscot "to the end." There would be no more politics. "I have a most thorough contempt for anything that smacks of politics," he said. "I shall in future keep clear of it." The political in-fighting within the Army sickened Hiram Berry as much as malaria.

In August of 1862, as promised, Berry got leave to return to Rockland. He was greeted by enthusiastic crowds. Yet, as the hometown *Gazette* observed, "General Berry appeared much fatigued and enfeebled, and at his request it was announced that in his present condition, he was unable to address his fellow citizens, as he desired."

*No more politics. Just more war.*

While Berry was in Maine, drinking in the salt air, his brigade fought at Second Bull Run. At Chantilly Phil Kearny was killed. Berry went back south to his embattled boys, his health somewhat improved but hardly great. "I find myself wishing to be at home rather than here sleeping on the ground again and living poorly enough for a hungry dog," he wrote home in September. He mailed back a couple photographs of Kearny, prized possessions, noting: "He was my friend and I had a great love for him, as I well know he had for me." He missed Phil Kearny badly.

After Fredericksburg, where the Fourth Maine suffered badly, Berry sought out his old regiment's camp. Approaching Colonel Walker, he cried on his friend's shoulder until aides pulled him away. And he wrote his daughter, "My hair is all out of my head and I have had it shaved. I hope it will grow again, as I look queer enough." Berry's mane of thick chestnut-brown hair and full beard were gone. *Gone like Kearny, gone like so many of his boys.*

But his heart still beat for the ordinary soldier. One frigid December night a Seventeenth Mainer was pacing guard outside Berry's tent when Berry emerged, a dipper in his hand. "Drink this," the general said, "it will do you good." The private gulped down the whiskey, and it did do him good.

With a new star, Berry parted with his brigade to assume command of Hooker's division of III Corps. It was a big division with an honorable record. Hooker, Berry's friend, replaced the unlucky Burnside as Commander of the Army of the Potomac.

In April there was a Grand Review with President Lincoln and the top brass watching Fighting Joe's reorganized army parade. Berry, gathering up some of his staff, slipped off to see "some boys who know how to fight." The Seventeenth Maine was delighted to see him, and he was comfortable with them, the only Maine regiment besides the Fourth Maine he had commanded. After saying a few words, he concluded, "And now, boys, let us give three cheers for old Joe and the next fight." They did "with a *gusto*," Lieutenant Charles Mattocks wrote, and then gave three more cheers for Major General Berry.

On May 1, in Washington, Secretary of War Stanton talked with Berry's adjutant, Hannibal Hamlin's son Charles Hamlin. Vice President Hamlin worked harder for Berry's advancement than for any other Maine officer. He was impressed by the big man, and so was Stanton. Now the Secretary told the Vice President that Berry "belongs to that class of volunteer generals destined to have the command of an army."

Back at Chancellorsville, however, Berry told his quartermaster that evening that he had a presentiment. He would not survive the coming battle. He entrusted to Captain James Rusling some papers and valuables, and asked Rusling to be sure his body was returned to Rockland. He was in a similar mood in conversation with Captain James Earle. Berry told Earle he was anxious to hear once more from his family. The captain volunteered at once to ride some eighteen miles to get the latest mail. Riding back into camp at two o'clock in the morning, he found Berry waiting. The general devoured the news from home by a campfire, repeating parts to Earle, and showing him photographs of his daughter that had been sent. Finally, Hiram Berry retired to his tent, saying, "Now I will try to get some sleep, as I look for warm work in the morning."

The "warm work," of course, came late in the afternoon of May 2. Berry's division was in reserve, stationed near Hooker's headquarters at Chancellor House. As increasing numbers of fugitives from Howard's XI Corps clogged the plank road, Fighting Joe called upon Berry to fill the breech.

---

The fate of the Army of the Potomac depended upon Berry. Yet he set about moving his division into line perpendicular to the road with the same calm, businesslike demeanor he had shown in the past. Breastworks were thrown up, infantry aligned, and artillery positioned to fire over the men's heads at the oncoming Confederates. With almost studied contempt, Berry's soldiers ignored the running men from Howard's shattered corps who burst through intervals in their line.

Darkness descended as advance units of Rebs bumped into Berry's skirmish line. One of the captured men turned out to be an aide of Jeb Stuart; another prisoner claimed General A. P. Hill was only a couple hundred yards off, on Berry's front.

What was not known was that Stonewall Jackson himself, with some staff, had been reconnoitering the federal line. He was shot by some North Carolina soldiers. Union skirmishers were within fifty yards of the wounded Confederate general before he was hastily, painfully, carried back. Hill, the same Hill who sent Berry his compliments at Fredericksburg, was also wounded, and command passed to Stuart.

It was about nine o'clock. Scattered Union resistance, disintegrating coordination of their advancing units, the loss of Jackson, and nightfall slowed the victorious Confederates for valuable minutes. Berry rode back and forth along his line, preparing to receive an attack.

Howard came up, depressed, bitter, with a remnant of his corps. According to Howard's recollection, Berry said, "Well, general, where now?"

"You take the right of this road and I will take the left and try to defend it," was Howard's reply. A less flattering version was that Howard said, "General Berry, I am ruined!"

Berry shot back, "Oh, no, General; I have a division that never was driven an inch; I will put them immediately into the breech and regain what you have lost."

Most likely what happened was that Berry asked Howard where the Union line could expect to be hardest pressed. Howard said the right, and Berry replied he would concentrate on that part of the line. Howard remarked to an officer after parting, "How noble was the bearing of General Berry."

The size and closeness of the Confederates was accentuated by the noise of many officers shouting orders and cursing in the woods. Moonlight revealed a large column heading down the road.

At 9:30 Berry's artillery opened up, with canister poured into the oncoming Confederates and shells dropped in their rear. The fire was very destructive, more than Berry realized, and the attack faltered.

An hour later, Stuart's men tried again. Heavy discharges of cannon and small arms from the Union line illuminated the night. And again the action was broken off.

Annie Etheridge, a young nurse who loved Berry like her father, took canteens of coffee to the front that night. Berry told her, "We are going to have a midnight charge," and directed her to a nearby house to attend to the wounded. He also asked her, if he was killed, to "go home with my body."

Berry was up all night, riding along his line, which was steadily augmented by other regiments and brigades.

Dawn came. Captain Rusling joked about the general's "presentiment." He was still alive, the line had held.

Berry, serious-faced, simply said, "Rusling, the battle is not over yet."

The Confederates resumed their attack with ferocity. Berry's division sustained heavy casualties, the heaviest of any on this Sunday. When the Third Maryland broke, Berry's left was exposed to a flank attack. While he sent one of his staff to Hooker to ascertain if he was expected to continue to hold his position, a lull in the shooting developed by seven o'clock in the morning. Berry decided to take advantage of it to talk with General Gershom Mott, whose brigade was on the opposite side of the plank road. He was used to communicating orders in person and, when his staff objected, pointing out there were Confederate sharpshooters in the woods beyond, he refused to let one of them deliver the order.

He proceeded across the road, conferred a few minutes with Mott, and started back. He was almost up to where his staff was standing when a puff of smoke in the trees was followed by the sound of a rifle crack.

Hiram Berry fell, a minie ball having plowed through his body, from shoulder to hip. "Poland! Poland!" the stricken man called to his chief of staff. Staffers scurried to the general. Captain Benedict took him in his arms as Berry murmured, "My wife and child!" His only other words were his last order: "Carry me off the field."

The damage was massive, and with one shudder, Hiram Berry died at 7:26 a.m.

He was 38.

In full view of many of his soldiers, the general's corpse was carried off and placed to the rear, under a blanket.

General Joe Hooker galloped up and, seeing officers clustered together by a body, he asked:

"Whom have you there, gentlemen?"

"Major General Berry."

Hooker quickly alighted from his horse. Hurrying to where Berry lay, he kissed the cold forehead. Hot tears running down his face, Hooker cried, "My God, Berry, why was this to happen? Why was the man on whom I relied so much to be taken away in this manner?"

There is little doubt that, had Berry lived, "Fighting Joe" would have given him command of a corps. Indeed, before fate intervened in the form of a piece of lead, Berry might have been destined for more.

Edwin Stanton told the Vice President it had been his intention to give Hiram Berry of Rockland, Maine, command of the Army of the Potomac.

*Hannibal Hamlin—Maine Historic Preservation Commission*

# Hannibal Hamlin
## *In the ranks*

General Hiram Berry's funeral procession moved from his flag-draped home to the Achorn cemetery on a cloudy, windy day. Thousands watched quietly as the funeral car passed, accompanied by Berry's horses, a military escort, over 300 Masons, and various dignitaries. The most conspicuous figure was that of the Vice President. The manner in which Hannibal Hamlin chose to honor Berry was likewise conspicuous, and aroused considerable comment.

The Vice President of the United States did not march with other prominent politicians, like Governor Coburn and ex-Governor Washburn. Instead, he marched in the ranks of the Bangor Fusiliers, Company A of the State Guards. The Rockland *Gazette* reported that there was criticism of Hamlin's action. It was more appropriate, people clucked, for him to appear in his official character as Vice President.

"He desired to render the highest honor in his power to the memory of General Berry, and he felt that he could best do this by serving in his place in the ranks of this company, in performing the last sad duties with which the soldier pays his farewell tribute to a fallen commander," the *Gazette* explained. Thus, with gun and knapsack, standing unmarked in the ranks, with tears glistening on his dark face, the Vice President bore homage to his dead friend.

It was unique in American history, but it was typical of the man. Hannibal Hamlin, born on Paris Hill in 1809, shared more than the year of his birth with Abraham Lincoln. Like Lincoln, he was a big, strong man with a swarthy complexion, who practiced a distinctly earthy, "down-home" type of politics. Both came to the Republican Party from other parties; Lincoln was a Whig before that party collapsed and Hamlin was a longtime Democrat, finally breaking with the Democrats over the slavery issue. Like the Illinois Republican, Hamlin was accused of being "black" in more than figurative terms. And like Lincoln, despite his folksy, understated style, Hannibal Hamlin definitely knew his mind and could be a very tough politician. But he never lost the common touch. He never developed "airs." What you saw was what you got.

Hannibal Hamlin had liked Hiram Berry from the start. Berry was his kind of man and his kind of general. He promoted the former Democratic mayor of Rockland harder than any Republican. And he knew exactly how to honor him.

Hamlin would maintain that he had never wanted to be Vice President. He had been in politics a long time, as congressman, governor, and senator; he knew he wielded much more power and influence as a senator than he would as Vice President. Aside from breaking a rare tie vote as presiding officer of the Senate, about the only power he had was over the Senate restaurant (where he prohibited the sale of booze). For a man used to power, the Vice Presidency was largely a frustrating experience in impotence.

Whatever the impact he had was totally dependent upon his rapport with a man he had never formally met until after they had been elected President and Vice President in 1860. Hamlin worked hard at developing a good working relationship with Lincoln.

He was named after a Cartheginian general, and when war came, no general could have been more vigorous in supporting the war. After Lincoln's April call for 75,000 volunteers, Hamlin, certain the President would have to call for more men when Congress convened in July, returned to Maine in May to see off the first regiments raised. Hampden, the town near Bangor where Hamlin had long resided (and where reformer Dorothea Dix was born), arranged a flag-raising ceremony to honor Hamlin's return as Vice President.

Hamlin took over direction of the event, making it into an old-fashioned muster. Musters were guaranteed to arouse patriotic sentiment. Hampden's own military history was hardly glorious; when British soldiers landed off the Penobscot one foggy day in 1814, the assembled militia scattered at the first shot. The redcoats had proceeded to march up to Bangor and occupy it for a few hours. But such history was banished on a fine May day, as good old Hannibal Hamlin fraternized with the home folk. The more discerning, however, noted that "there was an air about him that plainly drew the line between friendly and familiar advances."

Hamlin gave a short speech, saying: "There should be no temporizing now, no going back in this contest between anarchy and freedom." As the crowd cheered, the Vice President shouted:

"Now we will have a drill."

"But, Mr. Vice President, we have no arms," somebody noted.

"No arms?" Hamlin smiled. "Why, look at that fence. Let every man take a picket for a gun."

Hamlin ran to the fence, ripped off a picket, showing the way for the following crowd. The fence was quickly stripped.

"Take your places in line," the Vice President commanded. He proceeded to give the line of men what must have been for most their first exposure to the manual of arms.

Afterwards someone observed Hamlin's method was rather original, to which the Vice President responded, "Well, it was certainly an improvement over the 'hay-foot, straw-foot' plan."

What the thoughts of the owner of the picket fence were are not recorded.

Hannibal Hamlin was a Radical who believed in emancipation and the arming of freed blacks long before the cautious Lincoln supported such policies. When Lincoln finally decided upon emancipation, Hamlin was shown a draft of the Emancipation Proclamation a month before Lincoln announced his plan to the Cabinet.

When Hamlin spoke in Bangor on July 27, 1862, he knew where Lincoln intended to go on Abolition but could not say so. His remarks were really directed more at McClellan than at Lincoln, although it is understandable if they were misinterpreted. As his son explained: "He was more anxious to reach men who could carry only a few ideas than to deliver a polished effort for posterity to read."

"We don't fight the Rebels to save their property," Hamlin said. "We want to save our men as much as possible if it is done by men a little blacker than I am. I wish my voice could reach the officials at Washington. They are slow to move, but they must come to that position where they will seize everything to our advantage."

If that sounded critical of Lincoln, the fact was Hamlin *was* impatient, as a letter to Major Charles Hamlin after Antietam reflected. "How much do I wish the President had more energy, and would come up to the just demands of the country," the Vice President wrote.

When Lincoln issued the preliminary Emancipation Proclamation on September 22, Hamlin wrote from Bangor, "It will stand as the great act of the age." Lincoln replied that his expectations "are not as sanguine," given the slow enlistment rate. "The North responds to the proclamation sufficiently *in breath,* but breath alone kills no Rebels."

Of course black soldiers could kill Rebels. Selden Connor would later recount a conversation he had with Hamlin after the war, in which the former Vice President described how Lincoln came to order the raising of black troops. It was in January of 1863 when Hamlin's son, Captain Cyrus Hamlin, sent his card to his father's hotel room. Young Hamlin was requesting a meeting, along with some of his officer friends, on an important matter.

Hamlin assented to the meeting, and Cyrus brought along a dozen officers. They said it was time to organize black troops. They would accept commissions in black regiments at the same rank they were then holding.

"Well, boys, I will see what I can do for you," Hamlin said. He sent a page to the White House to arrange an audience with the President. The boy returned with a card from Abraham Lincoln setting the appointment for eight o'clock the next morning.

"Now, boys, you must meet me here at 7:30 tomorrow morning and I shall know that the man who is not at hand is not in earnest," Hamlin said.

Everybody showed up. They took carriages to the White House, and at eight o'clock Hamlin sent in his card. The small army was at once ushered in to meet Abraham Lincoln. "I could see that his countenance fell a little when he saw the brass buttons of my retinue, and the reason soon appeared," Hamlin later said.

Hamlin introduced them, saying, "Mr. President, these young men are friends of my son; some of them are Maine men and personally known to me; they are as good specimens of earnest, intelligent, patriotic citizens as can be found; some of them are graduates and other have abandoned their colleges to serve their country."

Lincoln displayed the "quizzical smile" Hamlin knew well. "How many of them," he said, "want promotions?"

"Wait a minute, Mr. President, and you will be informed on that score." Hamlin then repeated what the young officers had proposed.

Lincoln assumed a thoughtful demeanor, his chin against his chest. When Hamlin had finished, he said, "Mr. Hamlin, you have long been pressing upon me the duty and necessity of arming the colored men; but now when such young men as these take the same view and are willing to take service in colored troops without any increase of rank, the time has come for action. I will at once issue the necessary directions for organizing."

"How much of a matter is that?"

"Oh, only a line."

Rather boldly, Hamlin said, "Well, Mr. President, won't you write it now?"

Lincoln smiled. "Certainly, if you won't take my word."

The President scribbled, "The Secretary of War will at once take the necessary steps for organizing a brigade of colored troops."

"That will do, as well as a longer order," he said.

"Now, Mr. President, I do not ordinarily play messenger, but I should like to take that order myself and deliver it to the secretary," Hamlin said.

Lincoln slapped his Vice President on the back. "Oh, I have long suspected you and Stanton of being in a conspiracy on this subject."

Accompanied by his youthful entourage, Hamlin took the paper to Stanton's office.

"*His* countenance fell, too, when he saw me coming with so many young officers," Hamlin recalled. Stanton, too, figured they were after promotions.

"Without a word I handed him the order. He glanced at it, then turned it over on the table before him and looked at me. Then he picked it up, read it again, and came round to me and put his big strong arms around me and with tears in his eyes gave me a regular bear hug."

This was the origin of the "Ulmann Brigade," one of the regiments commanded by Cyrus Hamlin. Although its genesis was the first official directive from Washington to raise black troops, General Nathaniel Banks in Louisiana, the destination of the brigade, was also raising, apparently on his initiative, the *Corps d'Afrique* at New Orleans. Black solders participated in the May 27 assault on Port Hudson. I. S. Bangs, originally with the Twentieth Maine, was in charge of recruiting for one of the regiments.

Referring to Port Hudson, Bangs later wrote, "For reasons I could never learn, no flag of truce was ever sent to bury the colored soldiers who fell on that day, and their bones bleached in the sun (nearer the Rebel works than any white men fell) until the surrender." It was a tarnished start, but black Americans would play an increasingly important part in the Union war effort. It was a role Hannibal Hamlin helped make possible.

As with Emancipation, it was a policy finally dictated by military necessity more than Hamlin's advocacy. But he did what he could. He was always ready and willing to render aid to Maine soldiers. One example was recollected by Captain Frank Garnsey, a Bangor man with the Second Maine. When a friend of Garnsey's, Lieutenant Sumner Kittredge of Milo, held prisoner by the Rebs for over a year, was released, he was in bad shape. Trying to obtain his back pay to cover medical expenses, Kittredge was frustrated by a Federal payroll officer who refused to make disbursements between paydays. Learning of this, Captain Garnsey took the issue straight to the Vice President of the United States.

Hamlin asked where the bureaucrat was located, grabbed his hat, and went to the miscreant's office. "Vice President Hamlin simply eyed that man, and the look that came out of his big black eyes was sufficient to change the major's high-and-mighty appearance," Garnsey said. Hamlin then demanded that a check be made out immediately for Kittredge, and without delay. The nervous major made out the check and handed it to Hamlin "who was standing there as grim as an Indian sachem."

That was Hannibal Hamlin. No wonder he and Hiram Berry got along so famously. They were cut from the same cloth.

*Neal Dow—Maine State Archives*

# Neal Dow

*"There was no room*
*for excitement or enthusiasm."*

Neal Dow felt impotent, marooned on a sandbar in the Gulf of Mexico. On May 19 he had received a commission as brigadier general, but assumed he could not put it to much use. It looked like the war would end soon. He was ordered to occupy Fort Saint Philip, reduced to rubble by Farragut's guns and the corrosive hand of Nature, and then was sent to command at Pensacola. Both stations were distant from actual fighting, but allowed Dow to exercise considerable power. He continued to train fugitive blacks to fight for the Union.

And he continued to confiscate Confederate property, ostensibly for military reasons. It appears that old Neal had sticky fingers; Rebel furniture and silver was shipped back to Portland for his personal use. In fairness to Dow, he was hardly the only Union officer to engage in such activity. His correspondence to his wife indicated some qualms. And he was always courteous with Southerners, even when looting their property.

In July he was summoned to New Orleans, to command its defenses. He lodged at the City Hotel upon his arrival. The landlord paid the little man little initial attention, but a reporter, noting his shoulder tabs, told the proprietor he was hosting a brigadier general. The landlord at once sent an orderly to Room 21 with a mint julep, so chocked with greenery, it "looked more like a flower-pot than a genial beverage."

The black orderly lingered in the general's room, evidently waiting for Dow to gulp the drink. The general, however, asked him to leave the drink, which he did and left. Several hours later the waiter, whom Dow described to his wife as "a darkey" who was quite "a character," returned to announce that dinner was just about ready. The man saw that Dow's drink was untouched, its greenery wilted.

"Oh, dat's all dead now!" he said, according to Dow's account of the conversation that ensued.

"Well, I never drink at all."

"Ah, I tought you was one 'o dem dat indulged."

"No, I never do."

"Oh, all right."

"Yes, I mean to keep all right."

"Yah, yah!"

The waiter headed off with the dead julep. Dow expected the glass would be drained by the time it reached the bar. He was correct. What he had *not* anticipated was that a humorous story, written by the observant reporter who learned his identity, would be twisted by his political enemies (easily as numerous as Confederate adversaries) to make it look like Neal Dow was boozing in the bayous.

The mint julep story made the rounds, but was not as damaging as rumors that Dow was feathering his own nest. In early 1863 a plantation owner tried to take the general to court for confiscating twenty-four hogsheads of sugar and some silverware. Dow had a silver pitcher sent back from Portland, but otherwise insisted he was subject to military, not civil, law. He refused to appear in a Louisiana court, maintaining it would set a bad precedent. Many years later, the Supreme Court upheld Dow's stand. Ben Butler, himself nicknamed "spoons" for alleged pilfering, reprimanded

Dow, who blamed his embarrassment on Butler and his "rum clique."

Dow's brigade was made up of regiments from Michigan, New York, Connecticut and New Hampshire. The general got mixed reviews. The New England troops apparently liked him. At least one of the New Hampshire soldiers found Dow "very pleasant" compared to division commander General Thomas Sherman, "a stern-looking old fellow." On the other hand, a New York officer noted that it was "the greatest of all the many wonders we have how so thoroughly incompetent and unofficerlike a man should retain so high a position."

By this time Dow had a new commander, General Banks, another political general from Massachusetts who shared Dow's Abolitionist sentiments and Republican politics. Dow was disappointed to learn that Banks, once a Prohibitionist, shared Butler's tippling habits. In May of 1863 Banks ordered Dow's brigade to proceed up the Mississippi to assist in operations against the Confederate fortifications at Port Hudson.

Port Hudson was a smaller version of the Rebel stronghold upriver at Vicksburg; both deprived the Union of uninterrupted control of the Mississippi. When Neal Dow showed up with his brigade, the contending armies were trading heavy gunfire. The diminutive New Englander expected little more.

On May 25 he rather blithely called upon the brigade's band to play some patriotic tunes. When the band leader objected, warning this might draw enemy fire, Dow clucked, "If you're afraid to play, you'd better go home." The nervous musicians had hardly gotten into "Yankee Doodle" before a shell screamed in and exploded near Colonel Dow. That ended the music quickly.

Dow was patently inexperienced, but a West Point education was not needed to know that an assault on the well-entrenched Confederates was stupid. General Tom Sherman, who did have a West Point diploma, agreed with Dow's assessment. Nevertheless, the word was that Banks would order an assault. "I do not see any great urgency for it," Dow wrote home, "especially as we have entirely cut off the enemy's communication, and with the fall of Vicksburg, which cannot hold out much longer, this place must also come into our hands without bloodshed."

It was an astute analysis. Port Hudson would surrender four days after the fall of Vicksburg on July 4, 1863. But Banks could not wait. He ordered a general assault on May 27, hoping "some stroke of luck" might result in victory.

General Dow had no illusions. The attack would have to be made across an open plain, fully exposed to Rebel sharpshooters and artillery. A gulch had to be surmounted before coming up against a deep ditch in front of the Confederate breastwork. It was a daunting prospect for veteran troops, let alone an army which, for the most part, had never even been under fire.

Ordered to advance his brigade in a column, Dow took advantage of the discretion Sherman granted him in deploying his troops. He spread them out in four long lines over a broad front, to minimize the expected slaughter.

Before sending his men in, Dow rode along the front on "Billy," offering words of encouragement. He overheard one Michigan soldier say, "I guess it's all right, the old man is smiling."

It was not all right, and Dow knew it. But, with drums beating and flags flying, he marched his men out of the cover afforded by some trees. Bullets whistled by and artillery shells exploded; Dow was surprised and pleased that he was able to control his fear. In good order, his force moved out onto the plain. It was about 500 yards to the Confederate works. The brigade moved at double quick into a deadly crossfire. To Dow the rifle balls of the enemy seemed to fall on the field like "big drops of rain upon dusty streets."

An Arkansas colonel, watching Dow's movements, ascertained his rank, and directed a group of sharpshooters to concentrate their fire at Dow. Within about 300 yards of the Rebel works, after knocking down several fences that obstructed their progress, the brigade was sweeping forward when a spent ball hit the little general in the arm.

The impact made Dow sway in the saddle as his arm ballooned to twice its normal size. Assisted off a frantic "Billy," Dow continued walking toward the enemy.

It seemed like the Confederates had the range of every square yard of the field. There was no cover of smoke, since the Union troops were not firing. The object was to get close to the fort as soon as possible and engage the enemy there—if they could get there. "There was no room for excitement or enthusiasm," Dow thought, only a grim determination to push on.

Within eighty yards of the breastworks, the brigade received a withering volley. Dow urged his men on, but felt the sharp sting of another Confederate ball as it ripped through his left thigh.

Neal Dow's participation in the charge was done. Helped toward the rear, he painfully remounted his old pet and rode "Billy" away from the noise of battle. The dead and wounded were littered on the dusty ground. Soon the living were retreating over them.

The brigade had suffered 354 casualties, less than Dow had expected, but bad enough in a futile action. One of the wounded officers was General Tom Sherman, whose leg had been shattered. The old Regular sent word to Dow that he had never seen a better charge than the one the Maine general led. He also told the messenger to "tell General Dow that he is now at an age when an occasional glass will do him good."

While the pain in his arm was most acute, surgeons informed Dow that his leg wound was more serious. He had been lucky. If the bullet had strayed a bit on its path either the bone would have been hit or the artery severed. Either way, amputation probably would be necessary. Dow also learned bullet holes had perforated his coat and one of his stockings.

Advised to accompany other wounded officers to better medical facilities at Baton Rouge or New Orleans, Neal Dow insisted upon remaining at the front. He had hopes for further action and promotion to succeed Sherman as division commander.

# Joshua Chamberlain
## *"How I should enjoy a May-walk with you."*

During the months after Fredericksburg, Joshua Chamberlain sought to patch up conditions on the home front and see action on the military front.

In January, after the fiasco of "Burnside's Mud March," he requested a fifteen-day leave of absence to "attend to business in the state of Maine involving pecuniary and other important matters." Part of those "other important matters" involved a trip to Augusta to talk with Maine's new governor Abner Coburn. Chamberlain pushed several promotions in the Twentieth Maine, including that of brother Tom to the rank of lieutenant.

Evidently Chamberlain also made some headway with Fannie; he was back in the Army only a month after his February leave when he got another five days off in April to meet Fannie in Washington. In a subsequent letter to "my precious wife," he insisted he always thought first of her. "You were too sad, Darling," he wrote. He hoped she was "in a happier mood." Money matters weighed on him; he wanted to get back to Maine again as executor of a will yet was hesitant to leave the Army on the eve of another campaign. "I feel quite puzzled—'cornered' expresses it," he said.

"The most that troubles me now is that I may not be able to take part in the next fight," Chamberlain fretted. On April 22 the Twentieth Maine was removed a mile away from the rest of the Army of the Potomac on "Quarantine

Hill." The camp was surrounded by ominous placards saying "Small Pox." If a battle occurred and Chamberlain was
"left here in a pest-house, I shall be desperate with mortification."

Holman Melcher, recently made a lieutenant, echoed
Chamberlain's frustration. He was sure the Twentieth
"would have made a 'mark' against the Rebels," and believed the smallpox outbreak was result of a plot. "Murder!
Nothing more or less, only a little indirectly," he fumed. "It
is just what was intended by the villains that procured the
'matter.' It was probably done to cripple the Army."

Melcher figured Colonel Ames would leave the regiment to get field duty. "It is very hard for one so ambitious
to remain inactive at such a time as this," he observed. The
same could be said of Chamberlain. Ames got a staff position with General George Meade, commander of V Corps.
Chamberlain was frantic to get the Twentieth Maine involved in the Chancellorsville campaign. Apparently in all
seriousness he told headquarters that, if nothing else, the
regiment "could give the enemy the smallpox."

Finally, the Twentieth Maine was assigned the task of
guarding telegraph and signal lines. "Prince" was wounded
in the head; Chamberlain was on the fringes of the battle,
but not in the thick of it. Ames was promoted to brigadier
general, commanding a brigade in Howard's XI Corps.
Chamberlain became Colonel of the Twentieth Maine.

"I am in command here now," Joshua wrote his
brother John. The quarantine had ended, and Chamberlain
invited his younger brother to visit the regiment. He
promised John "would thoroughly enjoy it."

The new Colonel almost immediately had to deal with
the transfer to his command of about 100 men of the Second
Maine. The soldiers, veterans with a good record, believed—
rightly—that they had been misled about the term of their

enlistment. They were mutinous and Chamberlain was empowered to shoot them, although he was not about to do that to men from the Bangor region. He sympathized with them, unsuccessfully urging Governor Coburn to share his sympathy, "but while under my orders, they will be strictly held to obedience."

Writing to his daughter that May, Chamberlain said there had been a big battle and would probably be another one soon. It was necessary to "make those Rebels behave better, and stop their wicked works in trying to spoil our Country, and making us all so unhappy," he wrote. "I suppose Mamma is at home by this time," he added. Fannie spent time in Boston and elsewhere while either "Cousin D" or Chamberlain's sister took care of the family.

"It is very hot here, so that we can hardly bear to have our clothes on," the Colonel wrote his little girl. "But we do not have any Mayflowers here. All the ground is so trampled by the Army that even the grass will not grow much. How I should enjoy a May-walk with you and Wyllys."

By June the heat was stifling. And the Army of the Potomac was marching north again. Chamberlain was felled by sunstroke. While he recuperated—he was lucky to survive—the regiment proceeded on without him. He missed some skirmishing with Stuart at Middleburg; when he rejoined the Twentieth he was too sick to leave his tent.

A couple of days later, he got company. Brother John had followed the Army, after finding it had left the Fredericksburg area; he was himself lucky to avoid Confederate guerrillas. John, graduate of the Bangor Theological Seminary and member of the Christian Association, was already having a more exciting visit than anticipated.

*Bugler Charles B. Kenney, Company K—History of First Maine Cavalry*

# First Maine Cavalry

*"That First Maine Cavalry would charge straight into Hell, if they were ordered to."*

Colonel Hugh Judson Kilpatrick, 27, was noted for having a good time almost as much as he loved fighting. It was no surprise, then, that on June 8, "Little Kil" invited the officers of his brigade over to headquarters after the men had bivouacked to have some pre-battle fun. Kilpatrick's brigade of cavalry was part of the 11,000-man force under General Alfred Pleasonton's command poised to cross the Rhappahannock and attack a Confederate cavalry force under Jeb Stuart, reported to be in the vicinity of Brandy Station.

The officers found something covered by a poncho outside the Colonel's tent. The poncho, it turned out, covered a "vessel of some kind filled with a liquid mixture, which upon investigation proved to be 'whisky punch.' "

There were three regiments in Kilpatrick's command: the Tenth New York, Harris Light, and First Maine Cavalry. The Maine unit's members were called "Puritans." Their officers had signed temperance pledges. "However," recalled Captain Charles W. Ford, "there were a few honorable exceptions." The liquor flowed quickly, and a "pleasant hour" passed. When the happy party was breaking up, Kilpatrick called upon an officer of the First Maine Cavalry Regiment to deliver a parting toast. The Mainer said: "Here's hoping we will do as well at Brandy Station tomorrow as we are doing at Whisky Station tonight."

"Good, blamed good! Best thing I have heard tonight!" the Colonel laughed.

Kilpatrick would have reason to appreciate the First Maine the next day. It was a month after Chancellorsville, and although General Hooker did not know what Jeb Stuart was up to, he had learned where he was. On June 9 Stuart's 9,500-man command would be startled by the Union cavalry attack. Although some infantry—including a brigade under Adelbert Ames—was involved, the battle that ensued would be the biggest cavalry fight of the war. It also marked the beginning of the Gettysburg campaign, since Stuart was at Brandy Station to "screen" the movement of the rest of the Army of Northern Virginia to the west. Lee was heading north again.

The blue horse-soldiers started preparing to move before dawn. At daylight they splashed across the river at Beverly's Ford to the north of Brandy Station and Kelly's Ford further south. Kilpatrick's brigade was in Gregg's Division attacking from the south. The First Maine was the last regiment to cross the Rhappahannock; forming in a column four abreast, they galloped for four miles through a forest on a narrow road before coming up to the battlefield.

The horses were rested briefly before the cavalrymen remounted and trotted out of the woods. They beheld a large open area with a semicircle of hills in the distance: it looked like an amphitheater. Large numbers of blue and grey horsemen were performing, and clearly things were going badly for the boys in blue. Another of Gregg's brigades had taken a drubbing trying to take a key hill called Fleetwood with a few houses on it. One was Stuart's headquarters. Kilpatrick had sent in his New York regiments, only to see them "float off like feathers on the wind" after contact with Confederate units.

According to Kilpatrick, "I looked back with my heart swelling in my throat, sad for that day, feeling that we were defeated" when he saw the First Maine come up. He rode over to Colonel Calvin Douty and shouted in a loud voice, so loud every man could hear him: "Men of Maine, you must save the day!"

Another version has the brigade commander crying to the Maine colonel: "Colonel Douty, what can you do with your regiment?"

Douty said, "I can drive the rebels to Hell, sir!"

Whatever the exact words, the Maine regiment was ready, and thundered ahead. Their objective was a Rebel battery on Fleetwood Hill, and they galloped across the intervening mile or so oblivious to shells lobbed at them, musketry fire, and Rebel cavalry. A Virginia regiment of horse, which had scattered the Harris Light, charged the First Maine. The Mainers swerved to their left a bit and slammed head-on into the Rebels.

Although there were more Virginians, the Mainers' blood was up and, in brief, savage fighting with sabres, the First Maine overwhelmed the Confederates. The lusty cheering of the "Puritans" reverberated across the field. Sending about a hundred prisoners to the rear, the First Maine regrouped and charged on—without Colonel Douty. In the collision of the two cavalry columns, Douty and a few men were deflected from his command.

Without hardly pausing, the First Maine continued to head for the enemy battery. Confederates, mounted and on foot, fired at them from the hill, but their aim was poor and the Mainers were moving fast. They swept right over the cannon, scattering the gunners, and moved past the Barbour house, which had quartered Stuart. Their momentum carried them straight across a field beyond. Only when they ran up against woods did they wheel about.

*Calvin Sanger Douty—Maine State Archives*

Pride of Lions

It was one of the longest and most spectacular cavalry charges of the war. Years later one of the participants wrote: "Oh, it was grand, and many a man who was in that charge has at times fancied that if he were allowed to choose, he would say, 'Let me bid this world goodby amid the supreme excitement of a grand, exultant, successful cavalry charge like this.' "

However, at the time, the First Maine came to a sobering realization. They had no support, were way within the Rebel lines, and could be surrounded and cut off. The Confederates, who thought more Union cavalry *had* to be coming, awakened to the same reality. They started to rally and fire at the exposed blue cavalry in the field.

Lieutenant Colonel Charles Smith, who had assumed command once Douty had been sidetracked, ordered some of his troopers to dismount. Using their horses' backs to steady their aim, they returned fire with their carbines.

Rebels were back at the battery on the hill. Major Stephen Boothby ordered one of his sergeants to tell a captain to charge the battery. The sergeant, William Loud, a joiner from Richmond on the Kennebec, was older than most of the troopers, almost forty, and had a speech impediment. In the noise and confusion, he apparently misunderstood the major. Whatever the reason, he rode up to the Rebel gunners and shouted, "By orders of M-Major B-Boothby, I w-will t-take charge of this b-battery."

The Rebs weren't about to comply, and the sergeant spent a few months as a guest of the Confederacy at Libby Prison. Exchanged and returned to his regiment, he was asked if he really had demanded the battery's surrender. He replied, "N-no, it's a damned lie!" Maybe it was.

To extricate themselves from the bind they were in, the First Maine either had to go over the guns again, or around the Barbour House. Both were in enemy hands, but, reformed, the Maine men charged back. They headed directly for the artillery. Just as he saw the gunners starting to fire, Smith ordered his column to veer right, barely avoiding the whizzing shells. Then the First Maine moved sharply left, around the house, into the field beyond. The Confederate soldiers who swarmed about, trying to stop them, were brushed aside.

Amazingly, the regiment made it back to Union lines with only a handful of casualties. More than thirty men were taken prisoner. But the First Maine took twice as many prisoners, and probably inflicted many more casualties than it sustained. It also brought back a captured Rebel battleflag, of Hampton's Legion. The story that went the rounds was that Kilpatrick tried to get possession of the flag, but was promptly told if he wanted a flag to go back to Fleetwood Hill and get one himself.

The whole episode took about two hours. The fluid nature of the combat was illustrated by the experience of Captain Benjamin Tucker, who was separated from his company and captured. Escorted to the rear accompanied by three Rebs, one on both sides and another riding ahead, Tucker grabbed his left guard's sabre and dispatched the unlucky fellow with a quick thrust. A hard back stroke disabled the guard on his right, and by the time the gray cavalryman riding in front had turned, he was Tucker's prisoner.

Another trooper, weighing in at barely 100 pounds, confronted a Goliath-sized Rebel on foot and demanded his surrender. The big man grabbed the smaller cavalryman's foot and pitched him off the other side of his horse. When the horse between the two combatants trotted off, the Confederate moved ahead to finish off the little Yank. But a bullet from the Mainer's revolver creased his skull, knocking him down. When he regained his sense he felt a gun barrel against his bleeding head. "How are you, Uncle Johnny? Will you surrender now?" the Yankee David said.

Trooper Riley Jones, twenty-one, a sailor before he became a cavalryman, had some trouble navigating on the return charge. Veering too far to the left, he headed straight for the four-foot terrace of a big white house. With no time to change course, his horse cleared the obstacle with a flying leap—but landed stiff legged. Jones wrote, "the jar nearly drove me through the saddle, and I surely thought my backbone must be four inches shorter at night than it was in the morning." It can be assumed Jones walked like a sailor for awhile after this.

The First Maine had charged into and out of the jaws of death almost unscathed. Yet the hill remained in Confederate hands. At best, Brandy Station was a draw. But that was an improvement for the much-maligned Union cavalry. At Brandy Station Yankee horse soldiers showed they were equal to Southern cavalry. And the sarcastic quip that one never saw a dead cavalryman in the Army of the Potomac, commonly repeated by infantry, lost some of its edge.

June 17 was a "scorcher" of a day. The First Maine broke camp near Manassas Junction that morning and rode across the two-time battlefield, kicking up a column of dust. It was shaping up as a campaign enveloped in dust; after a six-week dry spell, the earth was parched. After twenty-odd miles in the saddle, the regiment reached the little town of Aldie. A cavalry fight had been raging all day, and now, in the fading light of late afternoon, it was going badly for the Union cause.

The Rebs were on a string of hills, crisscrossed by stone walls, just beyond the town. There were batteries on the elevated ground, and skirmishers among sheds and haystacks bordering the lower slope, along the Snickersville Turnpike.

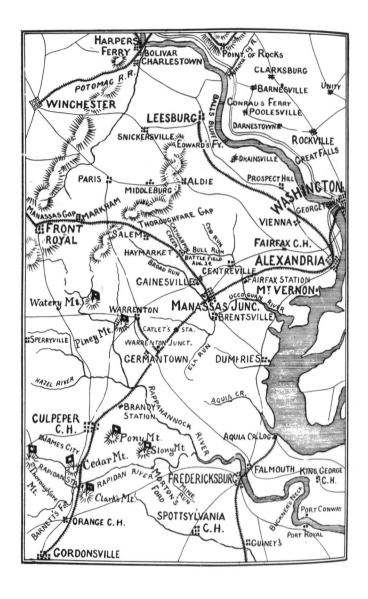

*Virginia Theatre of War, 1863. Brandy Station, Aldie and Middleburg were all scenes of cavalry battles, as Lee headed north.*

*—U.S. Army Signal Corps map*

Kilpatrick, now a brigadier general (He credited the First Maine's action at Brandy Station with winning him his silver star), had failed in assaulting these positions, and the regiments of his new brigade were falling back in confusion.

For "Little Kil" and the First Maine, history was about to repeat itself.

The First Maine's Colonel Douty took in the scene. It was nearing six o'clock, and the regiment, now in a brigade commanded by General Gregg's cousin, had been ordered in to relieve Kilpatrick. Douty was on the left flank, aligning the companies there in preparation for a charge, when Kilpatrick came upon Company H on the right. His brigade had been routed and Confederate horsemen were in hot pursuit.

Now he encountered an "unbroken front of live men, with glistening sabres drawn," and he reined in his stead.

"What regiment is this?" he asked, his face a mixture of sweat, dust and dejection.

"First Maine!" was the chorus from a dozen men.

Kilpatrick's face brightened. "Forward, First Maine! You saved the field at Brandy Station, and you can do it here!"

The Mainers let loose three rousing cheers, and moved forward against the Rebel cavalry behind Kilpatrick. A melee followed, and the Confederates retreated, with Company H hard on their heels. While Kilpatrick had initiated the charge, Colonel Douty lost little time in bringing up the rest of the regiment.

This was a lot of activity for a man of fifty, about three decades older than most of his men. But Calvin Sanger Douty was a big, hardy man, noted both for his abstinence and powers of endurance. When the war began, Douty was beginning his third term as Sheriff of Piscataquis County. A surveyor and "comfortably situated" farmer, Douty lived in the shire town of Dover with his wife and three surviving children. At first family and public responsibilities kept Douty away from the front, but after Bull Run even his wife's pleadings were inadequate to keep him from joining the First Maine assembling at Augusta.

Before he reached Virginia, death claimed two of his children. Shaken, he persevered in what he considered to be his patriotic duty. A prudent, almost stolid figure in his Maine habitat, he became a lion in the war zone. Jonathon Prince Cilley of Thomaston recalled that Douty, "scenting the battle from afar, seemed a different man from what ever appeared to us before."

At Brandy Station, Douty had been unable to see the charge through and Colonel Smith had taken his place. But Smith was detached with four companies on the other side of town when this charge began. The big man from Maine's back country would see this charge through to the finish.

But first he had to catch up with his troops.

At the outset, Lieutenant Henry Hall, exactly half "old man" Douty's age, found himself apparently in front of the rest of Company H thundering after the enemy cavalry. In the darkness and dust, it was difficult for the former student and teacher from rural Starks to tell friend from foe. Thus he started to swing his sabre at the first horseman in sight, realizing in the nick of time it was Private Isaiah Mosher, a twenty-two-year-old farmer and neighbor from Starks. Mosher had just been shot in the arm and was having trouble controlling his horse.

Several Rebs were hacking away at the disabled trooper, while another, probably the one who shot Mosher, was getting ready to pay Hall the same compliment. The Lieutenant knocked the revolver from the Reb's hand with his sabre, then whacked him on the side of the head. The man, clinging to the mane of his horse, ducked his head behind the animal's to elude Hall's blows. The Reb proved tenacious. Hall wrote: "I then thrust once, twice, three times, but I blush to confess that my sabre point was so blunt I could not pierce even his old gray coat, it was so thick and hard."

The charge of another, thick-set Confederate trooper diverted Hall's attention. When the Mainer turned in his saddle to do battle, however, the Rebel retreated. This interval—and all of this was occurring within seconds—gave the cavalrymen harassing Mosher time to ride off. Not seeing Mosher either, Hall was all set to return to pursuing the enemy when his horse fell, sending him flying over its head.

Landing in the road, Hall instinctively rolled into the ditch, just missing being trampled by the rest of the First Maine. Dusting himself off, he saw that his horse had disappeared and was somewhere in Rebeldom. Just across the road several troopers, including his older brother, Sergeant Daniel Hall, had captured a Confederate battle flag. They also nabbed a Reb riding a pale horse. Ironically a member of the infamous "Black Horse Cavalry" (Fourth Virginia), the Rebel was immediately given an offer he was in no position to refuse: "I told the rebel I would swap horses with him, and that I had already delivered mine." The Confederate, perhaps glad to be out of the fight himself, even helped Hall mount his horse. And he was off again.

Captain George Summat, like Colonel Douty, was not at the front of the action when it started. But like Douty, the thirty-three-year-old native of Konigsburg, Prussia, a Regular who had fought the Comanches, got there quickly. So did Kilpatrick, whose horse was shot in the neck at the beginning of the charge.

The First Maine had proceeded about a half mile when it ran into heavy fire from the enemy. The first two companies were hit by skirmishers in and around some haystacks at the base of a ridge. Charging in with four more companies, Major Boothby pushed the skirmishers back. Kilpatrick arrived and called out to the Lewiston clergyman's son: "God bless you, Boothby! Hold them! Hold them!" Henry Hall noted "the very air was blue with flashing words that fell from fearless Boothby's lips." These were presumably not words used in Pa's church.

As Rebels streamed up the hill, Colonel Douty charged after them. Kilpatrick joined in. Douty and his troopers reached the stone walls along the crest, behind which dismounted Confederate cavalry were able to cut up the attacking Yankees in a murderous crossfire. Kilpatrick saw Douty "go down in a soldier's death upon that bloody field."

At this point a reformed New York regiment and the rest of the First Maine under Colonel Smith cleared out the remaining Rebels.

The fight over, Colonel Douty, shot twice at close range in the side, was found lying near one of the stone walls. Nearby was the corpse of Captain Summat. Near some pines Charlie Decker, a private aged twenty-two, had a bullet hole in his forehead; no more farming for him. Jimmy Hurd, born and raised in Harmony, Maine, was also dead; a student, he had enlisted at eighteen. Captain Hall's brother, Daniel, died of wounds received capturing the Fourth Virginia's flag.

When a steward took a look at Corporal Abner Emery, he commented, "Well, they meant you this time." Emery, a farmer from Skowhegan had a bullet through his lungs, a wrist, and his arm, as well as sabre cuts on his head.

"Yes," the corporal replied, "but they didn't get me, and I shall soon be able to give them another trial, damn the Rebs."

That was the spirit. Corporal Emery would have a chance later to get some more licks in, but right now it was up to his comrades. They did not have long to wait. June 19 was another hot day in the Loudoun Valley, which bordered the Blue Ridge. Just beyond that ridge Lee's army was moving up the Shenandoah. It was to prevent Hooker from learning this that the Reb cavalry fought these fights. As long as Pleasanton's troopers were fighting, they were not getting the information on Lee that Joe Hooker wanted desperately. So, on a day when the thermometer hit 98$^{o}$, the Battle of Aldie was recreated at another small town with another hill held by Stuart's men.

Again the First Maine was called upon to charge Rebs behind stone walls. Led by Colonel Charles Smith, who had replaced Douty, the Mainers tipped the balance at Middleburg. It rained the next day, but on Sunday, June 21, another battle was joined at Upperville.

*Charles Smith—Maine State Archives*

Considerable infantry was involved in this fight, including Vincent's Brigade, that counted the Twentieth Maine among its regiments. The fighting in and around the town was inconclusive. As the day dragged on, General Pleasanton became increasingly irritated. When he fumed in Kilpatrick's presence about the lack of progress, "Little Kil," now a division commander, responded, "General Pleasanton, there is one regiment in the corps that can carry the town. Give me the First Maine Cavalry, and I'll do it."

Pleasanton directed General Gregg to let Kilpatrick use the First Maine; Gregg demurred. He was keeping the Maine unit in reserve; they had done more than their share of fighting during the recent battles. Pleasanton cut him off: "It is my order, sir."

And that was that. Kilpatrick's orders were for the First Maine to "charge the town, drive out the enemy and, if possible, get beyond." As the Maine soldiers trotted past headquarters, giving three loud cheers, "Little Kil" said: "That First Maine Cavalry would charge straight into Hell, if they were ordered to."

Kilpatrick called out to Captain George Brown, "Brown, do you sing any songs now?" Brown and Kilpatrick had sung a few songs together; now Brown expected to lead the two companies assigned to charge the town. But Colonel Smith rode up to the head of the column.

"Colonel, do not go with us," Brown pleaded, "we cannot afford to lose you today." Smith ignored him, saw some Rebs gathered about a field piece in the middle of the street, and shouted, "Charge!"

Startled by the suddenness of the onslaught, the Rebs fired high. Grape-shot hissed over the heads of the oncoming troops. One participant in the charge later admitted "I shut my eyes, as I did not wish to see who went down; but it was only for an instant, and then it seemed that I heard but the gallop of one mighty horse, as we thundered down the streets of that quiet town."

The horsemen went over and around the gun, scattered its supports, and swept through town. When Rebels tried to concentrate beyond Upperville, the First Maine horse soldiers broke them up.

Another successful charge. The Maine regiment's fame was spreading throughout the Army. They *would* charge Hell itself.

# Neal Dow

*"I'll surrender, sir."*

Neal Dow wanted to obtain a transfer, perhaps to Virginia. *Anywhere* but Louisiana. General Banks had thwarted Dow's hopes of succeeding the wounded General Tom Sherman to divisional command, and Dow exasperated Banks by requesting leave on June 12.

Banks was preparing another assault on Port Hudson, which Dow considered stupid and needless. Another attack on the well entrenched Confederates would, he thought, result in another bloody repulse. He felt "our true policy was to watch and wait for time and starvation to do their certain work." On June 14 the assault was made. Dow was right. Heavy Union losses translated to no gain.

Uncomfortable at the front, slowly recuperating from his wounds, Dow secured removal from the hut he occupied to a small house a few miles to the rear of the Union Army. Dow later claimed he was moved so that his rude lodging could be converted to field hospital, but it seems clear he sought better accommodations. The new house of a "Mrs. Cage" was more comfortable. It also was barely within Union lines and vulnerable to Confederate raiders.

Dow began to worry about his exposed location when a couple of his bodyguards were captured. He spent the evening of June 28 in a cotton shed. The next day he mounted "Billy" for the first time since he was shot, and spent the day with his brigade. He decided to move back that night, and rode back to the Cage house, unescorted.

Clad in white, like a Southern gentleman, the Yankee general was a conspicuous figure in the moonlight.

A squad of Confederates was prepared to try to nab him. Dow's whereabouts were betrayed by a "Mrs. Brown," who said he could be captured easily. She volunteered to lead soldiers to him. Mrs. Cage would cooperate by occupying Dow at a game of cards.

The squad was made up of a lieutenant on furlough from the Army of Northern Virginia, several members of the Seventeenth Arkansas, a young man living in the neighborhood, and a man known simply as "Tex," because that name was inscribed on his white hat. According to Jonathan Simms, one of the Arkansans, the squad arrived at Mrs. Cage's about ten o'clock in the evening.

The dogs immediately started barking, and the Confederate party quickly dismounted and rushed into the house. The general's orderlies, asleep in a hall, were grabbed. But General Dow himself was not there. The helpful Mrs. Cage had not played cards with Dow because there was no opportunity: there was no chance anyway. As Dow remarked later, "I have never played even one game since my early youth, and do not know a Jack from a King or Queen."

However, Mrs. Cage had learned where Dow had gone the previous night, and the squad had remounted to head there when Dow showed up, an apparition in white, in the dooryard.

Simms and fellow Arkansan John Petty rode up to the horseman, revolvers drawn, and asked if he was General Dow.

"Yes, sir."

"Surrender, or I'll kill you!" the Confederates shouted in unison.

Dow hesitated for a moment, as if considering his options. He was unarmed. At his age and in his condition resistance or flight were impossible. There were no options.

"I'll surrender, sir," Dow said to Simms. "I'll go with you."

The Confederate band galloped off into the night with Dow and his orderlies in tow. They travelled hard. Physical discomfort was, however, overwhelmed by Dow's absolute sense of mortification at allowing himself to be trapped.

Now the man so used to exercising control over others, either as a temperance crusader enforcing his reforms or a general issuing orders, was in the power of others. When the squad stopped for breakfast at a friendly house, Dow's most valued possessions were divvied up.

Simms, Petty, and John McKowen, the lieutenant from Virginia, divided the plunder. Drawing lots, Petty got first choice: he took "Billy." The magnificent chestnut sorrel was Dow's family pet. McKowen drew second choice and claimed the general's pearl-handled sword. Simm took Dow's brace of Allen-model revolvers in patent leather holsters.

The day after his capture, Neal Dow's journey to Richmond began. Lacking a uniform, Dow's best garment was "a long, much worn, travel-stained linen duster." Attired in this, Dow remembered starting out on horseback for the first 100 miles. After that, he could not recall his mode of transportation, most likely by wagon or train. "I had not sufficiently recovered from chagrin at my situation for such details to impress themselves upon my mind," he confessed.

He certainly *did* remember the "dirty room, without furniture of any kind," overlooking a pig pen, where he was kept in Jackson, Mississippi. He spent July 4, 1863, there, while the Union was celebrating Vicksburg and Gettysburg.

Port Hudson surrendered soon after Vicksburg's fall, as Dow had predicted.

As he continued his journey, Dow's "thoughts were far away, and I took little note of what I saw and experienced." He *did* notice that "the Confederate armies were as a mere empty egg-shell." It was apparent to Dow that Northerners lacked any idea of the level of sacrifice and suffering the war was causing Southerners to endure. Certain of Northern success, Dow began to consider his own troubles slight compared to those of the people he encountered.

Dow had no real sense of physical danger. People along the way were curious to see a man they associated with Temperance; the fact he was also a Yankee general and Abolitionist restrained their friendliness. He got along so well with his guards that when one evening they wanted to play cards, Dow volunteered to guard himself. When he reached the infamous Libby Prison in Richmond, Rebel officers crowded about "the Neal Dow of Temperance and Maine Law fame." There was good-natured banter; Dow begged the Confederates "not to let me wear my welcome out."

"At Libby I was as comfortable as could be expected," Dow admitted. He was treated better than the average Union prisoner, due to his rank (he was the only Union general at the time in Rebel hands) and fame. The other Union officers held at Libby likewise exempted Dow, partly due to his age, from "the drudgery of a turn at cooking or at keeping our quarters clean." He had a relatively quiet corner of one of the larger rooms, where he spent most of his time reading or writing. He was one of a thousand Union officers crowded into six rooms at Libby Prison. But he was viewed as special. He was, after all, *the* Neal Dow.

But Dow soon found himself travelling southward again, to Mobile, Alabama. He had no idea why. In fact, he was sent to Mobile where a military court was investigating charges that he had armed freed slaves while in command at Pensacola. The Confederate Congress had passed resolutions that the death penalty should be imposed upon any commissioned officer who engaged in such activity.

There was concern in Maine for Dow's safety. Thirty-three prominent citizens petitioned President Lincoln to take "special and exceptional" action on behalf of the Temperance champion. Public prayer meetings were held; in Portland Dow's cousin and long-time opponent, the writer John Neal, participated. After the riot Dow suppressed with force as mayor of Portland, Neal had said Dow should be hanged. Now he was worried that the Confederates might actually do so.

A number of Dow's former prisoners, like Judge Victor Burthe and the ex-mayor of New Orleans, testified on his behalf, citing his kindness to them. Burthe provided Dow with books, with which he whiled away his time in "a large, airy chamber with a wide view of town and country."

The officer in charge of his guard told Dow he was actually Unionist; one day he showed the prisoner a hole in the wall of the next room. It had been made by an earlier prisoner, and had not been covered since his escape. Returned to his room, Dow noticed his door was left unlocked. He assumed he was being given a chance to escape. But to attempt it "even if I had been young and in good health would have been foolhardy in the extreme," Dow concluded.

He was sent back to Richmond after a two-month sojourn in Mobile. On August 22 the court let Dow off the hook. It ruled that, because there was no proof of Abolitionist actions after the Congressional resolutions of May 1, it was not proper to take any action against him. Once again Neal Dow crossed the Confederacy. He had travelled now over 2,500 miles through Dixie, and nearly every mile further demonstrated "the utter hopelessness of the Southern cause."

On his way back to Libby, Dow learned that there was a possibility he might be exchanged for General John Hunt Morgan. The Rebel cavalryman had been captured while raiding into Ohio.

But when Dow returned to Libby, he was greeted there by none other than John Hunt Morgan.

"General Dow," Morgan said, "I am very happy to see you here; or, rather, I should say, since you are here, I am very happy to see you looking so well."

"General Morgan, I congratulate you on your escape," Dow replied, "I cannot say I am glad that you did escape, but since you did, I am pleased to see you here."

Dow got to see how much less genteel were the conditions under which regular Union soldiers existed when he was paroled to supervise the distribution of blankets sent by the Federal government to prisoners at nearby Belle Isle. Compared to the "very wretched conditions" at Belle Isle, whatever restrictions officers encountered at Libby "were as joys of Elysium."

Confederate officials claimed Dow violated the terms of his parole. Not only did he criticize the camp in his report, but he protested when a guard apparently started to use his bayonet against a half-naked prisoner.

For some time Dow had been secretly sending out messages from Libby Prison. Some were written on thin paper concealed in the military buttons of released prisoners. More often, Dow used the trick of writing messages to his family and the government in lemon juice on sections of letters written in ink that passed censors' approval. When heated, the lemon juice messages became legible. Dow sent out a steady stream of such letters before the practice was discovered.

The celebrated escape of a number of prisoners—including Colonel Tilden of the Sixteenth Maine—occurred while Dow was at Libby. Dow did not participate. "By that time my naturally strong constitution had been broken down, but the shattered wreck of my former strength remained." He was, however, well aware of the tunnel being dug in the basement.

Dow vividly recalled the consternation of the guard keeping tally of the number of prisoners the morning after the escape. As the ranking officer, Dow was the first to answer roll calls and usually then returned to his "quarters." This time "I stepped out first but stood close by the officer as he kept his tally. I saw by his face, when he counted up his marks, that he had noticed a discrepancy, but he said nothing except to order us back again to be checked out once more. He thought he had made a mistake."

As the guard retook the tally, men tried to confuse him by popping in and out of the line in order to be counted twice. They also stuck caps and hats on sticks to be recorded as heads. These games dragged the tally through the morning.

When the guard finally got the correct count, Dow found "amusing" the man's obvious amazement. "Why, it is a h-u-n-d-r-e-d and ten!" he gasped. At his first count, the poor fellow thought ten prisoners were missing.

After his return from Mobile, there was interest in Dow's impressions of the Confederacy. In all, he would give five talks on the subject. Whenever guards looked in, sometimes attracted by the applause his remarks elicited, Dow switched from talk of "rebels" to "rumsellers." This led guards to believe the "crank" was preaching prohibition to men with little food or water. The image of Dow exhorting starving men to abstain from alcohol that was not available has endured. Lieutenant Colonel James Sanderson, one of the leaders of the prison community, whom Dow considered pro-Confederate, portrayed his rival as an "old-womanish" fanatic.

By the beginning of 1864 Dow, in lemon juice, wrote son Fred in Portland that the Confederates might be willing to exchange him for recently captured General Fitzhugh Lee. If the Union preferred to keep Lee, Dow was "content" to stay at Libby. His great concern was that nothing be done that would in any way undermine the protection of black soldiers. Neal Dow's big concern was Abolition, not Temperance, at this point.

Fred talked with Maine's Senators and Vice President Hamlin about proposing an exchange, since the Confederacy would not initiate action. On March 14 the exchange was made. Neal Dow had been imprisoned for over eight months.

Dow's image as a martyr was marred when he insisted upon taking his blankets and hoarded provisions with him, instead of leaving them for other prisoners. And when, at City Point, Dow spotted a Federal sergeant carrying Lee's valise, he exploded: "When I left Richmond, the Confederates would give me no assistance, and you shall give him none!" The touchy general, who was tired and hungry, was overruled.

On March 15, as Dow stepped off the steamer *New York* at Fortress Monroe, he was "heartily" greeted by his old nemesis, General Ben Butler. Butler telegraphed Dow's wife to inform her of her husband's release.

A week later Dow was back in Portland, Maine. He had been gone over two years. He had left a tarnished politician, whose hopes for advancement had been blown away by the whiff of scandal. Even in the military, his reputation for a materialism almost as ferocious as his moralism had dogged him. But on March 23, at least momentarily, all this was stuff of the past.

As General Neal Dow entered City Hall, the Camp Berry band struck up a rousing "Hail to the Chief." Dow was showered with applause and cheers from the assembled crowd. The war, with the twin badges of wounds suffered in combat and P.O.W. status, had refurbished Neal Dow.

Yet he was so weakened that he nearly fainted at his hero's reception. A few months later Dow, at age sixty, resigned his commission in the Army. His illness persisted, and there were doubts he would live another year.

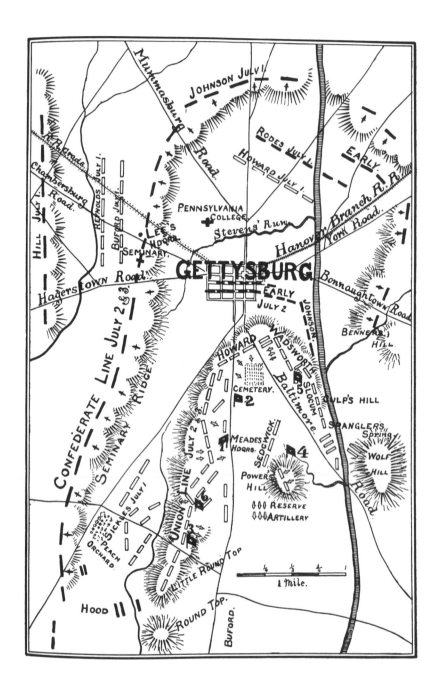

*Battlefield at Gettysburg, Pennsylvania—U.S. Army Signal Corps map*

# Oliver Otis Howard

*"God helping us, we will stay here until the army comes."*

"Probably there was no gloomier period during our great war than the month which followed the disasters at Chancellorsville," Oliver Otis Howard wrote. At a council of war on May 4 Howard argued to continue the battle, in part no doubt hoping for a chance to retrieve the reputation of XI Corps. It was about as low as possible—and so was his reputation.

On May 7, Hooker having ordered a retreat, soldiers of the Seventeenth Maine, passing XI Corps, "exchanged greetings of a highly uncomplimentary nature." John Haley thought that really the men were not the object of the Seventeenth Mainers' scorn. "General Howard should have been fully prepared, but he wasn't; hence these jeers."

Carl Schurz was convinced that the "Dutchmen" of XI Corps were being made the scapegoats for Union failure. And Howard was not showing much enthusiasm in defending his corps; when Schurz demanded an investigation of its performance, believing a military inquiry would clear XI's name, Howard replied he did not shrink from such an investigation. But, as Schurz tartly noted, neither did he actually request one.

Howard would never accept any personal responsibility for the disaster on May 2. There is no avoiding the fact that he did little publicly to try to refute the prejudice against his men. Thus the relationship between commander and men was unhealthy. Writing of the soldiers, Schurz said: "They had lost all confidence in the competency of their corps commander. It is greatly to their credit that, under circumstances so discouraging, they did not desert *en masse*." There were hardly any desertions.

Including Howard. About this time Republicans in Maine were trying to interest Howard in running for governor. If he had agreed, there would have been no tears shed upon his departure from XI Corps. But he decided to stick it out.

In June Lee moved north. Once again, the Army of the Potomac marched to intercept the great Confederate chieftain. The weather was, Howard thought, "too hot for campaigning," but with Lee on the loose there was no choice. There was no time to dwell on the recent ignominious past. Perhaps the new campaign would offer redemption.

Howard's XI Corps shared the Army's extreme left with Reynold's I Corps. John Reynolds, about a decade older and a senior officer, had urged Howard to take the Third Maine volunteers' command at the beginning of the war. The two worked well together. When, on June 28, Hooker was replaced by George Meade, Howard was hardly displeased.

Meade came across as cold but competent, with none of Fighting Joe's charisma. Howard considered the new commander to be "old enough to be my father, but like a father that one can trust without his showing him any special regard." Here was the kind of paternal figure the thirty-two-year-old Howard needed, and whose approval he craved.

Both Reynolds and Meade were Pennsylvanians. Lee was already in their state, apparently unconcerned about his communications, his Army of Northern Virginia living off the abundant grain and livestock of the region. By June 30

Federal cavalry had brushed with some Confederates at a crossroads town called Gettysburg. Calvaryman John Buford was sure Lee's army would concentrate here and, dismounted, his men assumed defensive positions north and west of the town.

Howard's headquarters were at Emmittsburg, just south of the Pennsylvania line in Maryland. Reynolds, at Marsh Run, about a half dozen miles off on the road that headed to Gettysburg from Emmitsburg, called Howard to a conference. In a back room almost devoid of furniture but filled with maps, the two men considered the meaning of the day's dispatches. It looked like contact would be made with Lee. Reynolds, Howard would recall, appeared depressed. The scattered condition of the Army of the Potomac and the apparent concentration of the Confederates somewhere nearby made the I Corps commander anxious.

Howard rode back to his more comfortable headquarters at a small Jesuit college about eleven o'clock. He was almost immediately asleep, only to be awakened about midnight with dispatches addressed to Reynolds. Howard perused Meade's orders before sending them to Reynolds. The Union Army was still feeling for Lee. The I and XI were to go to Gettysburg.

Early on the morning of July 1 Howard was ordered by Meade to come up within supporting distance of Reynolds. Avoiding the road filled with marching troops, Howard rode quickly through adjoining countryside. He arrived within sight of Gettysburg, on some high ground covered by a peach orchard, at 10:30. The temperature was hot, and so, apparently, was the situation. Howard saw rising smoke about a mile and a half to his left. The Confederates were opening their attack on Buford's cavalrymen. Closer, infantrymen of I Corps were crossing fields toward a seminary.

---

The Battle of Gettysburg had begun.

Howard was met by one of Reynold's staff; he asked where Reynolds wanted him to place his corps, about an hour distant. The aide said "anywhere," and Howard dispatched one of his own staff, Captain Daniel Hall, to get more precise information. He sensed waiting in support was not going to be enough.

Riding ahead to reconnoitre while XI Corps came up, Howard stopped at the highest point on a long ridge. It offered a panorama of the seminary to the northwest, where I Corps was located, the town below the hill, and the fields west of Gettysburg.

"This seems to be a good position, colonel," Howard said to Lieutenant Colonel Meysenburg.

"It is the only position, general," Meysenburg replied.

It was Cemetery Hill. Howard at that moment knew that it must be *the* position to hold until the rest of Meade's army arrived. That is what he would recommend.

Meanwhile Captain Hall returned from Reynolds. Howard was ordered to bring XI Corps forward to assist I Corps as soon as possible. That was it. No mention of a defensive position to fall back upon.

At this point, Howard was a general without his corps; he used his time awaiting its arrival by riding into the town of Gettysburg. He was looking for an observation point where he could better determine what was unfolding. He found it atop the Fahnestock building. As he was surveying the view with field glasses and consulting maps, some Confederate prisoners from Seminary Ridge shuffled by below. Then a young soldier rode up, saluted, and called up to Howard, "General Reynolds is wounded, sir."

"I am very sorry," Howard said. "I hope he will be able to keep the field."

A few minutes later Captain Hall rode up the street below. "General Reynolds is dead, and you are the senior officer on the field," his aide said.

That meant General Howard was now field commander. Displaying no outward anxiety, the Christian general thought, "God helping us, we will stay here until the army comes."

At this point his corps had still not arrived. Howard sent word to his division commanders to get to the front quickly. He also sent a dispatch to Major General Henry Slocum of XII Corps, four and a half miles off.

When Schurz, whose division was in the lead, got Howard's order, he was surprised, since no artillery fire could be heard from the direction of Gettysburg. Nevertheless, he ordered his men to march double-quick as he rode ahead to confer with Howard.

Meeting Howard on Cemetery Hill, Schurz could see I Corps in thin lines on and about Seminary Ridge and he could hear now the sounds of battle. Yet: "Of the troops themselves we could see little. I remember how small the affair appeared to me, as seen from a distance." But, as an ambulance passed carrying Reynold's corpse, the "awful significance" of what was happening was brought home.

Howard sent two of the XI Corps' divisions, those of Schurz and Barlow, north of Gettysburg, while I Corps, commanded by General Abner Doubleday, was to continue to hold its position facing west with Buford's cavalry. Schurz was put in command of XI corps. One division of XI Corps, Steinwher's, was kept on Cemetery Hill with some reserve artillery.

This would be the fallback. Howard was fighting for time, not a victory. It was increasingly apparent that the whole Army of Northern Virginia was converging on this sleepy-looking Pennsylvania town.

Around noon there was a lull in the fighting. This gave the two divisions of XI Corps time to deploy, but there was a gap between the two corps. To compound this, Barlow advanced too far, leaving another gap between his line and that of Schurz to his left. From two to four o'clock, the ever-growing Confederates pressed hard on the outnumbered Federals.

Howard again appealed to Slocum, now within a mile of Gettysburg, justifying, in Charlie Howard's caustic comment, the name "Slow come." Slocum promised he would send men forward, but he also told Charles Howard, "I'll be damned if I will take the responsibility of this fight." He outranked Howard and would be the commanding officer on the field.

Meanwhile, Howard was getting frantic calls for reinforcements from the two embattled corps. But the only available men left were on Cemetery Hill, and Howard did not dare weaken what he saw as the nucleus of the Union position.

By four o'clock he gave the order to retreat back through the town to Cemetery Hill. The columns of I and XI Corps became entangled in the narrow streets of Gettysburg. There was apparent disorganization, but it was not the rout Confederates (and critics of Howard) portrayed it as.

The much-maligned XI Corps had fought well, but its line had crumbled first and its 3,200 casualties included many prisoners captured during its confused retreat. Once again the corps had borne the brunt of a losing battle. Members of I Corps, which took over 5,700 casualties, would add to the criticism of the XI Corps. *This corps was damned.*

Howard could be justly criticized for not designating the most practical routes for a withdrawal, which would have reduced the actual confusion. It seems that he hoped for reinforcements from the rest of the Army of the Potomac until it was too late.

Yet when the army retreated, men were observed talking and joking as they headed through Gettysburg to the high ground beyond. Hardly a panic. And of forty-eight pieces of artillery engaged, only four were lost.

Howard had not displayed great tactical ability, but he had held off the Confederate onslaught as long as he could while retiring his defeated forces to a strong defensive position. It was his day. Even Schurz conceded Howard had done what had to be done.

Yet the end of the day brought humiliation. About 4:30 Winfield Scott Hancock arrived on the scene. Exactly what words passed between Hancock and Howard are disputed, but Hancock, Howard's junior in rank, told Howard he had been sent by Meade to assume command. Howard objected. According to the only observer of the exchange, a major from Doubleday's I Corps staff, Hancock told Howard, "I have written orders in my pocket from General Meade, which I will show you if you wish to see them."

"No" Howard replied, "I do not doubt your word, General Hancock, but you can give no orders here while I am here."

"Very well, General Howard, I will second any order that you have to give, but General Meade has also directed me to select a field on which to fight this battle in the rear of Pipe Creek," Hancock said.

The big man glanced about, and continued: "But I think this is the strongest position by nature upon which to fight a battle that I ever saw, and if it meets your approbation I will select this as the battlefield," Hancock responded.

Whatever was actually said, Hancock behaved as though he were in charge and Howard cooperated with him. There was no time for hurt feelings to interfere.

---

But Howard's feelings were hurt. Although he could not know it at the time, Buford had sent a dispatch to Meade claiming there "seems to be no directing person" at Gettysburg. Meade trusted Hancock and did not have full confidence in Howard. The father figure had rejected Howard.

When, finally, Slocum arrived, he assumed command. A message from Meade addressed to Hancock and Doubleday said Slocum should take the command when he showed up; Howard was not mentioned, adding insult to injury. Stung, Howard wrote Meade that he had handled the two corps "as well as any of your corps commanders could have done." Hancock "assisted me in carrying out orders which I had already issued," he wrote. He felt mortified and disgraced—again. "Please inform me frankly if you disapprove of my conduct today, that I may know what to do," Howard wrote.

Hancock had done little to affect the events of July 1, but his presence on the field revitalized the army. Unlike Howard, he was an inspirational figure. While Howard would be associated with another defeat at Gettysburg, Hancock would be viewed as contributing to the ultimate victory.

In fact, Howard had done much to set the stage for victory. Congress would specifically mention him in its eventual commendation and exclude Hancock. That was not fair either, but there was a certain irony to it all.

*Charles Tilden—Maine State Archives*

# Charles Tilden, Sixteenth Maine

*"You know what that means."*


The Sixteenth Maine Volunteer Infantry Regiment came close to being annihilated during the First Day at Gettysburg.

It had already made a name for itself, which it had done everything possible to shake: the Blanket Brigade. Mustered at Augusta in mid-August, 1862, the regiment had barely arrived in Washington when it was sent marching in the Antietam campaign. Tents, knapsacks and overcoats were, by order, left behind. The days were warm enough, but the nights were frigid. To keep warm, men wrapped up in their woolen blankets—thus the jeering name. At Fredericksburg the Blanket Brigade lost half of its men engaged, but gained respect.

When the Gettysburg campaign opened, the regiment was commanded by Colonel Charles Tilden, a handsome man from a Castine merchant family. Tilden had seen hard service fighting with the Second Maine, was cool under fire, and popular with his boys. The Sixteenth was in I Corps, part of a brigade including a Pennsylvania regiment and two New York regiments. The division commander was Major General John Robinson, a salty old soldier reputed to be "the hairiest general in a much bearded army."

According to Adjutant Abner Small (previously with the Third Maine) the Sixteenth counted 25 officers and 267 men when it encamped with Reynold's corps at Marsh Run on June 29. None of the "blanket brigade fellers" succumbed to the heat, which created casualties among many regiments. There had been hard marching; the Sixteenth made about forty miles marching twenty-five hours straight before reaching its bivouac near the Pennsylvania border.

When Reynolds was given temporary command of the army's left wing, Brigadier General Abner Doubleday became head of I Corps. Ironically, Doubleday was destined to be remembered for something he didn't do (invent baseball) rather than for what he did (fight well at Gettysburg).

Reynolds ordered Doubleday to bring I Corps up to Gettysburg on the humid morning of July 1; Robinson's division was eating the dust of the others. Word spread that Reynolds was killed; a black orderly bringing back a horse said it was the general's.

There was no time to grieve. When Robinson's Second Division reached Gettysburg, the other two I Corps divisions were fighting along a wooded ridge just west of the town and extending northward. This was Seminary Ridge. Robinson's men were placed in reserve in front of the seminary, where they busied themselves throwing up breastworks of rails and earth.

Then they waited for the order to go in. Small chatted with Captain Stephen Whitehouse of Newcastle. Smiling a forced smile, Whitehouse pointed to Tilden, and said: "Adjutant, I wish I felt as brave and cool as the colonel appears."

"Why, Captain," Small replied, "he is as scared as any of us. Cheer up, 'twill soon be over."

"Well, the colonel may be scared, but he *looks* as happy as though we were to have an old-fashioned State of Maine muster."

"I know that, Captain. No man ever saw him appear differently before a fight," Small said. That's why the boys idolized him.

*Abner Small—Maine State Archives*

It was about one o'clock and the anticipated order rang out: "Fall in! Forward, Sixteenth."

"Good bye, Adjutant, this is my last fight," Whitehouse said as he turned, bawling the command to his company.

Robinson's division was placed on the extreme right of I Corps. The Sixteenth Maine marched into position behind a rail fence almost parallel the Chambersburg turnpike, one of the roads that radiated out from Gettysburg like the spokes of a wheel. Confederates gathered behind another fence about 200 yards away, across a clearing, and opened fire on the Mainers. Several men were hit; Captain Whitehouse was shot dead.

Now the two lines fired away at each other. Colonel Tilden, the only man on horseback, was directing the Sixteenth's fire when his horse was hit. Animal and rider fell, but Tilden was up in an instant, unfazed. More men fell that didn't get up. Small saw a color guard topple. Captain William Waldron of Lewiston was hollering to his men to keep cool and shoot low when a bullet passed through his throat and into his lung. He tried to stop the blood gushing from his neck with his hand, stubbornly clinging to a tree with the other. He kept his place and refused to get medical attention.

Lieutenant George Deering of Saco sheathed his sword, grabbed a musket from a fallen soldier, and joined his company's line. More than a little excited, the officer forgot to remove the rammer after loading, and sent it flying. A witness to the event recalled: "The peculiar swishing noise made by the rammer as it hurried through the wood was laughable to the boys, and must have been a holy terror to the rebels."

"It was strange to hear laughter there, with dead men by," Small wrote.

The Confederates attempted repeatedly to charge, but were mowed down. Then Tilden ordered the Sixteenth to charge. His boys leaped over the rail fence, cheering, and ran toward their opponents. The Rebs decided it was an appropriate time to head for the woods to their rear. The Sixteenth was heading after them when they were recalled.

Trouble was developing to the right as more Confederate divisions kept arriving. Howard had dispatched two divisions of XI Corps to meet the growing threat, and Robinson's division was the extreme right of I Corps, next to the left of the XI Corps. The Sixteenth joined the rest of Brigadier General Gabriel René Paul's Brigade. Paul, grandson of an officer in Napoleon's army, gave another embattled brigade, Henry Baxter's, aid in repelling a Confederate attack at a stone wall near the crest of a hill. In the stillness of the oppressive heat, bullets whistled over the heads of sweat-soaked, dirty men who mechanically loaded, fired, loaded, fired. As Baxter's men ran out of ammunition, their brigade, badly shot up, pulled back and Paul's brigade tried to fill the hole.

Paul was blinded by a head wound, and three colonels in line to assume the brigade's command were also casualties. That meant the Sixteenth and other regiments of Paul's brigade were given orders by the division commander.

The Union line was being bent back and enveloped by Confederates who outnumbered them 2–1. When XI Corps began to retreat around 3:30, Robinson's division, the extreme right of I Corps, was exposed to Rebel flanking. Two of Dick Ewell's divisions hit the weakened line hard. As the other two divisions of Doubleday's I Corps pulled back, Robinson's men were left to confront the full brunt of the rapidly converging Rebels.

The order came to fall back. The Sixteenth was in the process of doing that when an aide of General Robinson's rode up to Colonel Tilden, who was walking near Second Lieutenant George Bisbee.

Bisbee had been a law student in a Dixfield law office on June 17, 1862, when Captain Daniel Marston showed up in the little village in a two-seated wagon. A fifer occupied the other seat; there was a boy with a brass drum in the back seat. "They immediately commenced to entertain us with their music." That drew a crowd and, after a few minutes of patriotic chatter with Marston, George Bisbee signed up. He recruited some more boys for the Sixteenth in Farmington and now, a little over a year later, he was party to a spirited conversation.

Robinson's aide gave Tilden an order to about face, lead his regiment back up the ridge, and assume a position as far north as possible. In other words, go back and face the advancing Confederates. Tilden kept walking when, a few moments later, General Robinson rode up and repeated the order. The Colonel tried to explain to the General that the Sixteenth was badly cut up and to stand against Rebels with overwhelming strength on both flanks as well as in front was hopeless.

The General did not want to hear it.

As George Bisbee recalled, "General Robinson, evidently feeling a little nervous over his own position as he perceived the flanking troops moving in, rose in his stirrups and with his hand extended towards Colonel Tilden, in a loud voice with some energetic words says, 'Colonel Tilden, take that position and hold it as long as there is a single man left.' The Colonel replied, 'All right, General; we'll do the best we can!' "

Francis Wiggin heard Tilden say, as he turned to his men, "You know what that means."

They knew but, when Tilden shouted, "About face, fix bayonets, charge!" they quietly headed back up the slope as if on parade. There were about 275 of them, heading into the proverbial jaws of Hell.

"The First Corps was being crushed between the blades of a pair of shears, and the Sixteenth Maine was ordered to move to the very acute angle of these closing-blades, and hold them apart till the shattered columns were safe," was how Wiggin described it. A sacrifice had to be made to buy valuable time for the Federal retreat.

The Sixteenth Maine went back into position at the low stone wall facing the Mummasburg Road. A Rebel battle line, flag high, loomed immediately ahead. An officer screamed an order to fire and the volley knocked down some of the Mainers. The Sixteenth fired back. The Rebel flag fell. So did the officer and a number of greybacks.

The Confederates regrouped and moved to surround the exposed little Maine regiment, its own flag hoisted defiantly. Long minutes passed. Abner Small later admitted he did not know how much time passed. He guessed it "was only a matter of minutes" before the Rebs threatened to crush them.

The Sixteenth looked back, saw no support, saw the rest of the army streaming into the town below, and started to fall back, shooting. For a moment a railroad cut seemed to offer some protection, but Rebs where hitting them in a crossfire from north and west.

It was time to surrender. The nearby Rebels demanded it, and Tilden shouted back he would. Then he drove his sword as far into the ground as his strength allowed, snapping it off at its hilt.

Neither, the men around him clamored, would the enemy get their battle flag. With the Colonel's consent, the silk was ripped off its stave and torn into shreds, distributed among the nearest officers and men.

Abner Small got one of the shreds, with a gold star, and, seeing a slim chance to escape, he took it. He was one of the few who did. Altogether only thirty-four men and eight officers made it to Cemetery Hill.

George Bisbee was one of the majority who did not make it. He could not see how a single man got away. That night, talking with his fellow prisoners, Colonel Tilden remarked, "Every man who did his duty was either killed, wounded, or captured."

That was not altogether true. Men like Small and Wiggin fought, and would fight some more. Daniel Marston, who recruited Bisbee, took command of the remnant of the Sixteenth. One of the wounded, Albion Stratton, spent the next few days laying on the pulpit of a church converted into a hospital. He watched the battle from a window and when, on July 4, the Rebels retreated they took with them all prisoners who could walk. Shot in the leg, Stratton could not leave, but he took no satisfaction seeing comrades marched off to Southern prison pens. "I guess the old Sixteenth is busted," said a man laying beside Stratton. But he was relieved to spend July 4 under the stars and stripes again.

And, through long months of captivity, boys of the Sixteenth Maine kept pieces of their flag on them. They never surrendered their flag.

Years later, the war over, Albion Stratton attended a meeting where a speaker recited the record of the Sixteenth Maine in glowing terms. "But I do not quite remember what became of their beautiful silken flag," he admitted.

No sooner had he said that than a multitude of hands were raised. Each held a piece of the flag. One veteran, long since a young man, said, "This piece went through Libby Prison, in the corner of my blouse."

Looking at the faded remnant, the speaker said, "Ah, I understand." No other words were necessary.

*Moses Lakeman—Maine State Archives*

# The Third Maine

## *The Peach Orchard*

In 1910, almost fifty years after the battle, Francis Wiggin would say, "The success of the Union cause in the battle of Gettysburg hinged on the bravery and devotion of small bands of men at two or three critical periods, and it fell to the lot of Maine officers and Maine troops in several instances to compose these small bands."

There were fifteen Maine regiments or batteries at Gettysburg, and although most saw action, a handful of them clearly fell within the category Wiggin described. In addition to the Sixteenth's sacrifice on July 1, five regiments performed significant roles on July 2—the Third, Fourth, Seventeenth, Nineteenth and Twentieth Maine Regiments.

The Third Maine was, of course, Oliver Otis Howard's first command. When he left it to become a brigadier general, he wrote a farewell order which concluded, "Gen. Howard owes much of worldly notice and position to this regiment, and he trusts he will never tarnish the reputation given him by any neglect or miscarriage on his part." After Chancellorsville, those rather pompous words assumed a certain poignance for Howard. But the Third Maine's own reputation was not hurt by its performance after the Christian General's departure. Indeed, it fought fiercely to reinforce the Union line at Chancellorsville around midnight on the fateful May 2.

At Gettysburg, the Third Maine was part of Ward's Brigade in Birney's First Division of the colorful Dan Sickles'

III Corps. Colonel Moses Lakeman of Augusta commanded the regiment which, after two years of fighting, was reduced to 196 men and 14 officers. General Sickles chose the tiny Third, together with a hundred sharpshooters, to "feel for, and find the enemy at all hazards" on the morning of July 2.

The Confederates started the day with a lively attack on the right of the Union line at Culp's Hill, but all remained quiet on the left and toward the center of the front, where III Corps was stationed. Sickles, remembering Chancellorsville, wanted a reconnaissance to find out where the enemy was.

The line Colonel Lakeman pushed out with the order "column forward" was small, but they were veterans, and they advanced defiantly across about a half mile of open land to the edge of dense woods. With skirmishers fanning out in front, Lakeman formed a line of battle and penetrated another half mile through the trees. The skirmishers collided with Rebel pickets and skirmishers and, exchanging fire, drove them back.

Moses Lakeman and his boys had located the enemy. They were gathering on his left, obviously getting ready to flank the Third Maine. The regiment repeatedly fired volleys into their ranks, oblivious to the fact they were heavily out-numbered. The fight raged for about thirty minutes, with Colonel Lakeman losing forty-eight men killed or wounded. The Third came close to being wiped out in this encounter, but retired in order. The bugle to cease firing was ignored, the Mainers continuing to unleash volleys as they fell back.

General John Ward was effusive in his praise of the Third Maine's conduct. "Colonel, I had to send three times to you, before I could get your regiment to retire," he told Lakeman. "I believe you intended to stop there all day; they did nobly, sir, and your officers and men are deserving un-bounded praise."

Sickles moved his corps forward to thwart whatever movement the Confederates were planning. It was a controversial move, not militarily sound or in compliance with Meade's wishes, since it broke the Union line strung out along Cemetery Ridge, leaving the hills to the south called the Round Tops unprotected. But it also created a salient squarely in the line of the massive Confederate attack on the Union left that Lee had planned and entrusted to his "old warhorse" James Longstreet. After the war, Longstreet told Sickles his "damned corps" had obstructed his attack long enough to deprive him of crushing the Union left.

Ward's brigade was sent up to the Emmitsburg Road with the Third Maine positioned in a soon-to-be-famous peach orchard. Throughout the day the Mainers kept up such a successful harassing fire on the enemy that the Rebel skirmishers were unable to secure a foothold. A series of Rebel charges were stopped in their tracks, and as Longstreet's men marched *en masse* toward their intended objective, the Union left, Lakeman's Third raked the Rebel flank.

Increasing numbers of Confederates were drawn off to silence the nuisance, and by five o'clock the struggle was heavy. For two hours Ward's brigade sustained what seemed to be crazed enemy assaults, which left their dead in piles. The Third broke into squads of about fifteen or twenty each, who fought like individual micro-regiments. When the rest of the brigade fell back, its left flank threatened, to allow a field of fire for Union batteries to open on the Rebel masses, the Third remained at its position. It did not fall back to rejoin its brigade until twilight. The men—those who were left—fell asleep almost immediately. General Sickles complimented the regiment, saying "the little Third Maine saved the Army today!"

*Elijah Walker—Maine State Archives*

# The Fourth Maine

## Devil's Den

Of course what could be said of other regiments could be said of the Fourth Maine. This was Berry's regiment, and led by Colonel Elijah Walker, Berry's old friend, it fought as it would if Berry had been there, which is to say brilliantly.

The Fourth remained a tough regiment after Hiram Berry left it. It was the last infantry unit to leave the field at Malvern Hill, Second Bull Run and Chancellorsville.

It was evening, July 1, when the 318 veteran scrappers arrived at Gettysburg. They were bone tired, but were sent out on picket during the first hours of July 2. Out beyond the Emmitsburg turnpike, the sounds of large numbers of men gathering in the woods to the west were clearly audible. General Sickles ordered the Fourth Maine to attack the Confederate pickets. This would be suicidal, Walker pointed out to Colonel Hiram Berdan, commander of the crack First U. S. Sharpshooters. Berdan concurred, and Sickles, as we have seen, sent Berdan's men with the Third Maine on a flanking movement into the woods.

The Fourth Maine was also in Ward's brigade. When early that afternoon Sickles sent III Corps forward, the Maine regiment was on the extreme left. They took their position in a ravine filled with a jumble of massive boulders. The locals called it Devil's Den. The little 124th New York was placed on a knoll further to the right, where James Smith's New York battery positioned some guns. Immediately behind the Fourth Maine, beyond a small stream called Plum Run, loomed two hills called the Round Tops.

Lieutenant Nathaniel Robbins was from Union, Maine, and familiar with hills. He was also a graduate of Bowdoin College, Class of 1857. But one did not require a college degree to realize the strategic significance of those hills. As Robbins looked west he could see lines of Confederate infantry forming on a ridge just beyond the Emmitsburg turnpike. He glanced behind him and saw nothing, "not even a picket line." There should have been at least a regiment extending from the Fourth's left to defend those hills! "Whose stupidity was answerable for this neglect I cannot say," Robbins recalled.

The Fourth Maine had not eaten a meal since its breakfast on July 1, only water. At about three o'clock the men began cooking some unlucky cows they had slaughtered, and heating up some coffee. They never got to eat much of the barely smoked meat. At about 3:45, apparently the time Robbins sent word of what he saw, the Confederate infantry, accompanied by artillery, started rolling out of the woods.

Captain Smith, on the knoll just beyond the ravine, was worried about his guns' flank, and asked General Ward for support. The General ordered the Fourth Maine to move back into Plum Run Valley. This moved the Mainers further away from the 124th New York, which bothered Colonel Walker, but he complied. At approximately the same time— things were happening quickly—Walker also dispatched seventy skirmishers directly into the boulder formation to his left.

Not one but two crises soon developed. Smith's battery banged away in an artillery duel with a couple of Confederate batteries. It did good work, and even may have been responsible for wounding Confederate General Hood, commanding Longstreet's onslaught against the thinly defended Union left. The 124th New York was soon pressed by the Third Arkansas and First Texas regiments. The battery was endangered.

Simultaneously the Forty-fourth and Forty-eighth Alabama were advancing on Devil's Den, heading for Little Round Top immediately beyond the rocky ravine. If the Confederates were not stopped in their steady progress, the Army of the Potomac would be flanked on its left and face defeat.

In those anxious moments, only a little Maine regiment stood in their way.

The skirmishers in Devil's Den waited until the right wing of the Forty-fourth Alabama was only fifty yards away. A couple of nervous Mainers fired prematurely, giving the Rebels a split-second warning before they were slammed by a volley that cut down a quarter of the Southerners. Stunned, they stopped and returned fire. Their momentum was slowed.

At precisely this time, the rest of the regiment, along Plum Run, saw blue infantry scrambling into position along the slope of Little Round Top. It was Vincent's brigade of V Corps.

Although Lieutenant Robbins, with the small band in Devil's Den, could not know it then, his former Bowdoin professor of logic and natural theology was busy only a matter of yards away readying the new extreme left of the army.

The Forty-eighth Alabama showed up on the Fourth Maine's left. The Rebs were within fifty yards before they discovered the Mainers' presence. Elijah Walker hurriedly reformed on his left and his regiment pumped over a half dozen volleys into the oncoming Rebels. When the gap was reduced to what the Forty-eighth Alabama's colonel estimated was only "twenty paces," the Rebels started firing back. It was close, deadly combat.

Colonel Walker, on horseback, felt the sting of a bullet severing his Achilles tendon and passing through his leg. The bullet killed his horse. Walker was quickly up, supporting himself with his sword, ignoring the pain. Casualties mounted on both sides in what would come to be called "the slaughter pen." Plum Run grew scarlet.

The situation was equally desperate on the knoll, where the 138 men of the New York regiment were pressed by at least four gray regiments. If the gallant New Yorkers fell, there went the battery. If the Confederates got those guns, the position of the Fourth Maine in the valley below would become absolutely untenable.

The 124th New York charged down into the First Texas, momentarily knocking the Confederates back. But the Federals were thinned by the fighting, and vastly outnumbered, they were driven back. There were too few of them left to support Smith's battery. Fending off the Forty-eighth Alabamians along Plum Run, Colonel Walker saw the cannon on the knoll above being abandoned.

Meanwhile, in Devil's Den, the Forty-fourth Alabama had regrouped. After a few futile minutes, the seventy skirmishers in the boulders surrendered. They had bought time for the Twentieth Maine and other Federal regiments on the slope of Little Round Top. But the immediate opportunity for the Alabama boys lay on the knoll. At this moment there was nothing directly between them and possession of Smith's battery.

Hobbling on his bleeding leg, Colonel Walker decided to get his Fourth Mainers to those guns first. He ordered them to pull about 100 yards away from the Forty-eighth Alabama on their left. The line reformed as he shouted to fix bayonets. Walker would never forget the sound, so prompt it seemed like one loud click, audible even amidst the general racket. He screamed: "By the right oblique, charge!"

The Fourth Maine charged out of the "Valley of Death," up the knoll, followed by the Alabama regiments. Strenuous work indeed in heavy, smoke-laden, 92° heat.

The Maine boys reached the guns first, joined the remnant of the 124th New York, and contested the Alabamians and Georgians climbing up the hill. The struggle was sharp and intimate. Walker's sword was wrenched from his hand, but retrieved. Color bearer Henry Ripley kept the regiment's battle flag from touching the ground, even when the rest of the color guard went down. When the staff was smashed above where he gripped it, the sergeant still would not allow the silk, perforated by more than thirty bullets, to fall.

*Action, brief but crucial, at Devil's Den—Sparks From The Campfire*

The Maine and New York regiments were almost engulfed when the Ninety-ninth Pennsylvania was sent into the melee. They waded into the roaring, shrieking mass shouting, "Pennsylvania and our homes!" Hundreds fell in hand-to-hand fighting. As the Fortieth New York and Sixth New Jersey piled into the fray, the Confederates were pushed back, down into Devil's Den.

But when another Confederate brigade slammed into the Union troops from the right, the pressure was simply too much. It was sunset now. Sickles' salient had collapsed, but not without a struggle. Weakened by pain and the loss of blood, Walker gave the order for his regiment to join the rest and retreat back to Cemetery Ridge. II and V Corps had plugged the gap there, if only barely.

For Elijah Walker it was impossible to move. He collapsed; enemy soldiers swarmed about him, taking his sword, this time for good. They almost took him, except for the intervention of two of his men, who went back to save their colonel and carry him to safety.

Hiram Berry would have been proud.

# The Seventeenth Maine

## *The Wheatfield*

Not only the Fourth Maine, but Berry's other Maine regiment, the Seventeenth Maine, performed heroically at a crucial point. Between the Peach Orchard, where the Third Maine fought, and Devil's Den, the Fourth Maine's position, lay a hotly contested wheatfield. This was the Seventeenth's ground.

*Charles Mattocks—Maine State Archives*

Captain Charles Mattocks was another Bowdoin student of Joshua Chamberlain's, Class of 1862. He went to war the same time his professor did. Young, ambitious and proud, Mattock did not allow his company to break when others of the Seventeenth and Fortieth New York did on that awful May 2 evening at Chancellorsville. General Ward, riding up alongside the young man, said, "Captain, your company stands its ground splendidly. I wish the rest would do as well." When the General complimented Mattocks in his official report as well, a puffed-up Charlie wrote his mother, "Can you wonder that I feel a little exalted?"

Chancellorsville, he wrote, was not like Fredericksburg. "There we fought with invisible foes, but here 'we came we saw' and whether we conquered or not is another thing. We killed more than they did." At Gettysburg, the Seventeenth Maine had another opportunity for up-close killing.

At Gettysburg, the Seventeenth Maine was in de Trobriand's brigade of Birney's division, III Corps. Philippe Regis Denis de Kerendern de Trobriand was a talented *bon vivant* born in France twenty-four years before Charles Mattocks saw the light of day. The Seventeenth's boys made predictable "Froggie" jokes, but de Trobriand was a respected "old" warrior. David Bell Birney was a lawyer, son of an antislavery candidate for president, and successor to command of Phil Kearny's division.

When Sickles established his salient, Birney put de Trobriand to Ward's right. An unoccupied wheatfield was between the brigades. When the Third Maine and other Union regiments in the Peach Orchard opened up a lively exchange with Confederates sweeping toward Ward's brigade, Lieutenant Charles Roberts of the Seventeenth Maine observed "the shots of the enemy [were] coming so uncomfortably near us that we deemed it prudent to seek the shelter of the woods where the regiment was lying, awaiting orders."

Those came quickly enough. De Trobriand sent the Seventeenth Maine to occupy the wheatfield. Running in a diagonal line across the yellow field, the Mainers took shelter behind a low stone wall. The wall faced thick forest—and allowed the Seventeenth to fire obliquely into the waves of Hood's Confederates. Stung by the Federal fire, the Third Arkansas took cover. But this practice was interrupted when Anderson's brigade came at the Mainers from the nearby woods.

John Haley remembered the Rebels' advance as "very impetuous," swatting aside the Seventeenth Maine's skirmish line "as chaff before a wind." Heavy infantry fire, supported by a battery behind the Mainers, slowed but could not stop the fury of the Rebel assault. To Haley "it seemed nothing short of annihilation would stop them." The Yankees did their best: "There was a dreadful buzzing of bullets and other missiles, highly suggestive of an obituary notice for a goodly number of Johnny Rebs, and we could see them tumbling around right lively."

Hundreds fell at the wall, many by bayonet.

According to Haley's recollection, de Trobriand came up and hollered, "Fall back, right away!"

" But we didn't *hear* the order," Haley recalled. "It isn't often that an order to fall back in a battlefield is disregarded. The old fellow didn't quite comprehend this state of ours. We had good reason for our action." The stone wall afforded good protection, and the Maine troops "knew the fate of the army hung on the result." This may sound like history in hindsight, but in fact, a hole punched in the Union defense at the wheatfield *would* have collapsed Sickles' position.

It is also true that the noise was deafening and orders were not easily heard. This became obvious when Humphrey's Second Division, to the Seventeenth Maine's right, started to fall back, creating the threat of a Rebel flanking attack. The Seventeenth Maine's commander, Lieutenant Colonel Charles Merrill, ordered the regiment to refuse its right. The "rattle of musketry and roar of artillery" drowned out Merrill's words, and Lieutenant Colonel Roberts went from company to company relaying the command. He had barely completed this work when the impact of a bullet hitting his right leg above the knee threw him, face first, to the ground. Merrill, standing nearby, at once cut a strap from his sword belt and tied it around Robert's bloody leg to stem the flow of blood.

The leg was eventually amputated. Roberts shared that experience with Dan Sickles, wounded a short time later.

But that was later; now the Seventeenth Maine's line was bent right and left. Repeatedly assaulted, the boys, in Roberts' words, "had no difficulty in holding our post." When some Georgians got close enough to stick their flag on the wall, the Seventeenth sent the Rebels reeling back under the pressure of a bayonet assault.

But sixty rounds of ammunition went only so far. Even with the assistance of Michigan and Pennsylvania troops, the dwindling supply of cartridges forced the Seventeenth to fall back. A Federal battery, Winslow's, fired point-blank at the pursuing Confederates. Then General Birney materialized and led the Seventeenth on another run at the Rebels with bayonets fixed. The sweaty, tired Rebels fell back to the wall.

They regrouped and went at it again. Without ammo, the Seventeenth fell back through the trampled wheat. According to Haley, de Trobriand, who earlier had urged retreat, now urged the Maine men to make a stand. With the added weight of some VI Corps troops, just arrived, the wheatfield changed hands again.

But it was a seesaw contest in which Confederate numbers were overwhelming. The Seventeenth Maine halted in the open field, ordered to await support troops that did not come. Exposed to the fire of Confederates who took cover in the woods, the ranks of the Seventeenth thinned.

The peach orchard and the wheatfield were swarming with gray and butternut-clad men now. Some of the boys of the Seventeenth Maine cried at the scene. The salient was gone, and soon the Maine unit joined others streaming to the rear. For two brutal hours they had slowed the Rebel juggernaut.

"Another terrible fight and yet I am safe," Captain Mattocks wrote his mother. "Our Regiment was in the thickest of the fight—close musketry—and lost over 100 men in one hour. I had three men loading for me, and I blazed away at the Rebs." His company went into the battle with forty muskets. Only eighteen could be stacked at the close of this bloody day.

# Joshua Chamberlain
## *"A hard day for Mother"*

On June 29 they made eighteen miles, but the next day there were twenty-three miles covered. On July 1, as the fighting escalated in Gettysburg, the Twentieth Maine entered Pennsylvania. By four o'clock in the afternoon, they had encamped with the rest of Barnes's division at Hanover.

But the tired men had hardly stacked their arms when they were ordered to resume marching. They knew where they were going: toward the sound of the guns. Of all the marches they made during the war, this one would stand out most vividly in their memory.

It was different on Northern soil, cheered and encouraged on, instead of receiving sullen stares. The rumor swept through the Union columns that McClellan, still the soldiers' favorite, was back in command. That news heartened the troops. Colonel Strong Vincent rode along the line, shouting, "Now boys, we will give 'em hell tomorrow." A report that even George Washington was in the saddle near Gettysburg also made the rounds. "I half believed it myself—so did the powers of the other world draw nigh," Chamberlain recalled.

Reaching the hills southeast of Gettysburg around midnight, the Twentieth Maine halted for a few hours' rest, then marched to the battle zone. Since the morning of July 1, they had covered thirty-two miles, fourteen of them in the dark. After spending the morning of July 2 near Cemetery and Culp's Hills, V Corps was moved left at noon to support

Sickles's III Corps. The Twentieth Mainers whiled away a few hours partially shaded from the burning sun in a peach orchard (not *the* Peach Orchard to the west). They made coffee and scribbled letters.

The long lull ended about three o'clock as cannon erupted. Barnes's Division moved down from Cemetery Ridge to the Wheatfield. The fighting in the Peach Orchard to the right and in Devil's Den to the far left was visible. The first two brigades were sent to plug the gap between the Wheat Field and Peach Orchard. Vincent's brigade was held in reserve; behind it loomed Little Round Top.

At about this time the realization was dawning on both sides that the hill, cleared on its west face, still wooded on its east side, could be the key to the battle. Meade's chief engineer, thirty-three-year-old General Gouverneur Warren, was worried. His professional eye immediately grasped the defensive advantage of the "rough" terrain. But was it adequately defended? At headquarters "very soon there was an uneasiness felt about the condition on our left." Reports of weakness in that area were coming in. As Warren wrote his young wife, "We are now all in line of battle before the enemy, in a position where we cannot be beaten but fear being turned."

That was it: if the Confederates took Little Round Top, they could enfilade the Union line with artillery and turn its left with infantry. "I have great anxiety in my mind, and never felt our cause so much endangered," Warren wrote.

He had to act. Warren believed that Chancellorsville was an unnecessary defeat, made possible by "a want of *nerve* somewhere" and "the incompetency of many of our corps commanders. I am almost in despair we shall ever get the right men in those places." Now, obsessed by Little Round Top, he got Meade's permission to ride down to that hill and look after its defense.

He found his worst fears confirmed: except for a handful of signalmen, the hill, key to the battle, had no Union soldiers on it. He could see the glint of thousands of Reb muskets in the woods beyond, to the west, massing to attack. Warren sent staffers galloping to Sickles and George Sykes of V Corps for troops. He personally flagged in a New York regiment and battery.

At the same time, Confederate Brigadier General Evander Law had sent Colonel William Oates' Fifteenth Alabama up Big Round Top. The sweaty, tired Alabamians, who had marched more than twenty-five miles since morning, were thirsty. Oates dispatched a detail to get water, and surveyed the scene from the hill's crest. Below was Little Round Top, virtually undefended. Beyond stretched the line of the Union left and center. It occurred to Billy Oates that he was in a position to determine the outcome of the Battle of Gettysburg.

Meanwhile, Colonel Vincent intercepted one of General Sykes's staff. Obviously something important was happening, and he demanded to know what. Learning of the crisis and Warren's frantic request for V Corps support, Vincent took the initiative. He ordered his brigade to turn around and head for Little Round Top.

They quickly crossed over a rough bridge spanning Plum Run, marched down the Valley of Death, moved up a rugged farm road to the hill's base, and then headed up the hill's slope.

Chamberlain was riding with brothers Tom and John when a Confederate shell whizzed by their faces. He immediately told them to disperse; otherwise it would be "a hard day for Mother."

It would be a day the Chamberlain boys would never forget.

---

# Joshua Chamberlain
## *"Boys, hold this hill!"*

Colonel Vincent had ridden ahead of the brigade scrambling into position along the boulder-strewn slopes of Little Round Top. When Joshua Chamberlain rode up to the extreme left, a rocky spur dotted with scrub oak, projecting toward Big Round Top not many yards southward, Vincent had dismounted. As Chamberlain joined him, the twenty-seven-year-old Vincent said, "I place you here! This is the left of the Union line. You understand! You are to hold this ground at all cost!"

Joshua Lawrence Chamberlain understood. If the Rebel onslaught already underway turned the Union flank here, the Confederates would be on the threshold of winning the battle and, quite possibly, the war.

It was as brutally simple as that.

The Twentieth Maine was to the left of the brigade's Michigan, New York, and Pennsylvania regiments strung out along Little Round Top's higher western and southern slopes. His 28 officers and 358 men must anchor the Union's left. And his own left was exposed. To provide some protection, Chamberlain sent Captain Walter G. Morrill's Company B hurrying to set up a skirmish line below him and at the eastern base of the higher hill.

Morrill was a tough customer; he and his men were crack shots. The area at the base of Big Round Top they went into was tree-covered, and as they disappeared from sight Chamberlain was left with 308 men. He augmented his line, which roughly conformed to the semicircular contour of the spur, with cooks, musicians, and anybody he could scrape up who could carry a gun.

For a fleeting moment he joined Colonel James Rice of the Forty-fourth New York further up the hill. Below them, in the Valley of Death, they saw masses of grey and butternut-clad troops "all rolling toward us in tumultuous waves." Several Texas and Alabama regiments were heading for the regiments to his right. Chamberlain hurried back to his line.

He had little time to wait for the wave to hit him. The Forty-seventh Alabama was moving on his right. And Colonel Oates's Fifteenth Alabama had descended Big Round Top and was about to smash into his center. Oates had wanted to remain on the higher elevation; with artillery it would command the smaller hill and allow Rebel guns to enfilade the Union line beyond. He heatedly argued his case with a staffer of General Law, but was overruled.

So down through the woods his regiment went. Spying a Union wagon train to the east, Oates dispatched a company to take it. This was an error, because it deprived him of about three dozen men who, along with the missing water detail, added up to fifty men he would badly need. Altogether, he had between 400 and 450 men.

Chamberlain's Twentieth Maine had barely aligned itself when Oates's Alabamians, screaming the high-pitched Rebel yell, emerged from the treeline about sixty feet lower and a mere matter of yards distant.

"Here they come!" several Mainers yelled.

Over the swelling noise of Rebel musketry, Chamberlain yelled, "Boys, hold this hill!"

No time for deep thought now. Did Chamberlain, aware of his heavy burden, have a plan? Doubtful. Did he remember another moment on a hillside in Maine when his father had issued a seemingly impossible command, and he had asked guidance, only to be chastised: *"Do it! That's how!"* Maybe.

The Twentieth Maine got off the first volley, always an advantage before smoke obscured moving targets. Oates was stunned. He had expected only to encounter some of the U. S. sharpshooters he had driven off Big Round Top. Instead, from a low elevation of ledge he was hit by "the most destructive fire I had ever seen."

The Confederates, although staggered, swept up the hill to within ten paces of the blue-coated line before being pushed back.

The noise of gunfire and men yelling, screaming and cursing was deafening. The inevitable gunsmoke clouded the hillside. Some officers ran up to Chamberlain, standing a few paces back from the color guard at the Twentieth's center. Something ominous was going on to the left. Chamberlain clambered atop a rock to get a better view. Visible through the trees were Confederates moving quickly, without firing. Oates was trying to flank the Union line.

Chamberlain immediately issued orders via his officers to refuse his line, lengthening it leftward to meet the threat. It stretched his line thin, very thin, and placed his left almost opposite his right. But it worked. The Confederate wave was again stopped.

The Alabamians regrouped and headed up the hill again. In the next hour to ninety minutes—time became confused, with minutes seeming like hours—the Rebels made several assaults. Oates counted five, Chamberlain three. Any semblance of regular lines on either side evaporated, with Rebs penetrating Union ranks at different points, only to be driven back in hand-to-hand combat, often solitary, always savage. "At times I saw around me more of the enemy than my own men," Chamberlain recalled.

---

*Little Round Top, near where Confederates almost turned the Twentieth Maine's left—Brewer, ME, reconstruction. Photo by author.*

The center was badly cut up. When the smoke briefly lifted, Chamberlain experienced an agonizing moment. The only blue soldier standing was Private Andre Tozier, holding the regimental colors in one hand and a rifle in the other. Chamberlain quickly sent brother Tom and some other men to fill the gap. The bullets were slicing through the overheated air so thickly he did not expect to see his brother alive again.

Whenever there was a lull in the fighting, the men scrambled to erect piles of rocks for protection as they lay prone. Others ran forward to retrieve the dead and wounded. They also sought Springfield rifles from fallen Rebs to exchange for their detested Enfields. As ammunition ran low, men emptied the cartridge boxes of the casualties.

Blood spattered the rocks, Oates would remember. His men were being pushed to the limit. He regrouped them for one last push, focusing on Chamberlain's left. By now Oates, who led the attack, discharging his pistol as he advanced, was attacking the spur mainly from the east. Up the hill, through the trees, no energy wasted on yells now, the Rebels grimly advanced. They pushed the Twentieth's left, commanded by Major Ellis Spear, back toward the right. The Maine men fell back from tree to tree; blue and gray smashed together in vicious combat. Oates would never forget the sight of one of his men driving a bayonet through a Maine boy's head in front of him.

The Rebels reached a massive boulder to the right of Spear's position. Oates felt a moment of exultation. *He had turned the Union regiment's flank.*

But it was a fleeting moment. The Mainers hit back with withering power. And Oates had no reserves. Chamberlain, who at the time thought he was fighting a brigade, later admitted that, with one more regiment, the Confederates would have enveloped his position. It may have been closer than that. If he had had his fifty missing men, Oates might have pulled if off.

Now he saw his men cut down, including his brother John—how ironic that both Colonels had brothers named John at Little Round Top! Oates's brother, pierced by seven bullets, would not survive the battle.

As the Alabamians fell back, Oates had to face a growing reality. His boys, never before defeated, were being whipped. He prepared to order a retreat back to Big Round Top.

At the same moment, Chamberlain did not realize he had won. A third of his men were down, his ammunition was nearly exhausted; he believed his Twentieth Maine could not withstand another furious assault like the last one.

Lieutenant Holman Melcher came up to the Colonel and requested permission to move forward with some men to retrieve the wounded lying between the two forces, crying for aid. Chamberlain hesitated, then informed Melcher that he intended to order a bayonet charge down Little Round Top.

It seemed the only option left. Chamberlain believed Vincent had given him discretion to do whatever was necessary to hold his position. And Chamberlain reckoned that the enemy must be exhausted and shaky also. The shock of an attack with cold steel might well tip the scales.

By the time the word "Bayonet!" was out of Chamberlain's lips, a number of his men were already in motion. Spontaneously, they had reached the same conclusion. Melcher, who knew Chamberlain's intent, was out front, waving his sword and shouting.

Many years later Theodore Gerrish, who was not with the Twentieth Maine that day, would write that the regiment momentarily hesitated to follow Chamberlain's command.

*Holman Melcher, who led the famous bayonet charge
down Little Round Top—Maine State Archives*

That was true only in the sense that, in the noise and confusion, few *heard* the command, and many wondered what was going on—but only for a few seconds, as men fixed bayonets and headed down the spur's rocky face with a yell. Spear, off to the left, had no orders, but seeing men to the regiment's right and center moving down at the Confederates below, went down with his men as well. Spear would later write that the charge was an example proving the statement that Gettysburg was fought by the men, not the officers.

Just as Chamberlain's men were acting out his decision, the Alabama boys acted out Colonel Oates's decision. Receiving a galling fire from his rear from Captain Morrill's men, aided by some U.S. sharpshooters and, probably, a few detached Michigan soldiers, Oates feared *he* was being flanked by Yankee regiments. He ordered a retreat; before the word was passed to all of his regiment, the Yankees came roaring down at them. As Oates later confessed, "we ran like a herd of cattle."

Since many of the Alabamians were hit on the east side of the spur they fell back toward a stone wall where Morrill's force was positioned. The Yankees stood up and fired a devastating volley into the now thoroughly demoralized Rebs. They fell back through the valley intervening between the Round Tops. Spear's left wing was in pursuit. Eventually the Union lines would align, so that the action resembled a perfectly executed "right wheel forward," similar to a door swinging in an arc—but not planned. After an incredible fight, things were falling in place for the Twentieth Maine.

Throughout the battle Chamberlain was an ill man; but he never showed it. He calmly and coolly gave orders, walking back and forth along the line during lulls in the action, offering encouragement to the living—and the dying.

Coming upon George Buck, unjustly demoted from Sergeant earlier by a bullying quartermaster, he leaned over to hear the badly wounded Buck whisper, "Tell my mother I did not die a coward." Moved, Chamberlain responded, "You die a sergeant. I promote you for faithful service and noble courage on the field of Gettysburg!" The twenty-one-year-old Buck died assured that the stain on his record was removed.

Twice Chamberlain was wounded. Earlier in the fighting, a bullet sliced the instep of his boot, causing him to limp as the battle progressed. Another bullet was deflected by his sword scabbard, bending it and causing a contusion on his thigh. Miraculously, he escaped any other more serious wound, although he was always in the open and clearly recognizable as an officer.

But when Chamberlain headed down Little Round Top's bottom slope, he found himself facing the gun barrel of a Confederate officer's revolver. The man fired point-blank at Chamberlain. He missed. As the Colonel brought his sword to the Rebel's neck, the man shrugged and handed Chamberlain the empty pistol. Chamberlain took it and continued downhill.

The 200 men who made the charge captured an equal number of Confederates. Chamberlain did not find it easy to halt his regiment. They were on their way to Richmond, they said.

It was sunset.

But the Twentieth Maine had more work to do that night. Chamberlain was ordered by Colonel Rice—the gallant Vincent had fallen—to secure Big Round Top. What was left of Oates's decimated regiment had skedaddled back up the hill. It was vital to push back the disorganized Confederates before they could haul artillery up the hill. At nine o'clock a limping Chamberlain led his Mainers, still without fresh ammunition, up Big Round Top and took it. Minimal Confederate opposition was brushed away.

In the darkness, atop the forbidding hill, the Maine boys waited to see what the dawn would bring. They did not realize that, for them, the Battle of Gettysburg was over. Yet in a sense it would never be over, after their ninety minutes of glory.

*Francis Heath—Maine State Archives*

# The Nineteenth Maine

*"They must have thought that God had suddenly raised from the earth an army."*

It was the Fourth of July, 1862. J. W. Spaulding helped his father drive some pesky cows out of the cornfield on their Richmond farm and repair the fence. These chores consumed two hours, enough time for young Spaulding, a Bowdoin graduate, to screw up his courage and declare, "Father, President Lincoln has called for 300,000 more soldiers. It is my turn now."

The older Spaulding, looking sad and proud at the same time, replied, "I have told you for the past year that there would be time enough for you to enlist, and you see I was right; but I agree with you now, though God knows how it pains me to say it, I think it is your turn now."

"From that moment," Spaulding would say, "I was a man." But not, apparently, man enough to enter the house and face his mother. He left that to his father. He went to Bath and signed up in the Nineteenth Maine Regiment.

A year later, he had truly grown into a man at Gettysburg. And the Nineteenth Maine had won *its* claim to saving the day.

But the regiment, which joined Howard's brigade, first won a different sort of fame. It happened on October 5, when the Nineteenth Maine camped on Boliver Heights, overlooking Harper's Ferry. A battery had recently occupied the high ground, and a goodly number of live shells remained. The Maine boys thought it prudent to pile them carefully next to the earthwork.

Spaulding and some other soldiers lit a fire to boil coffee for supper, then left it to scamper for their tents when a tornado suddenly came up. The fire spread into some brush and dry leaves—and, eventually, to the pile of shells. When they exploded, the division thought it was being fired upon. In the hands of the press, this incident was described differently.

The Philadelphia *Enquirer* said the loaded shells were set off when a hayseed from the Nineteenth Maine used them to rest a frying pan on. He built a fire underneath to fry some meat for supper when, Boom! Boom! Boom! Nothing was heard of the Maine soldier or his frying pan after that. It was too good a story; the Nineteenth Maine would become forever associated with that infamous frying pan.

The Nineteenth was also renowned for its foraging prowess. General Willis Gorman, who succeeded Howard in command of the brigade, said "the Nineteenth Maine if let alone would steal the whole Southern Confederacy in three months." Gorman, a St. Paul lawyer and politician, began the war as Colonel of the First Minnesota, a regiment which originally numbered more than 100 Mainers. In contrast to the pious Howard, Gorman was credited with such cussing power he could be heard a half mile away. He was sent west in November and replaced by General William Harrow, another Midwestern lawyer.

Apparently the Nineteenth Maine's foraging abilities were not limited to Rebel property. During the march to Gettysburg, the boys were involved in a raid on a Massachusetts battery's sutler. General William Hayes ordered out some artillery and infantry to disperse the raiders. But by the time this force was assembled, the sutler's tent was cleaned out and the takers had vanished. After that, it is reported the Nineteenth Maine was particularly well stocked with tobacco.

On July 1 the regiment reached Gettysburg and set up its tents about a mile southeast of Round Top. They were joined by the remnant of the Sixteenth Maine, and got "a very dismal account" of the afternoon's battle. The next day, their brigade was placed on Cemetery Hill, initially to serve as support for General Howard, if required. The soldiers were laying *en masse* in the cemetery, eating a dinner of hard bread and fried pork, when the Confederates sent a calling card. As Lieutenant Spaulding recalled, he had "taken but a few morsels of the palatable food, when a shot or shell came and cut off the leg of one of the Massachusetts boys, about a rod from me. I did not want any more pork that meal."

Captain Silas Adams thought, "What meaner place could man be put in?" They were sitting there, waiting and wondering when the Rebs would lob another shell into their ranks. It would be a relief to be "up and at 'em."

At two o'clock that afternoon, the brigade was moved, with other elements of Hancock's II Corps, to take a position along Cemetery Ridge, to fill the gap created by the III Corps movement to the west. General Hancock rode up, dismounted, and took the first member of the Sixteenth Maine he encountered, George Durgin of Company F, to a spot a little further to the regiment's left. "Will you stay here?" Hancock said.

The short, thickset Durgin looked up at the tall, florid Hancock, and replied, "I'll stay here, General, until Hell freezes over." Hancock liked that. He smiled, then told Colonel Francis Heath to dress his regiment on the spot where Durgin stood.

In a moment, Hancock was back on his horse and riding off. He left the Nineteenth Maine almost alone in its section of the long, undulating ridge. Other units of the brigade, part of Gibbon's division, were moved elsewhere. To the regiment's right were a couple of batteries, but no infantry. To the left, aside from two more batteries, there was only the First Minnesota, and that regiment was about sixty rods away.

From its vantage point, the Nineteenth Maine could see the battle develop below them. III Corps was getting pounded. Slowly, tenaciously contesting every foot of ground, Sickles' divisions were being pushed back. The battle was moving toward the Maine boys on the ridge. "We had been silent spectators all day," wrote Captain Charles Nash.

That was about to change. As the sky darkened, so did the Federal cause below. III Corps was falling apart, streaming up the ridge, followed by waves of victorious Confederates. Colonel Heath ordered his men to lay flat on their faces. A wave of disorganized men was heading for them.

Heath walked back and forth in front of his men hugging the earth. They were, he said, to stay there as the human wave washed over them. The Nineteenth Maine was in the path of Humphreys' division, blown out of the Peach Orchard.

As Colonel Heath remembered it, General Humphreys galloped up to where he stood. The general ordered Heath to stop his routed troops with the bayonets of his regiment.

Heath refused. "I told Humphreys to get his men out of the way and we would stop the pursuers. He did not seem to appear satisfied with that arrangement, but rode down the rear of my lines, ordering the men up. I followed him and countermanded his orders, he finally going off, his men with him."

This episode was vehemently disputed by the regiment's historian, and Heath himself sometimes said the officer he had words with *seemed* to be Humphreys. Whatever the case, some officer ordered him to try to stop the retreating men.

Instead, the Nineteenth Mainers lay prone as Humphreys' division scrambled over them. Some took the time to weave a path between the prostrate soldiers, but many did not interrupt their flight, stepping on, even falling over them. "Run boys, we're whipped, the day is lost," some men, mentally as well as physically beaten, cried as they passed. But others, undefeated in spirit, wept with joy when they saw the Nineteenth Maine keeping its position. "Hang to it boys, give it to them, we'll form in your rear," these soldiers hollered.

Not one of the Mainers broke ranks. As soon as III Corps had gone back, Colonel Heath shouted, "Give it to them!" Jumping to their feet, the long hours of inaction and tension culminating in a moment of supreme release, the Nineteenth Maine immediately fired into the Rebels thirty-five yards away—Wright's Georgia Brigade, intermingled with Florida soldiers of Perry's brigade.

They "must have thought that God had suddenly raised from the earth an army to oppose their march," Spaulding said. The impact of the unexpected shower of lead stunned the gray line, but they kept coming. The Nineteenth Maine's ranks were now thinned by the shooting of the Georgians and Floridians. "Oh, my God," Lieutenant Spaulding thought, "would they never stop!"

The Maine boys poured about eight rounds into the Rebs. Gunsmoke hung heavily in the humid dusk.

The Nineteenth Maine, pressured heavily on its left, pulled back a few paces, then reformed. There could be no retreat, or the Union line would be pierced and the Army of the Potomac cut in two. Again, the battle hung in the balance.

Their line readjusted, the Mainers peered through a brief lifting of the cloud of smoke. There was apparent confusion within the Confederate ranks. The Rebels were still advancing, "but," Captain Nash wrote, "slowly and hesitatingly, for in the space of five minutes their strong line had melted away, and there were only a few daring spirits left to encounter."

A Rebel color bearer waved his flag to buck up the courage of his comrades to keep going. Colonel Heath snapped, "Drop that color bearer!" Several muskets blazed and the man fell. Although it was not altogether clear, the First Minnesota had already started to charge, relieving pressure on Heath's left.

The Colonel immediately perceived the Rebel tentativeness; moving the Nineteenth back to its original line, he ordered bayonets fixed. He shouted, "Come on, boys!"

And down the slope littered with corpses the Maine boys charged, yelling like wild men. The Confederates fell apart. Many dropped their weapons and put their hands up; other scurried for cover behind rocks and bushes. Most ran. They dropped some battle flags on the field, but the Mainers, intent on the chase, did not stop to pick them up.

They pursued the Rebs across the Emmitsburg turnpike, back toward the Peach Orchard. An aide, presumably from Hancock's staff, galloped up and demanded where Heath was going. The Colonel replied, "We are chasing the Rebs." The aide cautioned the Maine man that, if he went further, he risked capture.

Indeed, although men back on the ridge could be heard cheering the charge of the Nineteenth Maine, none had joined the charge. Once the Confederates had time to regroup, Heath's regiment would be in trouble. The order to halt was given.

Silas Adams said, "We stopped, but we hated to do so, as we were enjoying seeing them run and scale a five-rail fence along the side of the road with the agility of a deer." Adams was distinctly less happy to look back and see a few hundred of Humphrey's division follow about a third of the way the Nineteenth had come and pick up a battle flag. "How kind they were to relieve us of the trouble of bringing in our trophies, so dearly and honorably earned," the captain observed.

When the Nineteenth Maine returned to Cemetery Ridge, they brought with them hundreds of prisoners, a stand of colors, three cannon previously lost by III Corps, and four caissons. One gun was so overheated its brass cannon drooped and was useless. The whole line cheered wildly. "It was the first time that I felt the regiment had done anything more than what might naturally be expected of any regiment," Adams said.

That night the Nineteenth Maine bivouacked near the point where they had launched their charge. Although victorious, Lieutenant Spaulding felt sad and nervous. He dreaded what the next day would bring. He was homesick. Lying on the ground in his blanket, Spaulding gazed up at the canopy of stars. The same stars would be shining just as brightly back in Maine over his home and that of the girl he left behind. Maybe *she* was looking at the same stars, reflecting the light in *her* eyes, he mused. "And when a moment later I saw what I thought was a roguish twinkle in one of them, I was satisfied that I was right, and I was happy and went to sleep."

It was not easy sleeping that night, with the screams of the wounded lying between the lines punctuating the stillness. There would be more noise and killing, and the Nineteenth Maine would be in the midst of it.

*Joseph Spaulding—Maine State Archives*

# The Nineteenth Maine

## *"Everyone wanted to be first there."*

Lieutenant Joseph Spaulding of the Nineteenth Maine was up early on the morning of July 3. The regiment was positioned to the right along Cemetery Ridge about fifty-eight rods, to a new position slightly to the left of a small copse of trees. Spaulding and his comrades were only yards from where, that afternoon, the "high water mark" of the Confederacy would occur. Again, the battle would come to the Mainers.

But until two o'clock, the hours ticked by without much activity. Four companies of the Nineteenth Maine were sent across the clover-filled pastures that separated the Union line from the Emmitsburg pike. Near the road these skirmishers lay flat and commenced their deadly game with Rebel counterparts. It was a scorching day, broiling the prone soldiers. But to raise one's head was to risk getting it blown off.

The torpor was shattered at two o'clock when Lee unleashed a barrage from about 150 cannon. "None of us, not even the oldest soldier, had ever seen or heard anything like this before," Spaulding noted. Obviously Bobby Lee was going all out for victory that day.

About half as many Union guns returned fire. For over an hour the biggest cannonade ever in the Western Hemisphere rumbled. Most of the Confederate fire centered on that part of the Union line where the Nineteenth Maine was. Like everybody else in the infantry, the boys of the Nineteenth lay flat on their faces. It occurred to Spaulding, hugging the trembling earth as shells exploded above him at the rate of about 200 per minute, that exposure to five minutes of *this* would shut up the most rabid warmonger.

For the skirmishers of the Nineteenth Maine between the lines, the experience was more immediate. They were closer to the Rebel cannon than their own, and they were getting the benefit of both sides' heavy metal flying over them. "The air seemed to be all in a whirl," Sergeant Adams thought. "All we could do was to flatten out a little thinner, and our empty stomachs did not prevent that."

About three o'clock the Confederate thunder stopped; the Union guns were silenced earlier. "It now had become a perfect stillness," Adams wrote. It reminded him of a quiet Sunday morning in Maine.

That comparison held for ten minutes. Then the Confederate infantry, a lot of it, came into the open. Lee was sending over 12,000 men against the Union center on the ridge. They moved forward in lines that seemed to extend a mile, tightly disciplined, as if on parade. It was an awesome sight.

For the skirmishers directly in the path of "Pickett's Charge," it was time to get the hell out of the way. But when Silas Adams tried to get up, he had the peculiar sensation that his legs were paralyzed. After lying for so many hours on the ground, they had "gone to sleep." After a few anxious moments, they started to come to, and he moved slowly back up the long open field leading to the ridge.

The Maine skirmishers fired a couple shots into the Confederate masses; the Rebels did not respond, but just kept moving relentlessly forward. Officers on the ridge yelled for the skirmishers to get back and out of the line of fire. Too late: mistaken for Confederates, they had to dodge bullets from their own side as they scurried back to rejoin their regiment.

The Union artillery punched holes in the Confederate ranks, but they were closed as the Rebels approached the Federal line. "When the rebel infantry came within range, we up and at 'em," Spaulding said. Despite heavy losses, the enemy persevered and collided with the Yankee troops to the Nineteenth Maine's right.

"Our line rolled back to the point where I was standing," Spaulding remembered, "very much the same as a piece of birch bark when one end is placed in the fire." The brigade nearest to the Mainers, Webb's, bore the brunt of the Rebel assault, and was reeling back from the impact.

Rebel yells pierced the general din, Confederate flags bobbed within Union lines near the growth of trees, and at that moment it looked like the Rebels were successful.

Colonel Francis Heath ordered the Nineteenth Maine into the gap. It was impossible to maintain order. "Everyone wanted to be first there and we went up more like a mob than a disciplined force."

Lieutenant Spaulding described the scene:

We were all loading and firing and yelling and pushing towards the gap now filled with the exultant rebels. Company, regimental and brigade organizations were lost, and we were a great crowd. We would load, run to the front and fire, then others would jump in front of us and fire, and the color bearers, always at the front, would toss their colors up and down to show the enemy that we were not going to give it up, and to encourage us on. I got a cartridge in wrong end first, and the only man of my regiment I could see fired off his rammer. He and I kept together. The ground was covered with arms of every description, and we had no difficulty in supplying ourselves.

In the mob of soldiers, the Nineteenth Maine boys pushed to the front. There was no time or room for loading and firing in the swirling, intermingled mass. They used bayonets. They clubbed Rebs with their muskets. They threw rocks.

Colonel Heath was hit, wounded in the shoulder.

*Pickett's Charge. Nineteenth Maine is to the left of the artillery*
*—Sparks From The Camp Fire*

Then, after about ten minutes, the hundreds of Confederates who had penetrated the Union line were engulfed. Abruptly, it was over. The Confederate tide receded. As Rebels retreated, men of the Nineteenth Maine followed them a way, firing parting shots.

At this moment, which historians would later identify as the turning point of the Civil War, as disorganized clumps of the enemy melted back across the field over which only an hour earlier they had marched so gloriously and picturesquely, Lieutenant Spaulding was thinking about food.

Like the rest of the regiment, he had not eaten a bite since morning. Now he was overcome by raging hunger. Broken Confederates were scattered everywhere about him. Their haversacks, unlike Spaulding's, were full. A Rebel boy at his feet was faintly praying to God to look out for his wife and child.

"I waited a few minutes till he was dead, then I removed his haversack and canteen, and feasted upon some fresh biscuit and honey that I found there." The Rebel must have been foraging in a nearby farm. Now, as dusk gathered at Gettysburg, the Maine soldier enjoyed the products of his labor. He was too hungry to be squeamish.

# Joshua Chamberlain
## *"I do not have much of the beautiful and spiritual here."*

It rained hard on July 4. The Twentieth Maine was sent forward to reconnoitre the area where III Corps had fought. It was a grisly spectacle. Everywhere, in every grotesque position imaginable, were the dead. Hundreds of dead soldiers were scattered amongst at least a thousand dead horses, bloated, rotting, the stench overpowering, amidst broken caissons and assorted rubble of war. Some lived, barely, crying, moaning, envying the dead. The Army of Northern Virginia was gone.

The regiment returned to Little Round Top, to bury its dead. Joshua Chamberlain scribbled a note to Fannie. He did not recount the scenes of the killing fields, but wrote, "We are fighting gloriously. Our loss is terrible, but we are beating the Rebels as they were never beaten before."

The Colonel was proud of his regiment. "The Twentieth has immortalized itself," he wrote. "I am receiving all sorts of praise, but bear it meekly."

Some of the praise had come from Brigadier General Adelbert Ames, whose division had defended Culp's Hill at the north end, or right, of the Union line. Ames had ridden over to his old regiment to tell them how proud he was of them. They had given the man they once detested three cheers. Chamberlain, so weak and sick he swayed in the saddle, had conducted himself on July 2 the way Ames did.

It soon became apparent that Lee was in retreat. Meade followed, but slowly. At Williamsport, the Army of Northern Virginia had its back to the swollen Potomac. Instead of attacking, Meade entrenched. Vice President Hamlin arrived from Washington. Meade's son wondered in a letter why the unimpressive-looking politician was in camp.

Years later it would be claimed that Hamlin bore a message from Lincoln. The President, frustrated that Meade was not moving to crush the Confederate army, supposedly wrote that if only Meade would attack he, Abraham Lincoln, would take full responsibility for the result. But Meade did not attack. Meeting a reporter he knew, the Vice President simply raised his arms in disgust at the situation, and walked away.

Lee finally was able to bridge the Potomac with pontoons and recrossed the river. Cautiously, the Army of the Potomac followed. The sun reasserted itself as the Federal army moved into beautiful, rolling, green country. Joshua Chamberlain's mood was not sunny. He had gotten a letter from Fannie postmarked New York. Brothers Tom and John knew she was there, but had not told him. Now he knew. She had not gotten his letter describing his finest hour, sent to Brunswick. *She had been shopping while he defended Little Round Top.*

Now, encamped in Maryland, he wrote again on July 17. "I was very much surprised to have a letter from you dated at *New York*. I wrote you on my knee in the battle of Gettysburg, after our terrible fight in which the Twentieth held the post of honor on the extreme left of the army where the fiercest attack was made." He recounted the story again, adding, "These prisoners of mine were fierce fellows from Texas & Alabama—they said they had never before been *stopped*."

"But New York! I am sorry you are there," he continued. The city was the scene of destructive draft riots after Gettysburg. "It is not safe to try to get away is it? I wish you were at home. You should have been there before."

By late July, Chamberlain, fevered and frustrated, was at the end of his rope. He requested leave from the Army; he could not continue his duties "without the most serious consequences." In Washington he got medical attention. His condition was attributed to "malarial fever," but he was also stressed out. The doctors recommended that he go home for a fifteen-day sick leave.

There is no remaining record of what happened in Brunswick, but things must, once again, have been patched up somewhat. He did apply for an extension of his leave that August, but he was needed in Virginia, to take command of the Third Brigade while his friend Rice took *his* home leave. Rice was promoted to Brigadier General and went to I Corps. The wounded Vincent had been promoted, but was dead by the time the promotion was made. Chamberlain would now be in charge of the Third Brigade.

At the end of August, he wrote Fannie. He was glad she was home and thought of "my little dear ones all nestled together—'all'—I paused over that word—the tears filled my eyes—a dull heavy pain flowed over my heart." He missed his "precious wife" and "sad mother," adding, "You were in 'two moods.' So I am, always, when I write you." He was that way, he said, when he began this letter after the bugle sounded time to extinguish lights. "You would not miss it at all if you were to *tell* me of the 'dreamy love.' If you are tempted to write of 'facts'—write about *that fact.* I do not have much of the beautiful & spiritual said or done to me here."

He wanted so badly for Fannie to say she loved him the way he loved her.

Autumn followed summer as Meade and Lee played a game of maneuver. On November 7 an attack was made upon a position Lee had fortified on the north side of the Rappahannock River. Some of the men of Chamberlain's old regiment, led by Captain Morrill, joined the Sixth Maine and other regiments in making the assault. Outnumbered, they nevertheless carried the Confederate works.

Impatient not to be in on the action, Chamberlain rode to the fringes of it and his magnificent new horse, "Charlemagne," was wounded in a foreleg.

Chamberlain was unscathed. However, a couple days later he slept on the ground with his men. There were no fires because Lee's army was close. During the night it sleeted and snowed, and the Colonel awoke encased in white. He shook it off, but could not shake off the chills and fever that ensued. He was dispatched to Washington in a rattling cattle car, attended by a doctor, slipping in and out of consciousness. He spent a month in the Seminary General Hospital. Diagnosed again as being afflicted with "malarial fever," he was released in December to return to Brunswick.

Home for the holidays. The Army of the Potomac and its Rebel counterpart went into winter quarters. There would be no more fighting, certainly no decisive battle, until the snows thawed. The war continued.

# Selden Connor
## *Into the Wilderness*

Selden Connor, one of the Boys of '61, was a Veteran of '63 at age 24.

After the Seventh Maine was chewed up at Antietam, Selden Connor was sent home to Maine to recruit men and rebuild the regiment. Recruitment was not easy, but a battalion of five companies, numbering 230 men, was scraped together, and sent back to the front.

Lieutenant Colonel Connor led the battalion in the assault on Maryre's Heights at Fredericksburg during the Chancellorsville campaign in May of 1863; he was at Gettysburg on July 3. After the battle, Colonel Edwin Mason resumed command of the Seventh Maine. That fall, Connor returned to Portland to serve on a general court-martial as Meade played cat-and-mouse with Lee in Virginia.

It was a chance for young lions and old to rest. Colonel Hiram Burnham, the burly, battle-tested commander of the Sixth Maine, presided over the court. Burnham, in his fifties, a lumberman from Downeast, was a character. Before the attack at Maryre's Heights, Burnham was alleged to have ridden up to his men and said, "Boys, I have got a government contract."

"What is it, Colonel?" they asked.

"One thousand rebels, potted and salted, and got to have 'em in less than five minutes," old Hiram said. Then he bawled, "Forward! Guide center!" The contract was fulfilled.

One fine winter's day, a captain of the Eighth Maine, also serving on the court, took Connor aside. "I went to Augusta yesterday and you cannot guess what I went for."

Connor could not, and J. H. Roberts continued, "I went to ask the Governor to appoint you Colonel of my regiment. Governor Coburn said he would appoint you to the next colonelcy, whether it should be the Eighth or the Eighteenth."

As it turned out, the next vacancy was in the Nineteenth Maine, when Colonel Francis Heath resigned. Coburn appointed Connor to fill the position on the first day of December. It took repeated requests, however, for Connor to extricate himself from court duty. He didn't arrive in Virginia until February 25, 1864.

His record was well known, and Connor was placed in command of a brigade which included the Nineteenth Maine and several other regiments. Later that wet and rainy spring, with a reorganization of the Army of the Potomac, Connor was back in command of the regiment. In the reshuffling, General Gibbon became commander of the Second Division of Hancock's II Corps, while General Webb was given command of the First Brigade, of which Connor's regiment was a part. The Nineteenth Maine had aided Webb's brigade at Gettysburg, and it would play a crucial role for him—and the Army—in the first battle of the new campaign that opened in May.

It would be Colonel Selden Connor's last battle.

The Union Army immediately moved into the Wilderness, crossing the Chancellorsville battlefield, still strewn with the ugly debris of the previous May. Skeletons amidst the scraggly trees and brush beckoned it onward. The blue columns crossed two roads, running parallel, east to west, the Orange Turnpike and the Orange Plank Road. Running north to south, the Brock Road intersected the plank road. II

---

Corps followed the plank road out of the weird, ominous woods to Todd's Tavern.

Then, on the morning of May 5, the sound of artillery behind them indicated that the anticipated battle had started. In fact, Warren's V Corps had collided with Ewell's corps of the Army of Northern Virginia on the Orange Turnpike. The Battle of the Wilderness had begun. Grant's army (Meade was technically in command, but every soldier knew who really was) outnumbered Lee's 2–1, but in the Wilderness that wouldn't matter any more than it had a year earlier.

Lieutenant Spaulding had survived Gettysburg. Now, as Hancock's 25,000-man corps was ordered back into the damned woods, Spaulding knew "a big fight was in store for us"—and he was scared. All the talk about valor, gallantry, pluck and heroism sounded great, he thought, "but to tell the truth it was nothing but cowardice that kept me in the ranks now. I hadn't courage enough to say that I was a coward, or to act like one, and for that very reason I did what I could." The lieutenant probably summed up the attitude of the 200,000 men who would do their best to kill each other in fifteen square acres of hell.

It was the shank end of the day when the Nineteenth Maine was posted in woods to the right of the plank road, near where it intersected with the Brock Road. Breastworks were thrown up along the latter road, which pretty much defined the Union line. Colonel Connor reported, as ordered by General Gibbon, to the commander of the Third Brigade. General Samuel Carroll said he expected to move forward at dawn on May 6.

That morning, the regiment, behind Carroll's brigade, moved in line of battle obliquely to its left, crossing the plank road. While in the third line at the outset, the Nineteenth Maine soon found itself to the left of the other soldiers. Almost immediately the Mainers were hit by fire from an invisible enemy. Connor, jumping ahead of his men, led them to a gully, which afforded some protection. Worried about his left flank, he requested support. It never came.

It was a grim business. Only low commands were spoken as men loaded and fired at an enemy they could not see, but whose bullets they felt. Spaulding had only a moment to see the man beside him fall, blood gurgling out of his chest, when "I was struck in the arm with such force as to swing me round and hurt severely." It felt like a rock had hit him. "I was happy. But further examination disclosed no blood. Then I knew it was only a blow from a spent ball and would not take me to the rear." He kept shooting.

The Nineteenth Maine was running low on ammunition when bullets started flying lengthwise into its line. They were flanked on their left; Rebs in the woods were moving to their rear. It was time to pull back.

On the plank road the regiment replenished its cartridge boxes and reformed. General Webb came up with the rest of the First Brigade, which the Nineteenth joined, moving forward again. IX Corps was also on the scene; hatless, General Burnside's dome glistened in the late morning heat. The Nineteenth Maine connected on its right with Burnside's boys. Soon they had worked back to the depression in the forest they had held earlier.

Another hot engagement with an unseen adversary commenced. "We were lying flat on our faces," Spaulding remembered. "We would roll over on our backs and load, then on our faces and fire, each man as fast as he could, without reference to anybody else." Another regiment, probably the Fifteenth Massachusetts, ran up to relieve the Mainers, who ran back.

They were short of ammunition once again. Connor reported this to General Webb, who directed Connor to take his men back to some ammo boxes about 125 yards to the rear. About this time Webb was ordered by General Wadsworth to another part of the field, an order Webb considered foolish but which he obeyed.

The general was thus absent from his brigade for about fifteen minutes. It was about noon, and General James Longstreet was hitting the Union line where II Corps was stationed. In Hancock's description, the assault would roll up his line like a wet blanket.

Connor had gone back to the ammunition boxes with Webb's adjutant, Captain Charles Banes, when the sound of firing in the woods to their left grew in intensity. It flashed through Connor's mind in an instant: This was bad, it meant the enemy was coming on in force. Indeed, at that moment, some 6,000 men were retreating back through the trees and thickets like jackrabbits.

Quickly, Connor told Captain Banes that he intended to place his regiment so as "to cover our people who were being driven back," and, with Banes at his side, he wheeled his Nineteenth Maine parallel to the plank road, which was at a right angle to the Brock Road.

As soon as Federal troops pouring out of the woods had passed his front, Connor ordered his men to fire at the pursuing enemy. In rapid succession the Nineteenth Maine poured volleys into the rebel division's flank.

The Confederates were disconcerted. *Was there a new Federal line? Was it a trap?* For valuable minutes they halted.

General Webb galloped back, saw the retreating army, the advancing Confederates, the little Maine regiment blazing away. Forty-five years later, he wrote, "What a grand sight that was! Your Regiment was to hold back that Rebel advance and I had the opportunity to be with you."

Connor, Webb said, "did exactly what was necessary. He prevented the enemy from seeing the rout. The road was jammed with troops and the rear of the column would have suffered terribly had not Colonel Connor stopped his regiment." The Confederate General Wilcox later told Webb that he lost twenty minutes following the Yanks. Without having to contend with the unexpected fire on his left, he would have barreled right into the retreating blue soldiers.

Changing fronts, the Confederates laid down a withering fire upon the exposed Maine regiment. Connor apparently moved into the road, directing his men to fire continuously, by file. Struck by "something like a sledgehammer," he instantly crumpled to the ground. Webb asked, "Are you hit, Colonel?"

"I've got it this time, General," Connor replied.

He was hit in the thigh, the bone of his leg shattered. Some of his men wrapped him in a blanket and carried him off the field, narrowly avoiding capture. "I weighed about two hundred pounds and the way was rough, so that a good many men took a hand," he recalled. The regiment fell back to the breastworks along the Brock Road.

They had to make a run for it; some Rebs almost cut them off. "If we had known at the time what great service we had rendered, we should have felt better," Spaulding said. Like his comrades, he felt the Nineteenth Maine was whipped. Casualties were as high as spirits were low.

They didn't know then that they helped save the Union Army from a decisive defeat. The Confederate juggernaut was checked. Trying to ascertain what was going on at *his* front, Longstreet, in a strange replay of events a year earlier, was badly wounded by trigger-happy Confederates. The confusion following the Rebel leader's shooting was another key factor in stalling his offensive.

It was dark as the survivors of the Nineteenth Maine sipped coffee and tried to sleep in their rubber blankets along the Brock Road. As troops passed in the road they called out, "What regiment?" Sometime past midnight, having answered "Nineteenth Maine" for what seemed the hundredth time, someone in a passing regiment hollered, "How about that frying pan?"

Everybody had a good laugh. Feeling better, the men of the Nineteenth Maine got some sleep.

Several days later, at Spotsylvania, General Webb was wounded by a bullet in the head. Taken to a hospital in Fredericksburg, he learned that Colonel Selden Connor was one of the other wounded men sharing the room. Something bothered Webb. He sent an orderly over to the Maine man to ask his pardon for not thinking to offer the use of his horse after Connor was hit. Selden Connor replied it was all right, there was no way he could have mounted a horse.

Connor would suffer great agony and there were fears for his life. He wrote a friend:

"I am still flat on my back in spite of which I am 'gay and happy' still. The fact is, my sinful hearer, your beloved pastor's *dancing days* are 'done gone.' At the best my leg be more for ornament than use. I should not be human if I did not at times bitterly regret that just as I am entering manhood, I am obliged to occupy the chimney corner and let the world go by."

While he was in a Washington hospital, President Lincoln commissioned Selden Connor Brigadier General of Volunteers. He was promoted to rank from June 11, 1864. It was a great honor to be a general at 25, but he could not exercise it. The vigorous Boy of '61 was the disabled Old Soldier of '64.

# Thomas Hyde

*"I would rather speak of lazy intervals,*
*exploring ancient Virginia mansions."*

Tom Hyde had left the Seventh Maine to serve on "Uncle John" Sedgwick's staff. On July 1, 1863, at Meade's headquarters to receive orders, Hyde was told to find the VI Corps commander and urge him to march to Gettysburg at once.

Riding through the night, the young staffer found his straw-hatted general and guided him along a shorter route to the battlefield. By helping get Sedgwick up quickly, Hyde was convinced he had helped win the battle. He dodged bullets at Little Round Top and witnessed Pickett's charge.

He was just about always in the thick of the action. On May 4, in the Wilderness, Hyde was again on his way to Meade's headquarters while an unseen enemy mercilessly pounded VI Corps with artillery fire. A New Jersey brigade hurried up to reinforce the line.

"I had dismounted to fix my horse's bit when a cannon-ball took off the head of a Jersey man; the head struck me, and I was knocked down, covered with brains and blood," Hyde remembered. "Even my mouth, probably gaping in wonder where the shell would strike, was filled."

It appeared Tom Hyde was done for. Looking up, he saw General Sedgwick give him "a sorrowful glance," as several friends rushed over to him. Hyde could get up unaided, but recalled he was "not much use as a staff officer for fully fifteen minutes." In the midst of confused charges and countercharges in a "bushy, briery labyrinth," Hyde lost any sense of direction, wandering about until the next day's dawning.

At about five o'clock in the afternoon, Confederate General John Brown Gordon's troops flanked the Union right. As Sedgwick tried to rally the Union line with his staff, Hyde pulled several hundred men together in a clearing. They had hardly formed when the Reb juggernaut struck. The line disintegrated. Throwing himself, Indian-style, behind his horse's neck, Tom Hyde narrowly escaped capture. Asking a colonel—whose face was a mask of terror—what happened to the line, he was informed it was gone. Where was the Seventh Maine? Wiped out, he was told. Hyde was later overjoyed to learn that, while the Seventh had lost half its numbers, his old regiment still existed.

The fighting moved out of the Wilderness to Spotsylvania. On the morning of May 9, VI Corps headquarters was situated near a crossroad. Reb sharpshooters were notably busy. Tom Hyde pushed out a picket line to deal with the deadly nuisance. Bullets whistled out of the woods, but Hyde accomplished his errand and returned to Sedgwick. He found the general sitting on a cracker box by a tree. Hyde remembered "Uncle John" set about "pulling my ears affectionately, and chaffing me a little as I was trying to fill my pipe," asking about his staffer's ride.

Some artillery was hauled up the road and positioned to the men's right. Sedgwick got off his cracker box perch and left Hyde, apparently to give the gunners directions. Almost immediately the staffer heard a voice cry out, "the general!" Running over to the source of the cry, Hyde found the general lying on his back. Blood trickled from a small but fatal wound under Sedgwick's eye.

There was limited time to grieve for a man the young officer loved. A bower of evergreens was prepared to rest his corpse upon, as the savage fighting ground on. It was particularly horrible at a breastwork of logs which Rebels repeatedly attacked but failed to carry. After the battle, Tom Hyde surveyed the human wreckage. Between the traverses the enemy was piled up four deep, the bottom tier nearly submerged in blood and water. The wounded writhed under the burden of the dead.

"I undertook to relieve a young officer, who was nearly gone, of the weight pressed upon him," Hyde wrote, "but he said, shaking his head, 'You have conquered; now I die'; and suited the action to the word."

The blue soldiers cluttering the ground behind the breastworks also presented a sad, grisly spectacle. Many were "nothing but a lump of meat or clot of gore where countless bullets from both armies had torn them" as they lay in the open.

And that was the way it was as Grant moved relentlessly south. Hyde would not want to recall all of the carnage he saw. "I would rather speak of lazy intervals, exploring ancient Virginia mansions, built when feudal magnificence held sway in these fertile valleys." Was he thinking of time past in this same area when he and Selden Connor explored an abandoned mansion, drank wine from fancy decanters, and galloped over the green countryside? Those days were gone for Connor, but Hyde still tried to recreate them.

War was an unusually grim business, but Tom Hyde soldiered on. The Seventh Maine was left with only sixty-five men in line after Spotsylvania. Hyde asked to be relieved from the staff. He thought it his duty to return to the command of his old regiment.

FROM A PHOTOGRAPH.

GENERAL WM. B. HAZEN. GENERAL W. T. SHERMAN. GENERAL HENRY W. SLOCUM.

GENERAL O. O. HOWARD. GENERAL JOHN A. LOGAN. GENERAL JEFF. C. DAVIS. GENERAL J. A. MOWER,

# Oliver Otis Howard

## *"Hood will attack me here."*

After Gettysburg, it was clear to Oliver Otis Howard that XI Corps simply was not going to get any respect. Endorsing Schurz' proposal to break up and disperse the corps in other commands, Howard wrote General in Chief Henry Halleck there was simply too much prejudice in the army to overcome.

"Personally, it will be gratifying to me to return to the Second Corps," Howard wrote, "but I do not feel dissatisfied with the Eleventh during the present campaign."

After visiting his family in Maine and seeing his newborn son Chancey, born during the Battle of Chancellorsville, Howard learned that he and XI Corps were staying together. He was ordered to report to Joe Hooker for instructions. At the Willard Hotel in Washington, Howard learned that Hooker was in overall command of XI and XII Corps; they were to proceed by train west to aid the Union army besieged by the Confederates at Chattanooga.

*William T. Sherman and his generals. O. O. Howard stands to the left (note empty sleeve). Seated next to Howard is John "Black Jack" Logan. Sherman (seated center) passed over Logan to make Howard commander of the Army of the Tennessee. Later, Sherman would give Howard command of his army's right wing in the Georgia "March to the Sea." Henry Slocum (seated to Sherman's left) would command the left. The three standing in the back are, left to right, William B. Hazen, Jeff C. Davis, and J. A. Mower*—Battles and Leaders, Vol. IV

Howard could have not been thrilled to be under Hooker again, and Fighting Joe hardly could have been pleased to have back the man he blamed for the fiasco at Chancellorsville. But they had one thing in common: the West gave them a chance to restore their tarnished reputations. Neither had much further promise in Virginia.

It was a long trip, especially on trains averaging about fifteen miles per hour. Howard, his moving headquarters in the rearmost train, grew concerned that some of the soldiers riding atop the freight cars were tippling and toppling off. He therefore arranged for liquor shops in towns along the route to be closed as they passed through. The crowds were enthusiastic, and Howard's spirits were lifted as he moved west. "I feel that I am sent out here for some wise and good purpose," he wrote on October 1. "I believe my corps will be better appreciated. God grant us success and a speedy close to the war."

Howard was struck by the poverty and ignorance of the denizens of the mountainous back-country of Kentucky and Tennessee. "The actual cause of the war was not known among them," he recalled. One local told Howard he had heard the war was started by a battle among the politicians in Washington (actually not as ignorant an observation as Howard found it to be).

Outside Chattanooga at Wauhatchie, Rebels made a midnight attack, which Howard's XI Corps helped repel. Even the mules, who broke loose, got involved. Howard figured the puzzled Confederates confused the animals for cavalry charging.

Howard saw little action at Chattanooga as, under Grant's direction, several Union armies lifted the siege. Hooker covered himself in glory by taking Lookout Mountain in the (according to critics, fabled) "Battle Above the Clouds." After this crowning success in the West, Grant was called east, and William Tecumseh Sherman assumed command of western operations.

On the face of it, Howard and Sherman were about as opposite as possible. In contrast to the straight-laced young Mainer, meticulous in his dress and habits, Sherman—who habitually looked like he had just gotten out of bed, scruffy and wild-looking—enjoyed the company of men who knew how to swear, drink and fight. Carl Schurz recalled one episode when he, Sherman and General Jeff C. Davis were relaxing in a roadside house. Howard entered, and Sherman greeted him with a hearty, "Glad to see you, Howard! Sit down by the fire! Damned cold this morning!"

Howard, squeamish at even the hint of profanity, replied, "Yes, General, it is *quite* cold this morning."

Sherman winked at Davis, the shadow of a sarcastic smile flickering on his lips.

Davis, a tough customer who had shot dead another Union general in a Louisville hotel lobby, was known as a world-class cusser. He proceeded to sprinkle his conversation with a string of profanities. Unable to change the tenor of talk, Howard excused himself. As soon as he had left, Sherman and Davis burst out laughing. Schurz commented upon Howard's obvious discomfort at their expense, and Sherman said, "Well, that Christian soldier business is all right in its place. But he needn't put on airs when we are among ourselves."

Yet Howard was a West Pointer, a professional and an obedient subordinate. Sherman, who, appearances to the contrary, had a passion for order, liked that. When the command structure was reorganized in the Spring of 1864, at the start of the invasion of Georgia, Howard was given IV Corps in Thomas' Army of the Cumberland.

Hooker commanded the new XX Corps created by merging the old XI and XII Corps. Schurz, who had criticized Hooker, was squeezed out. The other two armies under Sherman were the Army of the Tennessee, commanded by General James B. McPherson, and the Army of Ohio under General John Schofield.

Howard liked the methodical but competent Thomas, and "the Rock of Chickamauga" liked the Mainer. "General Thomas's characteristics are much like those of my father," Howard wrote. "While I was under his command he placed confidence in me, and never changed it."

Sherman liked him, too. When the army was bivouacked at Cassville in late May, several officers decided a drink was in order. One of Howard's division commanders, General Tom Wood, started joshing his superior: "What's the use, Howard, of your being so singular? Come along and have a good time with the rest of us. Why not?"

Before Howard could say anything, Sherman interjected, in a sharp voice, "Wood, let Howard alone! I want one officer who don't drink!"

In the campaign against Joe Johnston, Sherman almost always avoided a direct assault on Johnston's defensive position. Repeatedly he would take advantage of his superior numbers to flank the wily Confederate, forcing him to fall back through the mountains of northwest Georgia toward Atlanta.

Matters at Kennesaw Mountain, on June 27, were different. Impatient, Sherman attacked Rebel positions that Howard considered stronger than his position at Cemetery Hill, Gettysburg, had been. The result was similar. After a few hours and 3,000 casualties, Sherman broke off and resumed his usual flanking maneuvers.

Johnston evacuated Kennesaw Mountain, moving toward the Chattahoochee River. Howard stopped his corps at Smyrna Camp Ground and received a visit on Sunday, July

4, from Sherman. The tall, red-bearded general was anxious for Howard to move forward.

"Howard," he said, "what are you waiting for? Why don't you go ahead?"

Howard, standing with Sherman in a thin grove of trees near a farmhouse, replied, "The enemy is strongly entrenched yonder in the edge of a thick wood; we have come upon his skirmish line."

"Nonsense, Howard; he is laughing at you. You ought to move straight ahead. Johnston's main force must be across the river," Sherman snapped.

"You shall see, general," Howard retorted. He ordered his lead division's skirmish line doubled and moved forward.

The men seized some outlying rifle pits when "a sheet of lead" came from the point Howard had indicated. Several Reb batteries opened up, their shells landing uncomfortably close to where Sherman, Howard, and other officers had "formed a showy group." They scurried for cover as "Sherman himself passed from tree to tree toward the rear."

Sherman must have recalled that, a few weeks earlier, he had noticed a group of Confederate officers about 600 yards distant. Remarking, "How saucy they are!" he had directed Howard to open fire with his batteries. General Johnston managed to hurry for cover, but General Leonidas Polk didn't make it. The story circulated that Sherman had fired the gun that killed Polk. He had not.

About ten minutes later, astride his horse now, Sherman said, "Howard, you were right."

Johnston crossed the Chattahoochie and fell back to the defenses of Atlanta. He had fought a masterful retreat, keeping his army intact, but Jefferson Davis wanted a commander who was aggressive, willing to attack Sherman. When he replaced Johnston with General John Bell Hood, he got that kind of general. In a series of attacks around Atlanta, Hood used up most of the force Joe Johnston had preserved.

Hood had graduated in the same class at West Point as the 36-year-old James Birdseye McPherson. The Union major general had been first in his class, but his former classmate's assault on July 22, outside the Atlanta defenses, cost McPherson his life. Howard, like his brother officers, was saddened at the loss of one "so young, so noble, so promising, already commanding a department!" There was "a feeling that his place can never be completely filled."

But *someone* had to command the Army of the Tennessee. The dead general's corps commanders were all volunteers: Grenville Dodge was a railroad engineer from Massachusetts, Frank Blair was a prominent Missouri politician with Republican connections, and John Alexander Logan was an ambitious Illinois Democratic politician. Logan, called "Black Jack" due to his swarthy complexion, jet-black eyes, and thatch of black hair, was a popular, hard-fighting soldier. Having seniority, he took command temporarily of the Army of the Tennessee.

There is no doubt "Black Jack" wanted a permanent assignment, but, after conferring with Thomas, Sherman selected "the best officer who was present and available." He picked Howard. In his *Memoirs,* Sherman tried to explain his reasons:

> I wanted to succeed in taking Atlanta, and needed commanders who were purely and technically soldiers, men who would obey orders and execute them promptly and on time. I believed that General Howard would do all these faithfully and well. I regarded both Generals Logan and Blair as "volunteers," that looked to personal fame and glory as auxiliary and secondary

to their political ambition, and not as professional soldiers.

In other words, Howard might be rather dull compared to the dashing Logan, but he was safe. The British historian B. H. Liddell Hart, who admired Sherman and contributed mightily to his modern fame, was critical. Logan had "the driving power" Sherman needed to take Atlanta. But Sherman detested politicians, even though his brother was one.

Of course, there was a professional soldier available who outranked Howard. But Sherman never considered Joe Hooker. Stung, Hooker resigned and Sherman was relieved to see him go. The two powerful personalities had clashed from the outset.

For Hooker, the fact of being passed over was made absolutely unbearable by being passed over for Howard! He would always feel Howard was at the root of his failure at Chancellorsville; over the years his hurt would fester and focus upon Howard: "If he was not born in petticoats he ought to have been, and ought to wear them. He would command a prayer meeting with a good deal more ability than he would an army."

For Howard, the problem would be more exquisite: having to overcome the doubt that he could possibly have gotten command of the Army of the Tennessee without somehow pulling political wires. Many years later, in the next century, he was pointing to Sherman's *Memoirs* to "relieve me from any suspicion of self-serving in obtaining a promotion that, as every soldier knows, I would highly value."

He had to prove his worth, and thanks again to John Bell Hood, the opportunity soon occurred.

---

July 27, the day Howard assumed command, Sherman was moving to the right to sever Atlanta's rail communications. At about eight o'clock the next morning, Sherman rode alongside Howard, saying there was slight danger in moving straight along a road to Ezra's Church. "General," Howard replied, "Hood will attack me here."

"I guess not—he will hardly try it again," Sherman said.

Howard disagreed. He knew Hood. He would attack.

There was skirmishing ahead. Then Rebel grapeshot rattled in some trees close by, bringing some limbs crashing into the road. Howard ordered Logan's corps to halt. Quickly men gathered rails, logs and stumps to create breastworks. Sherman rode off, reiterating his doubts that a general fight would develop. If Howard did require assistance, he said, he would provide it.

"Thus," Howard observed, "he permitted me to conduct my first battle alone."

At about 11:30, with the now-familiar high-pitched yell, Rebels started rushing Logan's defenses. They were under the command of Howard's West Point classmate, General Stephen Lee. They had served together in Florida; now Hood sent Lee against the Union force at Ezra Church while General William Hardee, Howard's West Point commander, guarded Atlanta.

The fighting was hard as wave after wave of Confederates attacked. Whatever his personal hurt, Logan fought well, and Howard gave him a free hand to direct his corps. When some gray regiments started to move around Logan's right flank, Howard had twenty-six pieces of artillery sweep that sector. After about four hours it was over. The enemy absorbed a staggering 5,000 casualties and the Union held the field. Howard had won his baptism of fire as an army commander.

It was reported to Sherman that, after the shooting had ceased, Howard walked along the line, "and the men gathered about him in the most affectionate manner." He had won their trust, maybe even their hearts. Sherman was pleased. Like Howard, he felt vindicated.

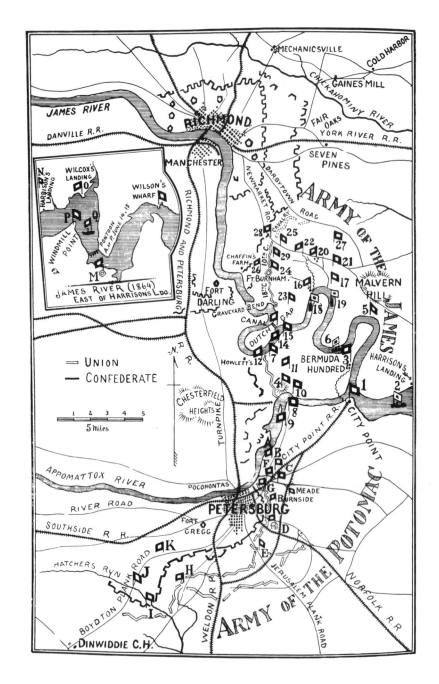

*Richmond-Petersburg area in 1864—U. S. Army Signal Corps map*

# Joshua Chamberlain

## *"I am lying mortally wounded the doctors think."*

Joshua Chamberlain did not rejoin the Army until the second week of May, 1864. After convalescing in Brunswick in December and January, he was assigned to court-martial duty in Washington and Trenton, New Jersey. Fannie joined him in Washington; she nursed him through recurrent, but less severe, bouts of fever. When he was up to snuff they took in some plays at the capital and, in April, she accompanied him to the Gettysburg battlefield. It was a long hiatus, and Chamberlain found it unbearable to concentrate on droning court-martial testimony as he heard reports of the great spring offensive underway.

"The week of active operations when I was kept out of the field was one of the most unhappy of my life," he wrote Governor Samuel Coney from Spotsylvania. "I am making up for it now however."

He missed the horror of the Wilderness, arriving in time for the end of the fighting at Spotsylvania. His brigade was now under General Joseph Bartlett, who had assumed command during his long absence. Chamberlain was put back in charge of his old Twentieth Maine; he accepted the demotion philosophically and was glad to be back with old comrades—those who remained. Many were gone, some killed or wounded, others just gone.

Governeur Warren was commander of V Corps now. The man who would forever be linked with Chamberlain by what together they had done to secure Little Round Top, thought highly of the Mainer's abilities. Chamberlain was hardly back when Warren gave him temporary command of a couple of regiments and asked him to seize an advanced position. Chamberlain accomplished the task although, unsupported, he had to surrender his gains. But he had demonstrated he still had it. Division commander Charles Griffin also esteemed the fighting colonel; he and Warren would urge his promotion to brigadier general.

During the next month, as Grant doggedly moved south by extending his lines to the left after each bloody battle, Chamberlain bounced back and forth between command of the Twentieth Maine and the Third Brigade. Bartlett was often ill and Chamberlain replaced him when he was. He was in action constantly, at places with unromantic names like Pole Cat Creek, and in dozens of places with no memorable names. It all merged into one continuous battle. Grant, Chamberlain later wrote, "was like Thor, the hammerer, striking blow after blow, intent on his purpose to beat his way through, somewhat reckless of the cost." There was a heavy cost. "The hammering business has been hard on the hammer," Chamberlain tersely commented.

On June 5, after Cold Harbor, General Warren reorganized V Corps. One of the changes was a new First Brigade of the First Division, made up of five veteran regiments from old I Corps, of about 250 men each, and a new regiment, the 187th Pennsylvania, of about 1,000 men. All of the regiments were Pennsylvanian and the new brigade was nicknamed the "Keystone" Brigade. Chamberlain was put in command of the new brigade. The veteran regiments had been taken from General Lysander Cutler's division, and he was unhappy to let them go. Chamberlain, however, quickly won the confidence of the regiments' officers and men.

Moving across the James Peninsula, not far from Richmond, the Union army was traversing the territory contested two years earlier in the ill-fated Peninsular Campaign. Grant's intention was not to repeat that history, but to cross the James as soon as possible and seize the key rail junction of Petersburg to the south of Richmond. If he could fool and elude Lee for a few vital days, he would be in a position to end the war.

Along the banks of the Chickahominy, Colonel Chamberlain performed some quick thinking of his own to elude capture. Riding his chestnut horse alone, he came upon a Confederate picket of about thirty men. Visions of Libby Prison passed through his mind, but Chamberlain resorted to his linguistic ability, faking a Southern accent. "Never mind the guard, it's after sunset!" he called out. Sword tucked under his arm, he gave a snappy salute and rode off. As he headed toward the cover of some trees he expected a bullet in his back any moment. None came.

But Chamberlain had a premonition that there was a bullet coming, one that would hit him in the abdomen. Gut-shot, few victims survived. Medical conditions in field hospitals were too limited and primitive to deal with internal injuries. Unlike cutting off arms and legs, gut wounds required skill, time and instruments usually unavailable. It was perhaps the wound soldiers feared most, and Chamberlain worried about it now.

He moved his blanket roll to the front of his saddle, guarding his abdomen, as the army headed for the James. V Corps was one of the last to cross, using steam transports, and then marched all night to take position left of the other corps before Petersburg on June 17. By then the element of surprise was lost. Union attacks on a Confederate line manned by a few thousand men were bungled, and Lee, finally aware of what was happening, was rushing the bulk of the Army of Northern Virginia to Petersburg's defense.

"So we had to take up the old game,—the eternal feeling to the left, with continuous, costly, fruitless engagements, in wearisome monotony," Chamberlain later wrote, summing up the Petersburg campaign. But in these early hours, with Grant anxious and Meade beside himself in profane fury as the chances of success dwindled away, the orders were always "attack!"

One of the regiments sent in to be mowed down was the First Maine Heavy Artillery. In a matter of minutes on the morning of June 18, about 600 men fell, neatly, in rows.

Not that far away, on the extreme left of the Union line, Chamberlain was approached about 10:30 a.m. by General Warren. The Rebels had fallen back to strong fortifications in the area of Rive's Salient. An artillery post was left on a crest before the approaches to the salient; it laid down a raking fire which Warren noted as "very annoying." He asked if Chamberlain thought he could take the Rebel gun position.

"I understood the purport of the mild inquiry," Chamberlain later recalled. " 'Thought,' indeed, was required; but the meaning was action." As Warren expected, the Maine Colonel acted, leading his Pennsylvanians in a flanking movement against the battery. He rode with his staff between the two advancing lines. A shell burst knocked them all off their horses, wounding Chamberlain's. Several men were killed and seven, including Corporal James Stettler, were wounded. The color-bearer being one of those down, the Colonel seized the brigade's triangular flag and carried it onward.

The battery was taken, but the position was exposed to heavy fire from the main Confederate works. Chamberlain pulled his men back enough to be sheltered by the crest they had seized, had some artillery brought up, and hunkered down for an anticipated counterattack.

The Rebel positions in front of him were formidable. Beside the breastwork immediately before him were several earthworks with cannon. Any attack would be subject to both frontal and cross fire. Worse, another fort, "Fort Mahone," was just across the Jerusalem Plank Road, with heavy guns capable of enfilading any movement against the earthworks. Chamberlain figured there were at least 3,000 infantry entrenched before him. About a mile in advance of the Union line, he awaited orders. He expected to be ordered to withdraw. An attack was out of the question.

An officer Chamberlain did not recognize, claiming to be from Meade's staff, rode up. He transmitted an order: attack.

In disbelief and unsure of the messenger's identity, Chamberlain scribbled a message of his own and dispatched it to headquarters. Taking an enormous risk, he questioned the order. Describing the awesome Confederate works, he also noted the "bad ground" his men would have to cover to get to them. There was a swampy, boglike area intervening before the sloping plain leading up to the Confederate guns and entrenched infantrymen. "From what I can see of the enemy's lines, it is my opinion that if an assault is to be made, it should be nothing less than the whole army," Colonel Chamberlain informed General Meade.

The staff officer came back. The attack was to be made, with the rest of the army. At three o'clock that afternoon the general assault would begin.

As other brigades moved into position, Chamberlain checked with General Cutler, whose Fourth Division was now formed several hundred yards in his rear, covered by woods. He assumed Cutler would be willing to give support on his exposed left when the attack began, but the crusty

Cutler informed him that, as the Colonel's senior, he would take no orders from him. "I shall know what to do when the time comes," he snapped.

As the time approached, a lieutenant in the 187th Pennsylvania, Ransford Webb, looked at the Confederate fortifications. "My heart dropped to my shoes," he remembered. "Cold drops stood on my forehead. I could still use my eyes, and turned them to the rear. Over a broad plain not a bluecoat was in sight. By this time my blood was frozen solid."

Chamberlain walked up and down the lines of men lying prone behind the crest, speaking to them. What they were about to do might decide the fate of the Republic. "We know that some must fall, it may be any of you or I; but I feel that you will all go in manfully and make such a record as will make all our loyal American people grateful."

The appointed time arrived. Positioning himself again between the two lines of battle, this time on foot, Chamberlain drew his cavalry sabre. He rattled off the commands: "Attention! Trail Arms! Double-quick, march." And to the sound of the bugle, the brigade advanced.

Yelling, they ran down the incline into a storm of artillery and musket fire. They did not stop to fire and reload. No time for that. Their only hope was to cover the ground between them and the enemy as quickly as possible. Scattered brush impeded their rush down into the more tangled growth at the bottom. In places it was an even worse morass of mud and brush than Chamberlain had imagined. His men could not afford to get bogged down in it. Case shot exploded above, spewing jagged fragments. Percussion shells exploded on impact. Canister and musket fire ripped through the air. Chamberlain, carrying the brigade flag, saw men falling everywhere.

To get past a particularly difficult area, the troops had to move oblique left. The din was too loud for commands to be heard. Chamberlain turned to indicate direction with his sabre.

And then it happened.

A Minie ball, hitting a rock, ricocheted upward and hit Chamberlain's right hip, burning a path through his lower abdomen as it moved diagonally, coming to rest near the skin of his left hip. An electric shock surged through him, the pain coming first in his back. The thought that came to him was what would his mother think, her soldier-boy shot in the back. Then he became conscious of blood pumping from his hips, running down his legs, and he was oddly relieved.

His mind shifted gears immediately to his men. They must not see he was wounded. He must not fall. Chamberlain drove his sabre into the mucky ground and used it as a cane. He remained standing as his boys broke ranks to pass him, rushing onward into the maelstrom of shot and shell.

Weakened by shock and loss of blood, he felt first one leg and then the other buckle. On his knees, he swayed and fell.

Two of his aides saw that Chamberlain was down and dragged him back to an only relatively safer position. Still conscious, the Colonel ordered them to tell the brigade's senior officer to assume command and to have Captain John Bigelow prepare his artillery on the ridge behind them for a Rebel counterattack.

Lieutenants West Funk and Benjamin Walters ran off to execute Chamberlain's orders. For the next hour, he remained alone, bleeding yet conscious, on the field.

Bigelow dispatched some of his gunners to remove him. Chamberlain, certain he was dying, ordered them to leave him and assist others who might survive. But he had given his last orders of the day, and the artillerists, under their own orders, loaded him on a stretcher and carried him back behind Bigelow's Ninth Massachusetts Battery. Artillery bursts showered them with dirt and mud.

Chamberlain's men, so close to the enemy lines that cannon could not be compressed to fire at them, hugged the bloody earth until three o'clock the next day. They then retreated to the ridge they had left twenty-four hours earlier. Many did not return.

Their Colonel was travelling a long day's journey into night. Several hours after he was shot he arrived at a division hospital three miles behind the Union lines. Corporal Stettler, the same aide wounded when Chamberlain assaulted the advanced Rebel battery, occupied the amputation table. When doctors started to remove him to make way for the Colonel, Chamberlain protested. "Lay me one side; I am all right," he said. "Go and take care of my dear boys."

The surgeons ignored him and began their grim business. It soon became apparent Chamberlain's internal damage was massive. He could not last the night.

But out of the darkness emerged brother Tom, who had learned of his brother's wounding and brought with him two doctors, Abner Shaw of the Twentieth Maine and Morris Townsend of the Forty-fourth New York. Tom and the two doctors had spent harrowing hours searching for his brother, from field hospital to hospital.

They were good at their trade, but the pain of their patient was excruciating. Unwilling to continue the torture, Shaw and Townsend put aside their instruments, only to be urged on by Chamberlain. They removed the bullet and did their best to sew together the vital organs it had mangled. When they put down their bloody tools for good, they informed the Colonel they believed his time was limited.

The next day had dawned. As Grant called a halt to the butchery, he received word from Generals Warren and Griffin, who had visited Chamberlain, of his mortal wounding. They urged him *now*, before it was too late as with Vincent, to promote Joshua Lawrence Chamberlain to Brigadier General. Grant "promoted him on the spot." The man who told a dying private at Gettysburg he was made a sergeant would die knowing he had won his star.

Writing painfully with a pencil on paper smudged with his own blood, Chamberlain set about saying goodbye to Fannie:

> My darling wife
> I am lying mortally wounded the doctors think, but my mind & heart are at peace. Jesus Christ is my all-sufficient savior. I go to him. God bless & keep & comfort you, precious one, you have been a precious wife to me. To know & love you makes life & death beautiful. Cherish the darlings & give my love to all the dear ones. Do not grieve much for me. We shall all soon meet. Live for the children. Give my dearest love to Father & mother & Sallie & John. Oh how happy to feel yourself forgiven. God bless you evermore precious precious one.
> 
> Ever yours<br>Lawrence

By the time Fannie received this letter she was probably aware that she was carrying another child.

---

# Joshua Chamberlain

## *"I believe in a destiny."*

Joshua Chamberlain was a goner, and everyone knew it. Except Joshua Chamberlain. He had received the "shattering" wound Professor Smythe had warned him of and Chamberlain had feared. But, with incredible determination and belief in Providence, he set about to put himself together again.

Transported overland by a stretcher team carrying him in relays, the wounded officer was borne to City Point on the James River. From there he travelled by water to Annapolis, Maryland. At the Naval Hospital he clung to the thread of life with a tenacity that impressed doctors, family and friends. Major Gilmore of the Twentieth Maine, stationed in Washington (he had a well-known and understandable aversion to the battlefield), stopped by his bedside with Chamberlain's commission as brigadier general. Shaken by the visit, Gilmore informed Maine's Adjutant General that Chamberlain's still partially severed urethra seeped urine into his wound, which dripped out of a gaping hole in his right hip. The surgeons feared infection would kill Chamberlain.

He had other visitors. On July 22 brother John reported that Chamberlain had weathered an acute crisis, and was regaining his strength remarkably. He was even talking about returning to the field!

And Fannie was there. They were never so close as they were now, wounded husband and pregnant wife. There is, of course, no record of their long bedside conversations. It most likely included the talk of the "dreamy love" he wanted to hear about.

Sometime in September, Indian Summer, he wrote his parents. He admitted "these terrible wounds must cast a shadow over the remainder of my days, even though I should apparently recover." Certainly his sex life would never be the same. Of course, proper Victorian, he did not say that. But he struggled to explain what had impelled him to place himself in harm's way. He could not say exactly what drove him.

"I haven't a particle of fanaticism in me," he said. "But I plead guilty to a sort of fatalism. I believe in a destiny." That destiny worked itself out not from his effort, but through the hand of God. "I have laid plans, in my day, & good ones I thought. But they never succeeded. *Something else, better, did,* and I could see it plain as day, that God had done it, & for my good."

Later that September he was back in Brunswick, in his home, his nest. But he did not stay. By November 18 he was back with the Army of the Potomac, still besieging Petersburg. Was it God or Joshua Chamberlain that brought him back—or both, intimately intertwined in his mind!

There was something heroic, tinged with sadness, about a man barely able to walk or ride back at the scene of his brush with death. And he came back to a new command—and a somehow new, more terrible kind of war. The brigade he was now in charge of was smaller than his old beloved Third. The new First Brigade was also different from his First Brigade that had charged Rive's Salient. It was composed of two big regiments, the 185th New York and 198th Pennsylvania.

It was not long before the new brigadier general was on campaign again, astride "Charlemagne." V Corps was sent south on a raid to disrupt the Weldon Railroad, a key rail artery sustaining beleaguered Petersburg. There was little fighting, but Chamberlain had to contend with unruly soldiers drunk on confiscated applejack, a biting December wind laden with snow and sleet, and stragglers who ended up bushwhacked. Their naked corpses, bloody gashes across their throats, incited acts of spontaneous and uncontrollable vengeance by bluecoats. In one area every house in sight spurted flames and smoke.

Chamberlain was intrigued by the business of ripping up railroad track, heating it, twisting it into useless junk. He described the scene as "grand," but the rest of the raid's fury repelled him. It was akin to what Sheridan's men were doing in the Shenandoah and how Sherman was making Georgia "howl." It was the inevitable nightmarish escalation of a war that had gone on too long. The grapes of wrath were being trampled.

On December 14 Chamberlain wrote his sister Sae that Rebel fire from houses along the Army's route elicited an indiscriminate response. It was unclear who was aiding the enemy and who was innocent bystander. To the blue soldiers there were no innocents. Chamberlain extended "the protection which every man of honor will give any woman as long as she *is* a woman." Yet he admitted women, good or bad, and children suffered. "It was sad business. I am willing to fight men in arms, but not *babes in arms*," he wrote. To brother John he was more explicit about his reaction to "war in its most disagreeable aspect," noting "for my part I had rather charge lines of battle."

He confessed to John that he had returned to the army before he was physically prepared for life in the field. He was probably in the saddle too much. He did not "feel right yet," and knew he would have to subject his body to the doctors' knife again. It was only a question of where and when. But he was confident that, if he left the army for another operation, his good friend General Griffin "won't let anybody come & rank me."

On that note, 1864—"that never-to-be-forgotten, most dismal of years"—ended for Joshua Chamberlain.

*Llewellyn Estes, looking older than he was. He was 20 at Flint River;
by 21 he was a "boy general."—Maine State Archives*

# Oliver Otis Howard

*"While General Howard sat at the table and asked God's blessing, the sky was red from flames of burning houses."*

Sherman had no desire to attack the Confederate defenses of Atlanta. Instead, he preferred to swing south, to cut Atlanta's supply line via Macon. The targeted place to do that was Jonesboro.

As Howard moved south, he cooperated with Sherman's new cavalry chief, none other than Hugh Judson Kilpatrick. "Little Kil" had also been sent west. Kilpatrick's personal habits were not Howard's, but the Maine general liked him; "we all liked his bright face and happy stories," Howard wrote. The colorful horse-soldier's job was to clear the way for the infantry, and in spirited competition with the Confederate cavalrymen, Kilpatrick performed well. Moving through fairly dense woods along narrow roads, Howard's Army of the Tennessee reached Renfro Place near sundown on August 30.

Howard's infantry was short of water, and the Flint River was only a half dozen miles distant. Howard was anxious to get to Jonesboro, on the other side of the Flint, as soon as possible. He asked Kilpatrick, "Have you an officer, general, who with a small body of cavalry can keep the enemy in motion, and not allow them to create delay between this Renfro Place and the river?"

"Just the man, sir," Kilpatrick said. He turned to his assistant adjutant, Captain Lew Estes.

Estes was a First Maine Cavalry boy, and he was about as much a boy as Howard could get. When Estes, of Old Town, had enlisted in the First Maine Cavalry in 1861, he had listed his age as 21. In fact, he was only 18. Kilpatrick was impressed with the Maine youngster. In May of 1863 Estes had volunteered to carry an important dispatch for General Hooker. Made prisoner by the Rebs, he turned the tables and captured his captors. When Kilpatrick, understandably enamored of the First Cavalry, asked Lieutenant Colonel Smith to suggest an adjutant, Smith had a man in mind. "Yes; there's Estes," he said, "he's smart and bright as a dollar, but he won't work in harness worth a cent."

For Kilpatrick, not exactly a working-in-harness type himself, Lew Estes was just right. On July 1, 1863—Day One of Gettysburg—Estes was appointed his adjutant general. A few hours later, Estes, with Kilpatrick's permission, participated in Farnsworth's charge as a volunteer aide. Farnsworth was killed. Estes went west with Kilpatrick and, aged twenty, he was approached by General Howard. Could he drive the Rebs across the Flint River, so Howard could get water for his army? Estes said he could.

"Try it," the general replied.

Estes led a squadron of cavalry toward Flint, first at a trot, then a gallop. Infantry followed. Howard, who rode ahead of the skirmishers, toward the river, said, "our infantry was so excited that they almost kept up with the cavalry." The Confederates retreated across the Flint.

Howard rode up to Estes and, complimenting his fellow Mainer, was asked by the young cavalryman, "Do you want me to take the bridge?" The Rebs had set fire to the bridge across the Flint, and were shooting from the opposite side. Estes' soldiers, using Spencer repeating rifles, returned a steady fire.

"Can you do it?" Howard asked.

"Yes," Estes replied. Howard shot back, "All right, go ahead."

Estes ordered the troopers of the Ninety-second Illinois and the Tenth Ohio to dismount, and charge the burning bridge.

The peppering of shots from the Spencers allowed Estes to send two companies of the Tenth Ohio running across the stringers of the bridge. The planking had been removed. Estes, revolver in hand, led the rush of men.

Driving the defenders off, Estes and his men put out the fire, and reached the other side. Soon Howard's skirmishers followed them across the dirty water of the Flint and occupied a nearby slope. The planking was replaced, and the oncoming infantry poured across.

Howard was one of the first troopers to arrive. He could not have been more pleased. Thanks to Captain Estes and his squadron, the bridge had been secured at a loss of four men killed and two wounded. As Howard would later recall, "the action was phenomenal." As night fell, the Federals were strongly positioned outside Jonesboro.

On August 31, two Confederate corps, totalling 24,000 men, attacked under the command of General William Hardee. Hardee, a Georgian, was the author of the 1856 book, *Rifle and Light Infantry Tactics*, which became the manual of both sides in the Civil War. While he was West Point superintendent, Howard had tutored Hardee's children.

The blue soldiers were entrenched on a ridge outside Jonesboro. Hardee sustained ten times as many casualties as Howard did. After holding off Federal counterattacks, the Confederates withdrew to Lovejoy's Station. The Confederates entrenched there, but evacuated Atlanta, which Sherman's army started to occupy on September 2.

It was a heavy blow to the Confederacy. Edward A. Pollard, a Southern journalist, wrote in his 1867 *The Lost Cause:* "The fall of Atlanta was a terrible blow to the Southern Confederacy; a reanimation of the North; the death of 'the peace party' there; the date of a new hope of the enemy and of a new prospect of subjugation."

When Hood moved north, trying to sever Sherman's rail link to Chattanooga, Sherman followed. In two months of chase, Hood was foiled in his objective. Leaving Schofield with an army in Tennessee to repel Hood, Sherman decided to cut loose from Atlanta and move to the Atlantic coast. Grant was bogged down in Virginia; Sherman viewed his famous (or, more accurately, infamous) "March to the Sea" as basically a change of base. "I simply moved from Atlanta to Savannah as a step in the direction of Richmond," he later explained.

After destroying anything of possible military use and removing part of the population, Sherman left Atlanta on November 15 with an army of about 63,000. The left wing, dubbed the "Army of Georgia," was led by Slocum, while the Army of the Tennessee, the right wing under Howard, moved more to the southeast. Howard figured he had command of about 33,000 men. Kilpatrick's cavalry, about 5,000, covered both wings. The "March to the Sea" had begun.

It was a big undertaking. 2,500 supply wagons, supposedly the minimum, accompanied Sherman's army. Altogether some 25,000 horse or mules, as well as 10,000 cattle, went along. "The army will forage liberally on the country during the march," Sherman said in Special Order Number 120.

To Georgians, that would be an understatement at best.

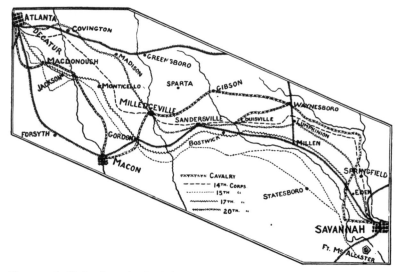

Sherman's "March to the Sea" from Atlanta to Savannah

—U. S. Army Signal Corps map

With Hood off in Tennessee, there was no significant Confederate force to contest Sherman. The closest thing to a battle occurred along Howard's route at Griswoldville. "It was an affair of one division," Howard later wrote. Actually, it was less than even that. The Rebel general, Gustavus Smith, pulled together about 4,000 effectives to oppose Charles Woods' division. General Charles Walcutt, with 1,513 men, many with Spencer repeating rifles, contested Smith. Entrenched behind "the usual cover of rails and logs," Walcutt's men, with two cannon, were able "to cover the approaches by using iron hail" and were "more than equal to 10,000 opponents, however determined they might be."

Starting at 2:30 p.m. and continuing until sunset, the Confederates launched three assaults. All failed badly, resulting in over 600 casualties, compared to a total Union loss of 84.

---

Oliver Otis Howard

Otherwise, the soldiers of Howard's army, like its left-wing counterpart, encountered little more than occasional skirmishing. Moving eastward, the Union invaders cut a wide swath of destruction.

Just how great the extent of pillaging and arson was has been a continuing subject of controversy. There is evidence that Sherman in 1864 did not live off the land more than armies had in previous campaigns. Yet, even at the time, one of Sherman's own adjutants, Major Henry Hitchcock, worried, "I am bound to say I think Sherman is lacking in enforcing discipline."

Sherman was quite emphatic with Hitchcock. *Nobody*, he said, tried harder to stop pillaging than he had during the first years of the war. "At the same time I don't think General would take same trouble now—indeed he admits as much—to hunt out and punish it," Hitchcock confided in his diary.

And what about Howard? Louise Cornwell, at whose Hillsborough home the general stopped on November 19, described the visit. "General Howard and staff officers came at tea time," she wrote. "We managed to have something to eat for that meal, which was the last for several days, and while General Howard sat at the table and asked God's blessing, the sky was red from flames of burning houses." It is a devastating picture of the Christian General.

But Howard did offer to post a guard at the Cornwell place, and, more than any other high-ranking officer, he showed concern about depredations against civilians. Even before the March started, he warned that foraging should be restricted. He repeated warnings against soldiers entering homes a few days later and, the day after the stop at Miss Cornwell's, Howard issued General Field Order No. 26: it authorized the shooting of pillagers. He also passed on his concerns to Sherman.

But nothing came of this. When one soldier actually was sentenced to death for plunder, Howard commuted the penalty to imprisonment. And when, at Gordon, an exasperated Howard threatened to shoot any soldier guilty of robbing or burning houses without orders, he was ignored. Most of the town was destroyed.

Except for the difficulty of building corduroy roads through swampy areas, the march was easily accomplished. Nearing the coast, troops moved through piney woods. By December 10, the outskirts of Savannah were reached. The indefatigable William Hardee defended the city, and Kilpatrick's cavalry was unsuccessful in attacking Fort McAllister, which guarded the mouth of the Ogeechee River. Possession of Fort McAllister would give Sherman's army direct communication with and support from a naval squadron offshore.

Howard asked Sherman to let him take the fort with infantry. When Sherman immediately gave his blessing, he assigned the task to the division commanded by General William Hazen. The attack was made late in the afternoon of December 13, with an anxious Sherman, Howard and other staff officers watching from a rice mill several miles distant.

Confederate Major George Anderson had worked hard on the fort's defenses. In addition to earthworks, the land approaches were protected by abattis and a wide, deep ditch filled with sharpened logs pointing outward like great spears. As an added impediment, "torpedoes" were buried in a line arcing in front of these defenses, set to explode when stepped upon. The fort had 21 guns of various sizes, and had repelled several attacks by ironclads.

However, while the heavier armament, pointed seaward, was protected, the 12 field pieces that covered the fort's rear were on ramparts exposed to sharpshooters' deadly fire. Anderson had about 230 men within Fort McAllister. When the woods to his rear became increasingly blue with the enemy, he started laying down sporadic fire on the assembling force under Hazen.

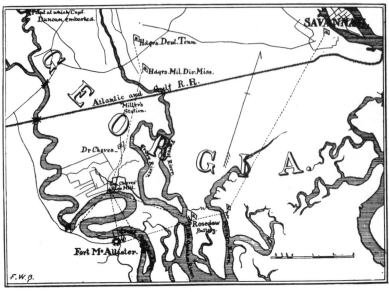

*Fort McAllister and Savannah. Note rice mill from which Sherman and Howard watched the fort's capture—U. S. Army Signal Corps map*

At 4:30 p.m. the Federal troops, deployed in three lines encompassing both of the fort's flanks, moved forward. Heavy fire from McAllister created puffs of smoke, visible from the rice mill crowded with Sherman's retinue. The blue lines seemed to be moving slowly. "Why aren't they moving at double-quick?" one officer wondered aloud. A few minutes later, it appeared to another safe but nervous officer that Hazen had been repulsed.

In fact, the Federal division was doing very well. Sharpshooters scattered Rebel gunners, and infantry quickly overcame obstacles to reach the fort itself. Major Hitchcock, talking with survivors after the fight, noted in his diary,

"The rebels inside were thunderstruck at the idea of such a charge. They say that they had confidently expected our line to be repulsed by the torpedoes alone."

It was all over in fifteen minutes. Hazen lost twenty-four killed and 110 wounded. Anderson sustained forty-eight casualties. Back in the rice mill, there was jubilation. Sherman grinned and repeated what a freed slave at a plantation had told him, "This nigger won't sleep this night!" For Sherman, who was not as sensitive to the plight of blacks as Howard, his "Day of Jubilee" had arrived. With the fall of Fort McAllister he had reached the sea. It was only a matter of time before Savannah fell.

General Hardee knew he would soon be bottled up; he moved quickly to escape the inevitable. On December 23, although Hardee and 10,000 soldiers had eluded him, Sherman took Savannah. He made it a Christmas gift to Lincoln.

The "March to the Sea" was viewed as a great triumph. The pro-Southern Pollard would sniff, "Where there is nothing to oppose an army, the mere accomplishment of distances is no great wonder or glory." Sherman himself would later downplay the march. It was, he said, simply, "a means to an end, and not an essential act of war. I simply moved from Atlanta to Savannah, as one step in the direction of Richmond." But it was a very big step, and the ease with which it was accomplished demonstrated that, as Grant put it, the Confederacy was a "hollow shell."

Sherman would achieve mythic proportions in the Southern mind as the ultimate Vandal. In the epic Civil War film, *Gone With the Wind*, Sherman *was* the wind. Never shown as a character, the name SHERMAN! emblazoned on the screen was sufficient. And yet it still remains a debated issue if the fierce-looking and harsh-talking general was intentionally cruel or simply a decent man made callous by years of warfare.

After Savannah fell, Howard, homesick and perhaps sick at heart about the suffering of noncombatants, went to Sherman.

"Now let me off," he said. "I don't ask but two days at home."

"General, I would give a million dollars, if I had it, to be with my children," Sherman replied. "Would you do more than that?" Permission for leave was not granted. There was a war to win.

Both warriors had a great desire to be with their children. Sherman visited the daughter of an old friend in Savannah. He had destroyed a railroad built by that friend, and the daughter's husband was with the Reb cavalry that harassed Sherman's army throughout northern Georgia. But no matter: the woman's children, particularly daughter "Daisy," reminded the grizzled conqueror of his own children. He told Howard of his visits and arranged for Howard also to pay a call.

It wasn't long before Daisy was on Howard's knee. At once she saw something was different. "Oh, you have only got one arm!"

"Yes, little girl," he replied. "Are you not sorry for me?"

"Yes, indeed," Daisy said. "What happened to your arm?"

"It was shot off in battle."

"Oh, did the Yankees shoot it off?"

"No, my dear. The Rebels shot it off."

"Did they! Well, I shouldn't wonder if my Papa did it," the little girl mused. "He has shot lots of Yankees!"

# Adelbert Ames

*"I shall have to do something brilliant
before we think of two stars."*

A day after Savannah fell, a massive federal armada of warships and troop transports commenced operations against Fort Fisher, North Carolina. The Confederate fort, considered to be the "Gibraltar of the South," guarded the approaches to Wilmington. This town of 10,000, about 250 miles as the crow flies from Savannah, was the last Rebel port open to blockade-runners. Without Wilmington, the Confederacy was doomed. Not only was it the lifeline to the outside world, but it was the key to the Cape Fear River, which extended inland to Fayetteville, the only other source of small arms and ammunition for Lee's army besides Richmond itself.

Overall command of the joint army-navy expedition to take Fort Fisher was entrusted by Grant to a general he didn't particularly trust: the brilliant but erratic Ben Butler. Butler's second in command was General Godfrey Weitzel; one of Weitzel's divisions was commanded by Brigadier General Adelbert Ames. Ames was to play a pivotal role in the Fort Fisher saga.

Since Gettysburg, where he defended Culp's Hill and won the cheers of his old regiment, the Twentieth Maine, Ames had gotten around. He participated in the siege of Charleston, including failed assaults on Fort Wagner.

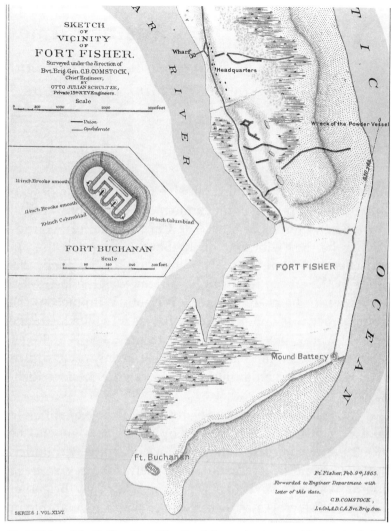

*Fort Fisher, North Carolina. The Confederacy's strongest fort extended across most of the peninsula, its works then facing toward the Atlantic to Mound Battery. Fort Buchanan was at the tip of the peninsula. Federal lines were to the north. Note site of the powder vessel's explosion.*

—Civil War Atlas

The harbor area was familiar. He had been there with Captain Jesse Ames before the war and West Point. Then, after some time at Fort Pulaski, Georgia, he was stationed in Jacksonville, Florida. Commanding black soldiers, possessing a buggy and yacht, and having "seven staff officers and any number of soldiers to do my bidding, I *should* be content, if I am not," he wrote home. "Father, I think you are right," he also admitted. "Florida is a place *into* which the rebels should be driven, not *out* of it. Everything will be concentrated in Virginia for a final struggle."

By April of 1864 the young brigadier general was back in Virginia, in General Butler's command. Early the next month, he was at Bermuda Hundred, opposite City Point on the James River. He was only across the river from the tramping ground of the ill-fated Peninsula Campaign. "How strange that I should be here a second time, after an interval of two years," Ames mused. His division included two Maine regiments, the Eighth and Ninth Maine, as well as several batteries of light artillery.

Butler was supposed to coordinate with Grant's overland campaign against Lee. As Ames summed it up, "Everything will depend on Grant." If Grant fared poorly, it seemed Butler's force would have to fall back. If Grant beat Lee, then Butler's army would join in the attack on Richmond. But Lee withstood Grant and Butler was "bottled up" (Grant's phrase) at Bermuda Hundred in the bloody, botched Spring of '64.

Ames got along with Butler. After a May 19 visit from the cock-eyed commander, Ames noted, "He thanked me for my efforts the other day—not that I did anything—but because I showed a disposition to do." Generally, he was guarded in his comments. "I say nothing, because it will do not good—rather harm me."

In a reversal of usual roles, son Adelbert lectured his father on the virtues of discretion. Jesse and Martha had moved west, and the former sea captain was not taking to farming; he definitely did not take to bankers. In reference to his father's desire to promote "the extermination of banks," Adelbert asked his father if he were familiar, as Del had been in his Rockland childhood, with *Aesop's Fables?* "Do you recall the one which showed the necessity of yielding occasionally? The *oak* was blown down—the reed yielded to the storm and lived to enjoy the sunshine. Father, please yield in this bank matter."

In Virginia, with the level of backbiting growing within the Union command in proportion to mounting casualties, Adelbert Ames learned silence could be truly golden. Grant, he allowed, was criticized "rather sharply," but he himself said nothing. With a surplus of senior officers in Virginia, "I was crowded down to a Brigade," but by summer he was in command of a division again.

No wonder he felt confident to advise his mother: "I wish Father was more of a philosopher. After a man does what he thinks is best, acting by the light he has, it is wrong to complain and regret he had not acted otherwise." When his father, in turn, wanted to know if son Adelbert was likely to become a major general, Del said flatly "there is not the least possible chance of my getting it at present. I shall have to do something brilliant before we think of two stars."

In the summer and fall of '64, as stalemate set in, Ames was confident time was on the Union's side. The Rebs were down to old men and boys. They couldn't replace their losses; if the Union could endure *its* losses a little longer by drafting more men, "I think permanent success will be the result."

In the heat and boredom, punctuated by moments of horror, that was Petersburg, he reported Aunt Mary, back in

Rockland, had written "an account of a stampede the Rock-landers had in consequence of an expected raid from a rebel pirate." It was a false alarm, but the activities of the raider *Tallahassee* led Ames to soothe his father, "You evidently left the sea at a very favorable moment."

Come September he was wondering, "Could I succeed in Minnesota? Could I work on the farm in the summer and be sent to the State Legislature in the winter?! Could I mix politics and money making in honest parts?"

He took part with some black regiments in a bold but bloody attack on Fort Gilmer. General R. S. Foster called it one of "those grand carnivals of death." Ames, whom Foster referred to as "that gallant young soldier and able officer," was sent with his men back to Bermuda Hundred. There was nothing to do but think about farming and politics in a cooler place.

Then, in the fall of 1864, Grant responded to pressure to do *something* about Wilmington. The Fort Fisher expedition had a number of problems. Primary among them was Grant's grudging interest and limited commitment of resources. Another was the bad chemistry between Butler and his naval counterpart, Admiral David Porter.

Butler, always innovative, came up with the idea of blowing up a tremendous amount of gunpowder on a vessel near the fort. It was a sort of Big Bang strategy. Admiral Porter liked it because it would give the Navy the primary role: at this time he was one of the few people who thought concentrated naval bombardment could reduce land fortifications. Between the Big Bang and his big guns, the navy could dispose of Fort Fisher.

The expedition got underway in late December, about the time Sherman's march to the sea was culminating. A decrepit steamer was loaded with over 2,0000 pounds of gunpowder—a third less than planned—and, without waiting for Butler's arrival, Porter had it set off. Detonated improperly, it turned out to be a Big Dud. The Navy then started firing everything it had at Fort Fisher, some 21,000 projectiles over two days.

At the time, Porter announced that the fort had been devastated by his barrage. In fact the Federal fleet sustained more casualties due to poorly constructed guns exploding. The naval gunners had an unfortunate tendency to shoot at Rebel flags, rather than direct their fire more precisely at specific points.

Troops were landed, primarily Ames', to assault the fort. Built over a period of four years, it was the biggest Southern fortification, with huge earthen walls protecting both its sea face and land approaches down Federal Point (dubbed Confederate during the war). The Cape Fear River to its rear was too shallow for serious penetration by boat. The fort commander, Colonel George Lamb, had every reason to believe that with proper infantry support, Fort Fisher's more than 40 heavy guns could withstand any attack.

Two days of bombardment had not knocked out many Confederate guns or killed many of the soldiers within. Moving up from the land side, Ames' lead brigade, under Colonel Newton Curtis, got so close to the Rebel parapets that a soldier was able to grab a Confederate flag shot away from its staff. Curtis said the fort could be taken, and Ames said go ahead. But Curtis apparently had second thoughts; neither Ames or Curtis realized that their superiors had decided to call off the attack.

Colonel C. B. Comstock, an engineer on Grant's staff, took a closer look at the fort with General Weitzel, and concluded "to attack with force would be murder." Weitzel, who had been in murderous assaults before, agreed. So did Butler, who also was concerned about reports that Lee had dispatched a division under General Robert Hoke to Wilmington. The danger loomed of Ames being caught between the fort and Hoke. And the army would have to act without much naval support; Porter was low on ammunition.

So Butler called it off. On Christmas Day, 1864, the Federals clambered back on their boats. Butler was in such haste, and the weather was so uncooperative, that 700 men, including Curtis, were stranded for two days. Critics of Butler's withdrawal, which was unpopular and embarrassing, wondered how they survived unmolested those two days. Curtis and others would insist Fort Fisher could have been taken.

Ten miles south of Cape Fear are Frying Pan Shoals, which had been the scene of an earlier fiasco in Butler's career. This time, in about the same region, Ben Butler was permanently grounded. Although recent historians have justified Butler's decision, it spelled an ignominious end to his military participation in the Civil War.

"I feel much disappointed and mortified at our failure," Ames wrote, "but have the consolation that the fault was not attributable to me in the least."

Unlike Butler, he would soon have a second chance.

# Oliver Otis Howard

*"It would be impossible to exaggerate
the horrors of that long night."*

It was not long before Sherman's army moved out of Savannah into the heartland of secession. "The truth is that the whole army is burning with an insatiable desire to wreak vengeance upon South Carolina," Sherman noted. "I almost tremble at her fate, but feel she deserves all that seems in store for her."

Howard, again in charge of the right wing, shipped his troops to Beaufort. From that South Carolina seaport he moved inland, toward Columbus, the state capital. What little restraint was exercised in "foraging" in Georgia vanished in South Carolina.

Oliver Otis Howard was a man of forgiveness, in an army apparently bent upon excess and vengeance. Major Hitchcock recorded an episode in Beaufort he considered characteristic of the one-armed general's character. Howard, Hitchcock and a Captain Duncan were rudely accosted by a civilian quartermaster's clerk at the dock; the man was upset because they were near some platform scales. Howard was mild in his initial response, but when the clerk persisted in his tirade, Howard's temper flashed.

As Hitchcock wrote: "H. broke out on him for a moment, ordered him in a sudden loud and peremptory tone to shut up (he ought to have knocked him down) and then suddenly turned round and walked rapidly away, evidently fearing to trust his own temper." The captain reported the clerk's behavior to General Rufus Saxton, commander in the area, and Saxton immediately dismissed the man.

The clerk apologized to Howard, who then personally requested that Saxton reinstate him. Saxton told Hitchcock, "Howard is a good man and sincere Christian, he is an instance that a man may be a good Christian and *yet a good soldier.*" Sherman was heard telling Howard that, if anything happened to him, Howard was to assume overall command. Of course, Sherman said similar things about Schofield who, having helped defeat Hood in Tennessee, would join the army as it moved into South Carolina's interior. Certainly Howard was viewed as more professional and stable than Logan and Blair.

"It was a winter campaign," Howard would emphasize. Nights were damp and cold. Roads were often soaked with rain. As they moved through piney woods and swamps, the blue troops were periodically attacked by Confederate cavalry. But Sherman's army was inexorable. General Hardee marvelled, "I made up my mind there had been no such army in existence since the days of Julius Caesar."

After some skirmishing in heavy fog on the outskirts of Columbus, the city fell to the new Caesar. On February 17 Sherman rode into the city of 14,000 with Howard at his side. What a sight the fierce-eyed Sherman with his stubbly beard and the slim, impassive general with one arm made! Howard must have heard the column behind them singing, "Hail Columbia, happy land/If I don't burn you, I'll be damned."

While white citizens were restrained in their welcome, blacks celebrated in the streets. The scene was so chaotic that Sherman had to ride along the sidewalk. Buckets of liquor were presented to soldiers who had marched since before

---

**Oliver Otis Howard**

dawn on empty stomachs. Their cheers for their commander were noticeably louder than usual.

Bales of abandoned cotton were everywhere, ripped open, the lint landing on houses and trees like snow. Some of the cotton was burning. In front of the new capitol building, a drunk decked out in a plug hat and long dressing gown staggered up to Sherman, sort of saluted, and said, "I have the honor (hic) General, to present (hic) you with (hic) the freedom of the (hic) city."

Sherman toured Columbus with Howard. He noted, seemingly for the first time, the drunkenness of many soldiers. Sherman warned Howard, who was put in charge of the city, of trouble.

"It would be impossible to exaggerate the horrors of that long night between the 17th and 18th of February, 1865," Howard would recall. The wind picked up and fires spread. The wind was not the only factor. Drunk soldiers, "army followers," and convicts who had escaped from the penitentiary "were doubtless guilty of all manner of villainies," he concluded.

Many South Carolinians, and Southern diehards in general, believed the burning of Columbus was intentional. Actually Sherman, Howard, Logan and staff officers worked with hundreds of soldiers through the night to stem the fires. Some men tried to set fire to Howard's headquarters in the McCord house. Major Hitchcock wrote, "Nothing was left undone to prevent and stop it but in vain. The guard was changed—*three times* as many men were on guard as were ever on guard at any one time in Savannah [and] our own officers shot our men down like dogs wherever they were found riotous or drunk."

"The very heavens at times appeared on fire," Howard wrote. Wide streets could not slow the spreading conflagration, with burning pieces of cotton, shingles and other debris borne by the winter wind. Before it was finally contained, the fire levelled about a third of Columbus, centering on the business district and most prosperous residential streets. It was a fire with a certain focus.

Louisa Cheves McCord, delivering a paper to Howard, found him in conversation with Sherman the next day. In a quiet but clear voice, Howard said, "You may rest satisfied that there will be nothing of the kind happening tonight. The truth is, our men last night got beyond our control; many of them were shot; many of them were killed; there will be no repetition of these things to-night."

And, as Mrs. McCord wrote, the next night was "peaceful as the grave, the ghost of its predecessor."

As XV Corps prepared to leave the devastated city, destroying assorted factories, railroad buildings and the like, a distraught mayor asked Sherman what he would do with the homeless and destitute. "Go to Howard," Sherman said. "Howard runs the religion of this army. He will treat you better than one of your own generals." Howard did what he could, giving the civil authorities of Columbus half his cattle and rations.

And then he left Columbus, "a sad retrospect to me, for I had never expected to leave such a wild desert."

What happened there was a more spectacular version of a series of acts of pillage. Howard was so upset by tales of robberies that he wrote Logan on February 20, "I am inclined to think that there is a regularly organized banditti. I call upon you and all the officers and soldiers under you, who have one spark of honor or respect for the profession which they follow to help me put down these nefarious proceedings, and to arrest perpetrators."

But Howard had no more impact than he had had in Georgia.

---

The level of outrages dropped off once the Federal army left South Carolina. Probably the attitude of most Northerners was that events like Columbus were justified, Sherman wrote. Yet he felt it necessary to add that Howard had responsibility for the city, as though that somehow shifted his own responsibility. The truth is that neither Sherman nor Howard could stem what had been unleashed. The Lord was trampling out the vintage of the grapes of wrath. Yet it was Sherman, not Howard, who publicly made *that* argument.

Isolated, Charleston, where the war began, fell. Sherman's army moved through North Carolina's pine forests, burning them. At Bentonville, on March 19, Joe Johnston, again in command, surprised Sherman by attacking his left wing under Slocum. Sherman, resting in Howard's tent at Falling Creek Church, received the news and was so excited he ran out of the tent without his pants on. Johnston did well at the outset; it was his best battle, the last hurrah.

Howard, also fighting his last battle, brought up the right wing with vigor and decisiveness. Impervious to danger, he was, seemingly, everywhere. And he was defeated. Not by Johnston, but by a teamster.

The major general, accompanied by a staff officer, came upon a teamster swearing at some mules entangled in their harness.

"Hold on, hold on there my man," Howard shouted.

Riding up to the frustrated mule-driver, the general took time out from the battle to ask the man, "Suppose, just as one of those vile oaths are issuing from your lips, one of those passing cannon balls should take your head off?"

"Well, General, it would just be my God-damned luck," the teamster replied. Turning back to his task, he hollered, "Get out of there, you God-damned bitch."

Howard confessed to his aide that he "was afraid that man was beyond redemption."

With Howard's reinforcements, the time seemed opportune to launch a smashing counterattack. But Sherman countermanded Howard's order and ordered a withdrawal.

Sherman later gave reasons. He thought Johnston's force was bigger than it was. Johnston would retreat anyway. And there had been enough bloodshed. The last probably was closest to Sherman's thinking. For all his ferocious talk and image, Sherman usually avoided pitched battles.

Howard, the fighting Christian, had sensed the moment was ripe for a decisive victory. None of Sherman's reasons for backing off satisfied him at the time, he admitted. Later he was "glad that this last battle had not been pushed to an extremity."

One aspect was a poignant reminder of war's harm. In the final phase of the fighting, General Hardee had allowed his son Willie to participate in a cavalry attack on Howard's line. Shot in the chest, Willie would die two days later. He was sixteen. At West Point, when Hardee was commandant and Howard a math instructor, the Mainer had tutored young Willie. Now word was delivered to him through the lines of Willie's death. Hardee's daughter Anna, "recalling old times," asked Howard to protect the friends who had nursed the dying boy. He assented.

It was good this war was almost over.

# Adelbert Ames

*"Thus was given me unrestricted command of the fighting forces."*

A few weeks after the first abortive assault on Fort Fisher, another Federal fleet arrived. It was bigger, better supported, and smarter than the first expedition. Butler was gone, replaced by General Alfred Terry, who had more troops at his disposal and coming. Grant had arranged for Schofield to come east with his army, to be used if necessary.

The capture of Wilmington assumed new urgency, with Sherman's movement north from Savannah through the Carolinas. It would be the Federal supply line's terminus when Sherman reached North Carolina. Thus Terry received a degree of support Butler never enjoyed. Wilmington was a top priority now. And lessons had been learned from the first failure. This time Porter's naval bombardment would be more focused and precise, and no Federal army would be attacking Fort Fisher without its rear adequately defended against Confederate reinforcements moving down Federal Point.

Once again Brigadier General Adelbert Ames was to play an important role. His division of 3,300 "picked men" would lead the army's assault. It was made up of three brigades, under Colonels Newton Curtis, Galusher Pennypacker and Louis Bell. Brigadier General Charles Paine's division, made up largely of black troops, would set up a defensive line north of the fort. Paine was supported by the

1,400-man brigade commanded by Colonel J. G. Abbott, with a couple of batteries of light artillery.

Porter still wanted the Navy to play a major role, and it would. In addition to the heaviest bombardment in U. S. naval history to that point, he landed some 1,600 sailors and 400 marines to assist in the attack. The sailors were armed with revolvers and cutlasses, as if they were boarding a ship as in days of old, and the marines had more modern, and somewhat more effective, carbines.

This time the fire of the sixty-four warships was centered on the land face of the fort, to be assaulted by the army. Starting on January 13 and continuing incessantly into the afternoon of January 15, the navy pounded away. It disabled most of the Rebel guns, severed lines to mines ("torpedoes"), and punched holes in palisades. The navy's fire also discouraged Confederate forces in the woods above the fort from contesting the landing of army and navy units of the Federal assault force. The landings, a couple of miles up the peninsula, assumed the character of a picnic.

In fact, this was when the invasion force was most vulnerable. But General Braxton Bragg, in charge of Wilmington's defenses, was stymied by the naval gunfire. During the bombardment more than 50,000 shells in all were fired.

Ames had another problem besides the Confederates—Colonel Newton Curtis. Still upset about the inadequate support he felt he had gotten in December, Curtis clashed with his division commander. According to Curtis's recollection, Ames joined the expedition a day after it started, coming aboard the *Atlantic* from a hospital boat. Ames, in Curtis's account made public three decades later, laid into the colonel "with bitter and insulting words alleging that I had been guilty of a 'shabby trick' in sailing from Hampton Roads without him." Ames supposedly accused Curtis of conniving to get leadership of the division away from him.

Curtis claimed he got, within an hour, an apology from Ames. Nevertheless, "his subsequent conduct compelled me from that time to refuse all intercourse with him, not required by the strictest official duties."

Ames filed grievances against Curtis to Terry, complaining that Curtis undermined him by consulting directly with Grant and failing to let him know the date of departure. Curtis raised innuendo-laden questions about Ames's "unexplained absence," saying even Ames's staff thought he was aboard the *Atlantic* when it set sail. Ames claimed he so completely distrusted Curtis and his brigade that "he would not be held responsible for anything they might be directed to do."

If Curtis found it hard to say anything good about Adelbert Ames, Colonel Henry Lockwood proved that the Mainer could be a hero to his *aide-de-camp*. Lockwood considered Ames "the beau-ideal of a division commander," with no equal for efficiency and gallantry in the Union armies. Whatever the level of enemy fire, Ames remained "cool, calm, and gentlemanly." As Lockwood put it:

"I often thought when I saw him under fire that if one of his legs had been carried away by a round shot he would merely turn to some officer or soldier nearby and quietly say, 'Will you kindly assist me from my horse!' "

On January 15, Ames planned to attack Fort Fisher in echelon, that is, to send in his brigades one after the other. Whatever his feelings about Curtis, that colonel's brigade was assigned to attack first, followed by the brigades of Pennypacker and Bell. The focus of the army attack was an opening in the fort's land face near the Cape Fear River, where the road from Wilmington, crossing a bridge in a marshy area, passed through the stockade. This point was defended by only one Napoleon.

And this would be the area Adelbert Ames would hit. Meanwhile, Admiral Porter, still eager to play the key role in this campaign, had landed *his* force. Apparently assuming the army would bear the brunt of the attack, first scheduled for two o'clock, Porter hoped his sailors could score the decisive blow. When the general signal for the attack came— the blowing of the fleet's steam whistles—the sailors and marines assaulted the sea face of Fort Fisher. But they had to hug the sand for an extra hour, as the army positioned itself. There was growing impatience to start the attack.

Ames sent a hand-picked group of skirmishers, including staffer Captain Albert Lawrence, ahead of Curtis's brigade to cut holes in the palisades. As the skirmishers moved forward, and the First Brigade got in position, Rebels fired artillery and muskets at them from the parapets. Frantically, the blue soldiers used their hands, tin cups, anything, to build little trenches in the white sand.

Ames met with Terry and his staff in an earthwork about 800 yards from the fort's land side. Terry would use this post as his headquarters during the assault on Fort Fisher. From here he could see the fort and also send signals to the fleet. Ames left the shelter to help position the troops. Lockwood marvelled how Ames could expose himself and emerge unscathed, "for he wore a brigadier-general dresscoat, and had made as careful a toilet as if he were going to review."

Preparations completed, Terry said to Ames at about 3:14 p.m., "General Ames, the signal agreed upon for the assault has been given."

"Have you any special orders in regard to it?" Ames asked.

"No, you understand the situation and what it is desired to accomplish. I leave everything to your discretion," Terry said.

"Thus was given me the unrestricted command of the fighting forces," Ames later wrote.

Leaving the earthwork to direct the attack, Ames said in a quiet voice to his staff, "Gentlemen, we will now go forward."

As the small group of officers came into the open, Confederates in the fort immediately focused their fire upon them. "We had better separate somewhat from each other," Ames cautioned, but by that time two members of his staff were already down.

At 3:30 the guns of the fleet suddenly fell silent and the steam-whistles of every vessel shrieked.

"I watched with anxious eyes the charge of the First Brigade," Ames recalled. But the attention of the Confederate defenders was drawn to the assault of the sailors and marines. They rushed forward as Confederates stood on the parapets to rain musket fire upon them. Robley Evans, one of the sailors, remembered the deadly impact—"the whole mass of men went down like a row of falling bricks." Another participant remembers the Confederates taunting the sailors to "come on" as they shot at them. "At this time there was no distinct sound of the bullets, but only a steady rush, and the water close to the beach was lashed to foam. I would not have supposed men could fire so fast."

Evans aimed his revolver at Colonel Lamb on the rampart, urging his men to kill the Yankees. Before he could snap a shot off, Evans fell, shot in the chest. Hundreds of other bluejackets fell. It was a slaughter. The Rebels thought they had repelled the main Federal attack, and were cheering when Lamb saw U. S. flags on the parapets to his left.

The First Brigade of Ames's Division had waded through marshes sometimes waist deep, then rushed through the stockade gateway, seizing the left bastion's first three traverses. Colonel Lawrence, in the lead, had his hand shot off as he attempted to plant the colors. But a foothold had been gained. Alerted to the new danger, Rebels in the fort rallied to stop it.

Seeing Curtis's assault stall, Ames ordered in the Second Brigade. As the men got up to move forward, they were sprayed by Confederate fire. Crossing the bridge, Pennypacker fell, badly wounded.

The prolonged and precise fire of the navy prior to the army's attack had knocked out most of the big guns on the land side of the fort. This was crucial in allowing the army to make a breakthrough.

But the Rebels were tenacious. Seeing the crisis, General William Whiting joined the gray soldiers rushing to plug the hole. He was the district commander, and early in the morning he had arrived at the fort. His greeting had been ominous. "Lamb, my boy," he said, "I have come to share your fate. You and your garrison are to be sacrificed."

"Don't say so, General; we shall certainly whip the enemy again," Lamb had replied. "Don't count on it," Whiting said. General Bragg, assigned to defend Wilmington, wouldn't commit infantry support for the beleaguered fort.

Now Union soldiers yelled, "Surrender!"

"Go to hell, you Yankee bastards!" Whiting shouted. A moment later, mortally wounded, he lay bleeding on the sand.

Ames entered the fort, sized up the situation, and ordered Bell's brigade up. Bell was shot dead, and his brigade became "somewhat disorganized," forcing Ames himself to form it "as best I could for the charge."

The fierce Confederate resistance limited the Union soldiers to only a portion of the fort. The ground was littered with debris of blown-up barracks and magazines. Confederates rallied behind interior breastworks and some cannon were redirected to fire at the Federals. Lamb was encouraged; the tide seemed to be turning.

Then the "remorseless fleet" started hurling shells, with great accuracy, ahead of the Union forces, into the Confederate positions. The fighting ground on. The Federals inched forward, the Confederates contesting them furiously.

Curtis would claim that Ames sent him messages saying the men were exhausted and entrenchments should be made. When an orderly brought an armful of shovels from Ames, Curtis threw the shovels over a traverse to the Confederates. Ames then personally told Curtis to stop ignoring orders and fortify the positions gained and await reinforcements. Whether or not this occurred as Curtis described, the colonel was approaching Ames about 4:30 when a shell fragment struck him in the eye. He threw up his arms and fell.

Colonel Lamb was also down. So was the sun. It was impossible to maintain the cohesion of brigades and regiments. The dispersed, often hand-to-hand "soldiers' fight" continued. With all of his brigade commanders dead or wounded, ten of his officers killed and forty-seven wounded, and at least 500 casualties, Ames requested Terry to join him in the fort. But Terry stayed put. The scene in Fort Fisher was "a perfect pandemonium."

Naval fire became less accurate at night, and in the confused fighting within the fort, it took a toll of Federal as well as Confederate soldiers. Ames sent a plea to Terry to signal the fleet to halt its fire on the fort's land face. This was done.

By eight o'clock Confederate resistance began to ebb. Ames called for reinforcements to press his advantage; Terry sent Abbott's brigade at about 8:45. By nine o'clock a general assault in the noisy darkness sent the Confederate garrison fleeing along the sea face of Fort Fisher. The Rebels retreated to Fort Buchanan at the tip of Federal Point.

Colonel Lockwood followed with Abbott's men. Learning he was a member of Ames's staff, the Confederates told him that, after seven hours of desperate fighting, they were ready to surrender. The news was communicated to Ames, then to Terry, and then to the fleet.

The celebrating warships fired off hundreds of rockets, illuminating the carnage in and about Fort Fisher. In a perverse finale, about 130 Federal soldiers were killed or wounded the next morning when the fort's magazine accidentally exploded. Altogether, the cost was more than 1,000 Federal casualties and about 500 Confederate. It was a victory made possible by incredible naval firepower and the failure of Bragg to attack the invaders. But in the end it was won by the troops on the ground.

The Fort Fisher campaign foreshadowed the army-navy amphibious operations of World War II. It also spelled the doom of the Confederacy. Within the week, Wilmington fell.

"My division did all the hard fighting and to it is due the credit of our success," Ames wrote his parents. "How I escaped unharmed I can scarcely imagine." Terry's initial report, to Stanton and the press, omitted Ames' role, giving himself the credit. Ames would not receive the public recognition that was his due. Whatever hopes he had of becoming a major general seemed to evaporate.

But he tried, as he had urged his father, to be philosophical. "As the case stands, General Howard is the only general from Maine who is ahead of me in rank or distinction. So I have done pretty well to say the least."

# Joshua Chamberlain

*"My dear General, you are gone."*

In mid-January of 1865 Chamberlain submitted to the knife in Philadelphia, and then returned to Brunswick to recuperate. A new daughter, Gertrude Lorraine, awaited. The college made it clear that a job awaited him as well. There were other offers, notably the position of customs collector at Bath. It was a good patronage job with little heavy lifting, second only to the Portland collectorship then occupied by former Governor Washburn. In urging him to take it, his mother wrote, "Surely you have done and suffered and won laurels enough in this war to satisfy the most ambitious."

But Chamberlain was a lion restless to return to the hunt. "I am anxious to be back with my command; if I am to hold my position there I want to be at any post," he informed his father. "The campaign will soon open, and it will open strong." His mind, and heart, were with the army outside Petersburg. Come spring, he knew the final campaign would be fought. He *had* to be there.

Chamberlain did not want to go back to academia's shaded groves; this February he talked of resigning his professorship in the summer. He was already looking beyond the war to a military career, which he admitted was "most congenial to my temperament," or some "other enterprise of a more bold and stirring character than a College chair affords." There was no mistaking his priorities. Joshua Chamberlain was not about to "back out just at the decisive moment, and leave the rewards and honors of my toil and sufferings to others. I had a great deal rather see another man in that Custom House, than see another next commander of the First Division."

On February 21, 1865, Chamberlain left the house on Potter Street for the first time since his return a month earlier. He was heading south again. If his wife and little family accompanied him to the train depot, it is not recorded.

He came back to an army anxious to end the long months of stalemate. There was a nagging fear that, somehow, Robert E. Lee would pull off another of his bold strokes—perhaps a break-out to join forces with Joseph Johnston's army in North Carolina. There was also the galling rumor that Sherman was coming up to Virginia to do the work the Army of the Potomac had so far failed to accomplish, depriving it of the ultimate victory. There was a pervasive sense that the endgame was near. Probably one last bloody battle loomed.

On March 25, a few weeks after Chamberlain's return to the ranks, Lee made his move, sending a division under General John B. Gordon to punch a hole in the Union lines at Fort Stedman. The fort was seized, and momentarily the Federal line near the key supply base of City Point was breached. But Gordon did not have the strength to follow up and strike at that target. Instead the inevitable counterattack sent the Rebels back, with a staggering loss of 4,000 men they could not afford to lose. For Lee, there were no master strokes left.

Grant aggressively pushed further to the left. He could extend his lines better than Lee, with his smaller army, could. Grant looked to either cut Lee's remaining lines of communications or turn his right. Either way, the Rebels would be forced out of their entrenchments. If Petersburg fell, so would Richmond. But Richmond was not the objec-

---

tive: it was the Army of Northern Virginia. Grant would make Lee fight or run.

The area Grant focused upon was to the southwest of Petersburg, a fairly flat, wooded area, swampy and bisected by numerous streams. The spring rains turned it into a mucky morass, difficult but not impossible to move through. By this time the soldiers in blue were well acquainted with the Virginia countryside. A number of plank roads were located in this area, as was the Southside Railroad, the still-open rail artery to Petersburg from the west.

When V Corps was set in motion on March 29, it headed up the Quaker Road (perversely also dubbed the Military Road) which led to the White Oak Road. That westerly running road bisected with several others at a juncture called Five Forks, just to the south of the Southside Railroad. This was the area contested, as Grant sought to turn Lee's right flank or break his communications. Exactly which was the priority became unclear, causing confusion and the abrupt end of General Warren's command of V Corps.

Chamberlain's First Brigade of Griffin's Division was small. At about 1,750 men, it was roughly comparable to Gregory's brigade and half the size of Bartlett's. However, since Chamberlain would practically direct Gregory's actions and would consistently have Griffin's support, he would actually be commanding several thousand men.

Coming up to the stream called Gravelly Run, Chamberlain found the bridge destroyed and Confederates dug in on the opposite bank. Without hesitation—his promise to Sae Chamberlain forgotten—Brigadier General Joshua Chamberlain attacked. As eight companies commanded by General Sickel laid down fire across the swollen stream, Chamberlain led other companies across Gravelly Run to charge the right flank of the entrenched Rebels. In spirited fighting his boys forced the enemy to retreat about a mile up the Quaker road to the vicinity of the Lewis Farm.

Chamberlain's hard-charging troops, their general in the thick of the fight, cleared the field beyond the farm buildings. In the woods beyond the Rebs hunkered down behind breastworks of earth and logs. Their withering fire drove Chamberlain's assault back, and they counterattacked. As General Griffin rode into the field blanketed in gunsmoke hanging in the humid air, Chamberlain was embarrassed that he had been repulsed. Griffin was visibly anxious to drive the Confederates out of their position.

With General Sickel leading his right and Colonel Sniper his left, Chamberlain charged the Rebel center "almost in cavalry fashion." His charge centered upon a big pile of sawdust, near an abandoned sawmill. His boys rushed ahead pell-mell, only occasionally stopping to shoot. It was work for the bayonet.

"Charlemagne," his blood up like his rider's, raced ahead of Chamberlain's infantry. The general tried to rein his stead to slow its momentum. "Charlemagne" reared as a Reb fired at close range at Chamberlain's breast, his chestnut neck taking the bullet. It plowed through the horse's neck and hit Chamberlain just below his heart. A leather field order case and brass-mounted hand mirror in the Mainer's breast pocket absorbed some of the Minie ball's impact and deflected the lead along Chamberlain's bridle arm. Exiting, it banged against the pistol in his aide's belt. The impact threw the man out of his saddle.

Stunned, Chamberlain slumped against his horse's profusely bleeding neck. Also in shock, the horse stopped in his tracks as Chamberlain's soldiers rushed up to and over the Confederate breastworks. Struggling to regain consciousness, Chamberlain felt a kindly arm about his waist and a soft voice saying, "My dear General, you are gone."

It was Charles Griffin. He thought his comrade was dead. Hatless and smeared with "Charlemagne's" blood, he appeared gone, but Chamberlain, his mental fog lifting, heard piercing Rebel screams to his right and saw his line there faltering.

"Yes, General, I am," he replied, spurring his mount toward his threatened right. In a moment, he was "gone" to rally his boys.

As he rode up he could tell the 198th Pennsylvanians "thought me a messenger from the other world." Certainly it was hot as Hell. Sickel fell from his horse, his arm shattered. Major McEuen, gallant boy, within arm's reach, was swept beyond reach of this world. The line rallied, throwing the Rebels back to their earthworks.

Spotting swirling confusion around the sawdust pile, Chamberlain galloped back to the center. "I was astonished at the greeting of cheers which marked my course," he recalled. "Strangest of all was that when I emerged to the sight of the enemy, they also took up the cheering. I hardly knew what world I was in."

"Charlemagne," weakened by loss of blood, sank to the ground. Afoot, the general waded into the melee just as the Confederate tide was ascendant. He found himself surrounded by men in gray, bayonets encircling him.

But he realized his identity was as unclear as the fight's progress; his tattered, dingy, bloody uniform was practically gray. Resorting to his linguistic virtuosity, he once again mimicked a Southern accent responding to demands to surrender.

"Surrender? What's the matter with you?" he scolded. "What do you take me for? Don't you see these Yanks right onto us? Come along with me and let us break 'em." Brandishing his sword he led them to their own capture.

The sawdust center regained, Chamberlain saw Colonel Spear of the Twentieth Maine materialize and proffer a drink from a ginger bottle filled with wine. He took a swig, a big one as Spear's expression reflected, and then was back in action. Now his left was endangered. Sniper's men were falling back. From somewhere somebody brought him a "dull-looking white horse." Chamberlain swung into its saddle and, looking like an Apocalyptic figure, he rode to the aid of Sniper's regiment.

Again Griffin joined him, offering a battery if Chamberlain could somehow hold the embattled line for ten minutes. With that assurance, Chamberlain yelled above the racket of killing, "Once more! Try the steel! Hell for ten minutes and we are out of it."

Within the allotted time, barely, the promised Napoleons were brought up by horses, nostrils steaming, spraying dirt as they rapidly wheeled the guns into position. The shells crashed into the trees above the Confederates, sending branches and splinters raining down. In desperation the Rebels tried to charge the deadly guns.

Again Griffin checked on Chamberlain, who looked strained, on the verge of collapse. "General, you must not leave us," Griffin said. "We cannot spare you now."

"I had no thought of it," Chamberlain said.

Letting Chamberlain continue to command his fight, Griffin fed in some regiments. The action ended with the Rebs withdrawing north toward the White Oak Road. Chamberlain always appreciated his divisional commander's "noble sense of fairness" in allowing him to win the fight he started.

Chamberlain would learn that he had been fighting four Confederate brigades; even with reinforcements, he had been outnumbered 3–1. It was a costly success; casualties were heavy, particularly among officers. Riding over the field, Chamberlain was troubled by the sight of hundreds of broken bodies. *Was this God's will or should men tremble in hope of God's forgiveness for so marring God's handiwork?*

Still trying to cheer the wounded that dark night, he came upon the mangled but feisty General Sickel. "General," Sickel said, "you have the soul of the lion and the heart of the woman."

# Joshua Chamberlain

*"Don't let anybody stop me but the enemy."*

On March 30 it rained nonstop. The ground became so soaked that soldiers joked about Grant sending them some gunboats. What the supreme commander was sending was Phil Sheridan and his hard-riding cavalry to cut Lee's communications to the west. II Corps was also up, but like V Corps, mired in mud.

Chamberlain, tired and sore, his bridle arm bruised and painful, rested in his tent on a bed of straw.

The next day the movement toward the White Oak Road was renewed. It was a bad day for V Corps. Lee was determined to beat it up, and was well on his way. Ayres' division was knocked back into Crawford's and a demoralized mass from both started breaking through Griffin's right in their rout. Chamberlain, as usual on the extreme left, heard the noise of battle grow. He was still recuperating when he had visitors.

They were Generals Warren and Griffin. "General Chamberlain, the Fifth Corps is eternally damned," Griffin exploded. When the battered man attempted to calm Griffin with a pleasantry, Griffin brushed it aside. "I tell Warren you will wipe out this disgrace, and that's what we're here for."

Until now silent, the corps commander, dark-faced, tense, said "General Chamberlain, will you save the honor of the Fifth Corps? That's all there is about it."

Untypically, Chamberlain was speechless. Finally he said his brigade needed a rest after its hard fighting. Why not send in Bartlett's bigger brigade, which had seen relatively little of the recent combat?

Warren's response was direct: "We have come to you; you know what that means."

Chamberlain did, and by making his part-plea, part-command on the grounds of honor, Warren had precluded any other response than the Maine general's ultimate one. He would do it. But, he added, "Don't let anybody stop me except the enemy."

Warren, the engineer thinking, promised to throw down a bridge in an hour to facilitate Chamberlain's advance across a rain-swollen tributary called Gravelly Run. Chamberlain refused. He would have his brigade wade across the waist-deep stream at once.

Shortly he was riding "Charlemagne," also injured but ready for more action. It felt right. "We belonged together," Chamberlain believed.

Chamberlain's brigade swept ahead, regaining the lost ground, driving the Confederates back to breastworks in woods shadowing the White Oak Road. With their main position on his right flank, Chamberlain believed it imperative to take it. But orders came from Warren to stop—precisely what he had not wanted—until the Rebel entrenchments were reconnoitred.

Chamberlain proposed that Gregory's brigade, moving under cover of trees, get in position on his left to divert the Rebs. He would charge the works frontally once Gregory demonstrated.

Once again he was putting himself in harm's way. He felt that seizure of the position on the road could be the lodgement needed to turn Lee's right flank. Robert E. Lee himself shared that view. Unknown to Chamberlain, Lee was personally directing the Confederate brigades in the area.

With Warren's blessing, spurred onward by his "youthful impetuosity," Chamberlain moved to the attack. After some desperate, close-in fighting, the Rebels scurried out of their fieldworks.

The First Brigade had won a hard fight that he and Warren believed set the stage for the ultimate big battle. But in the distance, to the west in the direction of Dinwiddie Court House, they could hear the sounds of another battle. Sheridan's cavalry had run into trouble. Big trouble.

*Jonathan Prince Cilley—Maine State Archives*

# Jonathan Prince Cilley

## *"Rear be damned!"*

March 31, 1865, was a hard day for the First Maine Cavalry. The horse soldiers who fought more battles than any other Maine regiment were in the toughest one of them all. They could not save Phil Sheridan from defeat, but they saved him from a rout. And they did it dismounted.

Dinwiddie Court House was a sleepy old hamlet, its most imposing feature a brick courthouse. Strategically, it was insignificant, with no rail connections; but it lay on a road leading north to Five Forks, next door to the Southside Railroad. That morning Sheridan's cavalry, the extreme left of the Union advance, swept into Dinwiddie, shattering it bucolic quiet with the thunder of hooves. It was a bright spring day.

The First Maine was part of Charles Smith's Third Brigade of cavalry. Just a day out of winter quarters, the regiment was spanking clean, looking like it was on holiday parade. Its commander, Lieutenant Colonel Jonathan Prince Cilley, recalled that the First Maine's veterans were "armed like an arsenal with saber, pistol, and repeating rifle." These rifles, shooting seven or sixteen shots, would play a key role in the fight looming.

Cilley was a short, energetic man with a bushy beard, the son of a Congressman from Thomaston who was a Bowdoin classmate and friend of Nathaniel Hawthorne. The elder Cilley was shot dead in a duel with a Kentucky Congressman outside Washington in 1838, when Jonathan was a mere child. Northerners, often taunted by Southern counterparts to prove their manhood by the *Code Duello,* usually refrained. But not Congressman Cilley, maneuvered into a challenge through the machinations of Southern politicos, notably the fiery Henry Wise of Virginia. He said he fought for the honor of New England; Hawthorne thought he was a damned fool. The blood of the elder flowed in the veins of the younger Cilley, and it was hot blood indeed.

Typically, Jonathan Prince Cilley was the first volunteer to sign up in the First Maine Cavalry and, typically, he was the first wounded. A Reb cannon shot knocked him out of action for a full year. But he came back and fought with a bravado the old man would have appreciated. It was a wonder he was still alive. Sam Merrill, the regiment's chaplain, observed that Cilley "is a small man in stature, and it is well for him that he is, for if his person had presented a target of the usual size, he could not have escaped the enemy's bullets."

At about noon the First Maine, sabers and swords jangling, moved out, heading up the road toward Five Forks, 500 men strong and itching for a fight. They soon detoured about thirty rods to the west, reaching a glen framed by pale green pines, along a creek called Chamberlain's Bed.

As Joshua Chamberlain and V Corps were fighting off to the east along the White Oak Road, Sheridan's Cavalry was about to be hit at Chamberlain's Bed by Fitzhue Lee's Cavalry, backed up by Pickett's Division. Robert E. Lee intended to smash the Union cavalry and solidify his position at Five Forks.

The advance of the First Maine had just splashed across the creek when it ran into large numbers of Confederate horse and infantry. They forded the Bed again, pell-mell, with the Rebs in hot pursuit. As they galloped back up the slope they had minutes earlier descended, the rest of the regiment responded to the command, "Attention! Prepare to fight on foot! Fours right! March!" The men in their bright blue uniforms scrambled, double-quick, to a slight rise dotted with a few pines that interrupted the downward incline. Two battalions commanded by Colonel Cilley were armed with Henry repeaters, Spencers, and Remington Army revolvers.

They let loose an awesome volley. Cilley's shrill voice was heard above the noise: "Charge! Charge!"

The Mainers headed down the slope, shooting, hollering, right at a mounted detachment of the Tenth Virginia with Sharps carbines, and dismounted troopers of the Fifth North Carolina with muzzle-loader rifles. In a brief, savage encounter the Rebs were forced back across Chamberlain's Bed. Many did not make it, including the North Carolinians' colonel, shot dead.

At the outset of the fighting, the regimental band provided musical accompaniment. A Southern band joined in. During the afternoon "Yankee Doodle" competed with "Dixie" in a strange battle of the bands.

From about 12:45 to 5:30 two lines of battle dug in on either side of Chamberlain's Bed. They were hardly a dozen rods apart, but, screened by cone-shaped trees, the enemies rarely saw each other. "Thousands of bullets flew across this stream during that time, and men were killed or mangled on both sides, and yet all must have been chance shots fired at random through the dense scrub," Sergeant Jeff Coburn concluded.

As the day wore on, the level of firing fell off. During one lull, a Reb shouted over to the opposing Yanks in one sector, "Oh, Yanks over there, have you all orders to fire?"

Someone from Company A of the First Maine called back, "We're firing because you are."

"Well, let's all stop firing and give warning to each other before commencing again."

"All right, it's a bargain."

After that piece of common soldier diplomacy, both sides fired a steady banter across the creek.

Mike Durgin of Company A, an Irishman with the wit Irishmen often seem born with, was particularly vocal. A Tarheel imitating an Irish brogue conversed with him. Among other topics, they debated which side a true Hibernian should be fighting for. After interminable chatter in this vein, a low voice was heard on the Reb side: "Hush up, men, let the Irishman alone. Lieutenant, don't let that occur again."

"Beg pardon, Major, but Erin's Saint over there—"

Durgin, sitting on the ground nursing a pot of boiling coffee, piped up: "Faith and the same I am, or divil a bit I would have minded to be invitin' ye to a sup of me sthamin' coffee and to have a dinnie wid me foine frinds in the Union, and not be a aitin' raw corn loike the pigs yees—"

This irritated a Southerner sufficiently to let fly a shot across Chamberlain's Bed. Either the aim was unerring or it was one of those lucky random shots Sergeant Coburn noted. The bullet sent Durgin's coffee tin and its contents flying, scalding a half dozen of his comrades. Some had been sleeping during his dialogue. They were awake now and wild, kicking him, sticking a hot poker down his collar, and otherwise showing their affection. Screaming "Howly murther," the Irishman grabbed for his weapon.

At this moment, a big, burly man with a mass of black hair materialized, fists clenched. "By the gods men," Captain John Freese said. "Lay low and keep quiet."

He stalked over to where Sergeant Coburn crouched.

"Very quiet on the left, Sergeant?"

"Apparently, yes; unusually so, Captain."

Arms folded, Freese gazed across the creek. Then, a tad melodramatically, he unsheathed his sword and wiped its glistening blade with a silk handkerchief.

"As I was observing, Sergeant, it is very quiet indeed on this part of the lines."

"As I was observing, Captain, apparently yes."

"Ah, yes, apparently, as you observed, thank you; and by the way, Sergeant, if another rebellion become imminent on this side of the Run, kindly let me know, as the one over there is all we can manage just at present, apparently."

Freese strolled off. Before he disappeared among the pines, he turned and waved his cap to Coburn.

The day dragged on. As the sun began to sink, a feeling of impending danger rose. Keeping their bargain, a Reb hollered, "Look out, Yanks, we're coming."

In the ensuing rush of men and swelling, ceaseless roar of companies firing volleys, no commands were needed or could be heard. A thick cloud of smoke drifted down the slope, filling the glen, obscuring the enemy. Men kept up a heavy fire into the smoky wall. Here and there, as the smoke lifted, Coburn could see shadowy forms emerging from the woods below. Stopping only to replenish their repeaters' magazines, the First Mainers kept shooting.

Under pressure from Pickett's infantry, the Union right started to crumble. Colonel Cilley got orders to do his best, as he fell back toward Dinwiddie Court House. "So the fight was simply a dull, heavy rear-guard, fighting by dismounted men whose duty was to fall back as slowly as possible," Cilley realized.

There was blood on both sides. Cilley, turning as he ran among the pines, felt a sharp sting and clapped his hand on the wound. He was shot "in an unspeakable part of my anatomy, which, from its locality, caused me to repeat some of Sheridan's oaths."

Seeing the colonel was hit, one of his men unwisely enquired if he should not remove himself to the rear.

"Rear? No! I am hit in the rear," the little man roared.

His pants stained red, Cilley continued to rally and direct his men. Seeing a man actually heading for the rear, he sternly rebuked him, only to learn it was a bugler from another regiment. The fellow had joined the action "for the fun of it" and was carrying orders to his own colonel. Later, Cilley's hat was blown away "in a quick, unexplained manner." The same bugler would return the hat, perforated by a bullet hole.

"Here, colonel, is your ventilated hat," the wag said, "which proves I was at the front after you left."

Cilley was afoot himself. "My orderly, in his anxiety to save horse flesh, had left me without a mount when the shower of bullets crashed through the trees." As he watched Confederates dart ahead, from tree to tree, one of General Smith's orderlies rode up and offered Cilley the use of his horse. Mounted again, the colonel spied four men lugging a wounded man across the field.

When the retreat started, Lieutenant Leander Comins was badly wounded. Seeing his crumpled body, Sergeant Coburn assembled several volunteers to rescue Comins. They were his brother, H. S. Coburn, Corporal C. A. North and Otis Lufkin. Despite a field swarming with more and more Reb cavalry and infantry, the little group hurried forward to where Comins was writhing on the ground, picked him up and started moving as enemy skirmishers closed in.

Heading through the pines, trying to use the bigger ones for cover, they were slowly making progress when rifles cracked. "It was over in half a minute," Coburn recalled.

Comins was hit again and a bullet ripped through Otis Lufkin's heart. Lufkin sprawled over the wounded man who tumbled to the ground.

Sergeant J. D. Waller of the Thirty-second Virginia saw what had happened. He shouted, "For shame, don't shoot wounded men." Then, to Coburn's party, "Take him on, Yanks; we all won't fire."

At this juncture, Colonel Cilley rode upon the scene, looking for stragglers. How in hell the colonel could be riding about when "a first-class wild-cat show was coming up" was beyond the sergeant's comprehension.

"Light out of here, Colonel, you're a candidate for Lee's rear," Coburn cried.

"Rear be damned," Cilley replied. "Queer advice for you to be giving just now. Whom have you there? What! Comins?"

"Yes, Colonel; lend us your horse and we'll save him yet."

Cilley immediately dismounted. Coburn saw blood on the saddle but did not ask questions. He later learned the meaning behind the colonel's oath about "the rear."

It was a strange scene. As scattered shots flew toward Coburn's party, Rebs shouted to errant comrades, "Wounded man on the horse, don't shoot him, don't shoot, look out, men." And about 500 Rebs acted as special protectors for a wounded Union officer.

Comins was delirious. He issued commands to divide cartridges, to club with rifles, to hold on. He addressed words to loved ones, sang snatches of an old hymn. Atop the horse, he righted himself for a moment, swaying, and surveyed the situation. Then he said, quietly, "Well, boys, I must say we make a good rear guard." It dawned upon him in the dying light that the hundreds of nearby Rebs were not firing at them. Slumping against the horse's mane, he murmured, "Thank them, thank them for me."

Meanwhile Cilley, afoot again, found himself between the two lines, if they could be called that. He could not run.

He walked painfully up the incline, unloading his Remington as he fell back. Fred Giles of Company G ran up. He had just removed another wounded man from the field. Removing the fellow's cartridges, he came back to do some more fighting. Learning Giles had about forty cartridges, Cilley directed him to take cover behind some bushes and hold off the enemy to the best of his ability. Giles did so and, surrounded by Rebs, waited until darkness to leave his forward position. He located his regiment sometime after midnight.

Jeff Coburn got Comins off the field. As his party approached some barricades where Union guns have been wheeled in place, the frantic gunners roundly cursed them. They could not fire until Coburn's group got out of the way.

Behind the barricades, Jeff Coburn got his first glimpse of Phil Sheridan. "There was something positively startling in his appearance," Coburn thought. The man's eyes burned like hot coals. Agitated, Sheridan raised himself in his stirrups to get a look at the oncoming Rebs beyond the smoke-shrouded trees. He settled back in his saddle, with a relieved sigh.

Coburn would wonder what that little scene meant. He decided Phil Sheridan had ascertained that the Rebs were not strong enough to overwhelm him.

At the time Sheridan cast a sharp glance at the wounded Comins slumped on the horse, then another down at Coburn.

"Well, boys, you've had rough work this afternoon," he said, "but damn 'em, I'll drill 'em for you tomorrow."

Leander Comins had exactly ten tomorrows. His body was sent back to Eddington, Maine, for burial. Sixteen men of the First Maine were killed at Dinwiddie Court House, seventy-five were wounded, of whom nine died. Seven men were taken prisoners, including two wounded. A hard day's work.

Late in the battle, Cilley observed Custer's cavalry trot upon the field in full view of the now-dirty dismounted troopers of the First Maine. With his red cravat and golden locks flowing as he mounted a charge, Custer was quite the glory boy. However, after crossing a couple of acres of soggy soil, the charge ended "in a mixture of mud, men, and horses like a porridge in midair, from whose upper surface flashing sabers gleamed like breaking bubbles of hot steam."

Jeff Coburn figured the dependable First Maine, by fighting its heroic rear-guard, had halted the Rebs an hour. The Mainers prevented the battle of Five Forks from being fought and won by the Confederates on the Dinwiddie plateau.

Sheridan had had a setback, but he would drill 'em the next day, April Fool's Day.

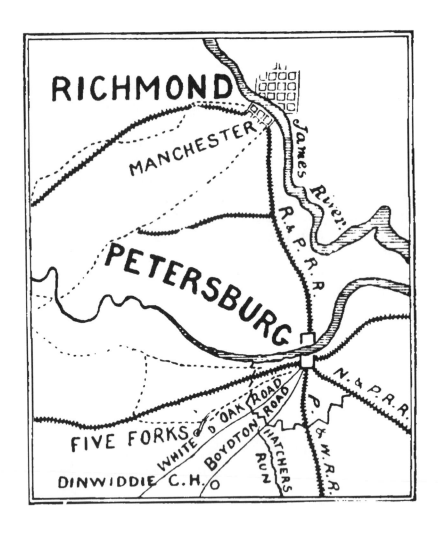

*Five Forks battle area outside Petersburg, Virginia.*
—*U. S. Army Signal Corps map*

# April Fools

Five Forks would turn out to be a smashing Union victory that sealed Bobby Lee's fate. Since it was fought on April 1, the men made the usual jokes. They did a serious piece of work nevertheless; it was the generals who acted like April Fools.

The seeds for the tragicomedy were planted on March 31. Having secured a foothold on the White Oak Road at heavy cost, Warren and Chamberlain figured the cost was justified if it set the stage for the decisive battle. When they heard the rumble of battle to the west, they wondered what its message was.

It must be Sheridan. Warren wondered aloud to Chamberlain if Little Phil was in trouble. If so, what should V Corps do? Reminding Warren that Grant looked out for Sheridan, Chamberlain observed that if "we" did not go to the cavalry's support, V Corps would catch hell.

"Well, will you go?" Warren asked.

"Certainly, General, if you think it best; but surely you do not want to abandon this position," Chamberlain replied.

"In our innocence we thought we had gained a great advantage," he remembered wistfully years later.

Darkness came and, besieged at Dinwiddie, Sheridan did his own wondering. Where the hell was V Corps? The more he wondered, the angrier he got.

In the dark, Chamberlain and Warren crawled on their hands and knees to get a better look at the Confederate defenses. A burst of firing gave them a good idea of their strength. Chamberlain spent most of that particularly black night on the picket lines with Gregory.

Messages and orders, often contradictory, busily flew back and forth between Grant, Meade and Sheridan through the night. One thing was increasingly clear: Grant's thinking had shifted to aiding Sheridan. Within the span of two hours Warren received orders to move elements of his corps in four different directions. V Corps was transformed, Chamberlain recalled, into a shuttlecock. No wonder Gouverneur Warren was beside himself.

Certainly Sheridan was. Grant sent him a message that Warren would come to his aid by midnight. It was impossible, but as the nightmare night wore on, Sheridan was blacker than the surrounding darkness.

An explosion was coming; later Chamberlain wondered if he had set the fuse. He was the one who exceeded his orders on March 31 at White Oak Road. He worried that he had got Warren "into this false position across the road, where all night, possessed with seven devils, we tried to get down to Sheridan and Five Forks." Warren dispatched Bartlett's brigade, then sent Ayres' division toward Dinwiddie as well. The presence of Bartlett was enough to convince Pickett *he* was endangered. He left Dinwiddie and pulled back toward Five Forks. So the pressure on Sheridan was relieved.

But that was not good enough. Sheridan was convinced that, his having drawn the Confederates out, they could have been whipped if V Corps had come in force. Now he prevailed upon Grant and the virtually neutered Meade to have the infantry leave its position on White Oak Road and join the cavalry. Under *his* leadership the army would "drill 'em."

"Instead of the cavalry coming to help us complete our victories at the front," Chamberlain would complain, "we were to go to the rescue of Sheridan at the rear." Of course it was more than that. Just as V Corps fought to regain its honor on March 31, Sheridan was determined to retrieve the cavalry's on April 1.

The morning of that day Chamberlain, moving to link up with Sheridan, encountered him leading a cavalry column near Gravelly Run. Saluting, Chamberlain was formal. He kept his feelings to himself. "I report to you, General, with the head of Griffin's division."

The little horse general made no effort to suppress *his* feelings. "Why did you not come before? Where is Warren?" he said in accusatory, staccato bursts.

"He is at the rear of the column, sir."

"That is where I expected to find him," Sheridan snorted.

The tension within the Union command was electric. If Sheridan was in a foul mood, so was Warren. He was doing a slow burn, his alternative to profanity. The aristocratic Warren was reputedly able to out-cuss even Sheridan and the legendary master of profane invective, Meade. Now he sulked. "Were Warren a mindreader he would have known it was time to put on a warmer manner toward Sheridan,— for a voice of doom was in the air," Chamberlain sagely recalled.

Charles Griffin took Chamberlain aside. He had learned that Grant had given Sheridan authority to remove Warren from command of V Corps if he felt it necessary. He warned the Maine general "we should see lively times before the day was over."

The Confederates had set up defenses at Five Forks. Pickett had preferred to stand beyond Hatcher's Run, but Lee had overruled him. It took Warren until about four o'clock in the afternoon to align his troops to attack. Sheridan paced back and forth, intermittently swearing, at headquarters near Gravelly Run Church as Warren sat "like a caged eagle," grimly silent.

If the Union command was unbearably tense, the Reb generals displayed a cavalier lack of concern. Apparently convinced a battle would not come off on April 1, Pickett joined Generals Rosser and Fitz Lee for a leisurely shad bake at Hatcher's Run. None of these gentlemen thought to leave word with their officers as to their whereabouts. Shad is a bony fish unless cooked just right; these shad, probably washed down with liquor (the boys not known as teetotalers), would stick figuratively in Pickett's throat for the rest of his life.

The Federal battle plan was masterful in its simplicity, as described by Sheridan with his saber in the dirt. There was a "return," or bend, in the Confederate line of entrenchments at Five Forks. Ayres' division would strike the angle of this "return," while Crawford and Griffin's divisions would sweep around to the right in an arc, enabling them to flank the Reb position. Sheridan's cavalry would keep the Confederates busy further down their line.

A diagram of the proposed movement, sketched by Warren, was distributed to the corps' commanders as they set out. It looked faulty to Chamberlain, and it was, a surprisingly sloppy piece of work by a famed engineer. "We will not worry ourselves about diagrams," Griffin counseled. "We are to follow Crawford. Circumstances will soon develop our duty."

This, too, was amazingly cavalier. Predictably, the unimaginative Crawford, doggedly following the diagram as he understood it, passed over the White Oak Road without seeing the "return's" angle. Encountering some enemy fire, actually from detached cavalry, he moved in its direction—and further away from the Reb entrenchments.

Meanwhile, a heavy burst of shooting to Chamberlain's left convince him Ayres was engaged. With no superiors at hand to order him, Chamberlain on his own initiative moved past Crawford's left toward the sound of guns. When he spotted Griffin riding near Ayres' line, he was reassured. With Gregory following as usual, he moved his brigade across a muddy brook and over a ravine. He came upon a Confederate line perpendicular to the main one on White Oak Road.

Waved on by Griffin, Chamberlain's men burst out of a bramble-covered gully and volleyed at close range at the surprised Rebs. This effectively ended a crossfire cutting up Ayres' division. At this opportune time, Sheridan spotted Chamberlain and yelled, "By God, that's what I want to see! General officers at the front. Where are your general officers?"

Chamberlain had hardly mentioned sighting Warren's flag in a field to the north when Sheridan said: "Then you take command of all the infantry here and break this damn—."

The Maine general was off before the sentence was completed. He was busily rallying troops when Sheridan, black-faced, rode up again and shouted, "Don't fire into my cavalry, I tell you!" When Ayres joined them, Sheridan lit into him too. "We are firing at the people who are firing at us," Ayres growled. Chamberlain admitted to himself that maybe his soldiers *were* firing into Union cavalry. If so, that was because the cavalry were not where they should be. He was more worried about his own left being exposed to Ayres' fire.

The mercurial, omnipresent Sheridan yelled, "We flanked them gloriously." Bullets were slicing the air and

Chamberlain, concerned for Sheridan's safety, urged him to get out of the exposed position. Little Phil gave Chamberlain a look that "seemed to say he didn't care much for himself, or perhaps for me." Then he galloped straight into the complained-of triple crossfire. But Chamberlain noted that the general ordered *his* cavalry to stop shooting in the direction of the infantry attacking the Reb breastworks.

There was confusion as soldiers in blue tried to avoid the fire of other soldiers in blue. As hand-to-hand fighting developed, Chamberlain found his brigade flanked by some Confederates. Turning their backs on the enemy ahead, his men prepared to fire at the onrushing Rebs. But the Rebs dropped their muskets and surrendered.

"It was a whirl. Every way was front, and every way was flank," Chamberlain would write.

In the midst of this confusion, Chamberlain, irritated by resistance at his left center, impulsively said to Major Edwin Glenn: "Major Glenn, if you will break that line you shall have a colonel's commission!"

Glenn led his men at once, on horseback with flag in hand, toward the breastwork. Three times Chamberlain saw the flag sway, fall, and rise again through the swirling battlesmoke. At last it waved from the captured works. He rode over to congratulate Glenn, but encountered the major being carried, bloody with a mortal wound, from the field. "General, I have carried out your wishes!" That was all he said.

"It was as if another bullet had cut me through," Chamberlain thought. "I almost fell across my saddle-bow. My wish?"

Leaning over the dying boy, the general said, in a choked voice, "*Colonel,* I will remember my promise; I will remember *you!*" And he would. Glenn's death at his wish would haunt him until his own death.

It was at about this point that Chamberlain learned of another casualty. Griffin was in command of V Corps! Chamberlain knew what this meant: Sheridan had pulled the trigger of the cocked pistol Grant had given him in the form of a note in the night.

Of course Sheridan showed up as Chamberlain was digesting this information. "I felt a little nervous because I was alone with Sheridan," he confessed. But Little Phil was flushed with battle, driving to complete the issue at hand. Waving his porkpie hat, he screamed at the men gathered about: "I want you men to understand we have a record to make, before that sun goes down, that will make hell tremble!" Pointing at the Confederate breastworks, he roared, "I want you there!"

And there they went—cavalry, infantry, Griffin and Chamberlain. A bullet hit Charlemagne's leg, but over the breastworks he went. Griffin stopped to squabble with cavalry officers over who deserved credit for taking the cannon there.

A frazzled Warren, having spent most of the battle searching for Crawford, finally found him. He sent his division down upon the Rebel rear, smashing it to pieces.

Belatedly Pickett, oblivious to the nearby struggle due to an acoustical oddity, saw blue ranks near his shad repast. Riding Indian-style through a hail of bullets, he arrived upon a lost battlefield. Leaderless, his men fought bravely. But, broken up in fragments, they were mopped up.

There remained a pocket of resistance in some woods at the edge of farmer Gilliam's field. Grabbing the corps flag, Warren led his last charge straight into Confederate fire. The position was taken, Warren narrowly eluding death. Perhaps that was not how he planned it. Returning, he was presented the official field communication relieving him of his command.

Riding up to Sheridan, he urged him to reconsider.

"Reconsider, Hell! I don't reconsider my decisions. Obey the order!" the little general snapped.

That night, on a field strewn with corpses and reputations, Sheridan approached the officers of V Corps. He apologized for speaking harshly to some of them. It was in the heat of battle; they must understand how it was. They were taken aback, seeing Sheridan in a different light.

There was no light for Warren, riding into the darkness. Griffin and Ayres thought he had sacrificed himself for Crawford. Privately, Chamberlain thought Warren's real failure was not being properly positioned to command his corps effectively. But he felt Warren had been dealt with unjustly. He would try to rectify the wrong done the man whose name, with his, was forever to be linked to Little Round Top.

Union losses at Five Forks were not much more than 800 men. The Confederate casualties, killed, wounded and captured, were near to 4,500.

# Thomas Hyde

*"And who was the officer on the gray horse?"*

Tom Hyde was back in the thick of it. Grant planned a general assault upon the Confederate lines protecting Petersburg by dawn of April 2. General Horatio Wright's VI Corps would start the attack in a wedge-shaped formation. Hyde's Third Brigade of Getty's Second Division would be the point of the wedge.

It was not a case of Hyde having a vacation since Grant's Overland Campaign in the Spring of '64. General Wright, who had replaced the fallen Sedgwick, had acceded to Hyde's request to return to command of his old regiment, or what was left of it after Spotsylvania. With the Seventh Maine, Hyde spent some time in the Shenandoah Valley, fighting under feisty little Phil Sheridan. Tom Hyde liked Sheridan and his no-nonsense, hard-driving approach to war.

And he had more escapades at the edge. One late summer day Hyde and Arthur McClellan were riding ahead of a dusty column of VI Corps infantry in the town of Middleton. The young bucks could not help noticing that the girls peeking out windows were not making the usual faces at them. Instead, they appeared "vastly pleased about something, but this did not warn us." The cause of the Reb girls' amusement became apparent when, just outside town, heading toward Fisher's Hill, the two riders were halted by a half dozen cavalrymen in dirty gray uniforms. Seeing their blue uniforms under open privates' overcoats, the Confederates blasted away at close range with six carbines.

As the balls missed and peppered the old boards of a nearby mill, Hyde's first thought was, "What a wretched weapon!" His next thought was to get the hell out of there. The Yanks were "blessed by our pride in having good horseflesh," and easily jumped a fence that proved too much for the Reb riders. A race back toward Middleton ensued with the pursuers on one side of the fence a ways and the pursued on the other. The gray cavalrymen did not have time to reload their carbines; Hyde and McClellan pulled pistols from their boots "and emptied them gayly. Walls and fences were nothing to us."

Another day, again riding in advance of the army, this time alone, Hyde decided to settle down for the night in the parlor of a Unionist doctor's house. He piled up some music books for a pillow, but was awakened to see a troop of gray cavalry ride by. It was a long line and Hyde spent anxious moments, revolver in hand, worrying that his horse, in the doctor's barn, might whinny and give him away. The animal kept quiet and when the Confederate column—which turned out to be the dreaded Mosby and his men looking for stragglers—was out of sight, Hyde began a long, circuitous ride through the mountains to get back to his command.

"These little adventures were heightened in excitement by a belief that capture would be followed by instant execution," Hyde recalled. That belief was often justified in the savage competition between Sheridan and Jubal Early for control of the valley.

Just as the Seventh Maine's tour of duty ended and the regiment was starting to head homeward, fighting flared. The Seventh stopped, Hyde wrote, for "our share of the fight," and then marched off.

Autumn found Tom Hyde back in Maine, pushing the politicians in Augusta to grant him colonelcy of the newly-organized First Regiment of Maine Veteran Volunteers. It had a definite seasoned look, made up of companies of the Fifth and Sixth Maine and reenlisting vets of the old Seventh. All were veterans; most had their "red badge of courage."

Hyde returned to the valley after Sheridan's famous Ride to Cedar Creek. The countryside looked the way he imagined Germany must have appeared after the Thirty Years' War. He was personally devastated by the thought that he had, while in Maine, missed the opportunity of his lifetime for promotion.

But he returned to command of the Third Brigade in Getty's Division. "It was a proud thing for a boy to command a brigade, and a good brigade too." It was made up of six regiments, including the new-old First Mainers. By mid-December VI Corps was ordered to return to the Army of the Potomac encircling Petersburg.

Enroute to the front, Colonel Hyde stopped by to visit Brigadier General Selden Connor in Washington. Connor was still hospitalized from his wound in the Wilderness. It was questionable if he would walk again. Hyde, still unscathed, rode south. He was excited by the prospect of one last great campaign. Maybe he, too, would be a Brigadier General yet.

Which brings us to dawn, April 2, 1865. The ground Hyde, at the point of the VI Corps attack, had to cover was burned over and obstructed by five lines of abattis. However, pickets informed Hyde that Rebs regularly used an opening in the abattis to come out to either go on picket or cut wood. A campfire beyond, near the Confederate forts, was in a straight line with the opening. Hyde determined to set the course of his attack toward that campfire.

---

At midnight he brought his 2,000-man brigade into position and peered through the chill darkness. The campfire was burning. The night rumbled as 100 Union guns celebrated Five Forks. Hyde fretted whether he would be able to make out the signal gun for his advance if the racket persisted. And it did through the night.

General Getty verbally gave Hyde the go-ahead. The artillery stopped. In as low a tone as he could manage, the colonel ordered the charge to begin. It was not yet light, and as the "last line of black forms in the blacker darkness were over the (rifle) pits, I followed as fast as possible, greatly regretting I had been so foolish as to have left my horse."

Moving ahead on foot, Hyde gave orders to send captured Rebs to the Union rear as his soldiers cleared their pickets' rifle pits. The blackness of night was turning into the gray of a misty dawn. The air hummed with enemy shot and shell passing a few feet over the advancing brigade; in the artificial light created by this artillery fire Hyde worried that his attack was veering off course. Lieutenant Webber of the First Maine guided the men up to and through the opening in the abattis.

Jumping into and taking a waterlogged ditch, the heavy-breathing men grabbed a moment's rest, then headed at a run for the main works. Surmounting them, there was a brief contest with the bayonet. Still-hot Rebel cannon were seized, turned and fired at scurrying Confederate survivors.

In the weird half-light of dawn, Colonel Hyde's horse was finally brought up and he galloped onward to catch up with his men. They were pushing toward the Southside Railroad. In a boisterous mood, the boys were rounding up Confederates, mules, *everything*. Some men dressed up in captured Reb uniforms. Others busily tore up track. Nothing could stop them.

---

Reforming his brigade and joining the rest of the division, Hyde and his soldiers swept leftward, pursuing the skedaddling enemy. Moving quickly through some woods, they came upon a sizable clearing. At its edge they spotted some mounted men, no doubt officers. Shots rang out, and one of the riders toppled. Hyde would later guess that this was where General A. P. Hill was killed.

Reaching a rain-swollen Hatcher's Run, Captain Merrill of the First Maine crossed with fourteen men on fallen trees. He came back with seventy-nine prisoners, Confederate sharpshooters.

The assault had extracted a price. Two regiments lost their commanders, two other regimental leaders were wounded. In one of Hyde's regiments, the Sixty-first Pennsylvania, 300 draftees and substitutes had taken cover, leaving it up to 200 veterans to take two of the five Rebel flags captured by the Third Brigade. Hyde felt those men should get big pensions. As for the rest, he wished them to be shot or hanged.

Returning to the forts and camps they had taken earlier, passing and cheering Grant's cavalcade, the First Maine took some fire from a remaining Rebel battery on a hill before Petersburg. Irritated by the guns' enfilading shots, the Maine regiment charged it several times, forcing the Confederate artillerists to change position. Hyde noticed a "fine-looking old officer, on a gray horse," apparently directing the movements of the troublesome battery.

Now no less than three brigades tried, unsuccessfully, to take the Rebel guns. Hyde dispatched Captain Nichols of the First Maine with fifty men to move around the hill, through a waist-deep swamp, to shoot the battery's horses. Shortly, as hundreds of men directly assaulted the hill, Hyde made out the crack of Nichols' rifles in the din.

He knew the cannon would not move.

After the battery was taken, with the dust still settling from the fight, Hyde asked a dying Confederate officer the identity of the battery. He learned it was Pogue's North Carolina battalion.

"And who was the officer on the gray horse?"

"General Robert E. Lee, sir, and he was the last man to leave these guns."

Hyde cursed the opportunity lost of grabbing the greatest trophy of war possible on the field.

And then Colonel Hyde went back to making war. His tired yet beyond tired men pushed now for the Appomattox River. Captain Whittlesey of the First Maine threw together a makeshift raft, crossed the river, and sent the few Rebs opposing him running.

The spires of Petersburg were outlined against the dying light of day—and the dying Confederacy. General Penrose arrived with his New Jersey brigade from another division of VI Corps to relieve Hyde's brigade. Two last enemy shots killed Lieutenant Messer riding by Tom Hyde's side and knocked General Penrose out of his saddle. He was lucky; the bullet was deflected by his belt buckle.

Hyde and his brigade, after nineteen straight hours of marching and fighting, were too exhausted to celebrate the victory. Without supper or blankets they collapsed into sleep on the battle-scarred earth.

*Sewall Pettingill. Photo taken when the native of Wayne, Maine, was an old veteran—Pettingill, Memoirs*

# Sewall Pettingill

*"The bloodiest mess I have ever seen."*

Sewall Pettingill of the Eleventh Maine was back in the Petersburg lines on April 2. He had not enjoyed his first stint, and today would be even less enjoyable. Stationed at Petersburg from August to October of 1864, he remembered it was "as much as your head was worth to raise it above the breastworks" and that Petersburg "was the worst place for picket that we struck during the entire war." On some days the firing was sporadic, but on others it was so intense "we had to run in zigzags or under cover to avoid their bullets and could relieve our pickets only at night."

On a September day Private Lewis Wing, from Pettengill's hometown, became the first man who had signed up to go to war from Wayne in the summer of '62 to die.

Often suffering from illness, Pettingill was officially off duty much of the time. That did not necessarily lessen the odds of sharing Wing's fate. "Actually the front was almost as safe as the campground," he wrote, "especially on the days when the Johnnies shelled it."

Pettingill had seen a lot of the South and war since his enlistment. He had not signed up for romantic reasons or to free the slaves, nor had he exactly rushed to the colors. Married in 1860 after briefly attending Maine Wesleyan Seminary, he worked on his widowed father's farm summers and taught in the Wayne village school winters. In August of 1861 his infant son died; his wife followed the boy to the grave in March of 1862.

At twenty-two Sewall Pettingill was at loose ends; he took a job in Lewiston, then helped his father with haying at the farm in June. When a friend showed up with enlistment papers, Sewall made them out in the kitchen. His father silently got up and left the house, crying. "These were trying days for parents," Pettingill recalled.

He went down to Portland expecting to join the Twentieth Maine. Pettingill spent some time there with other volunteers from home, found the Twentieth full, and was sent back to Wayne. "Like the boys that we were, we had great fun telling everyone that we had crushed the Rebellion and were returning home with honors aplenty." That August the boys were mustered into the Eleventh Maine and sent off to war for real.

Sewall was a musician. As a fife player he participated in continuous rounds of funerals. At his first post, Yorktown, most deaths were from disease. But dead was dead. The Eleventh Maine spent some time on the North Carolina coast, the Florida coastal island town of Fernandia, and besieging Charleston, before returning to Virginia.

His first experience under fire came on June 2, 1864. On August 18 he saw more action at Deep Bottom when Rebs attacked. "The charge was in a pine grove, and the pine needles, cut off by the bullets, dropped to the ground like snow flakes."

After the fight, the dead were stretched out in rows, and Pettingill was part of a detail walking along them to identify anyone from the Eleventh Maine. In addition to grotesque bloating and stinking, none of the dead were fully clothed, having been stripped by the enemy. Some had only a shirt or drawers, others were fully naked. "I remember I bit off a huge chew and braced myself well before I started on this disagreeable duty," Pettingill would write.

---

After several months in the trenches at Petersburg, the Eleventh Maine endured a bitter winter at Johnson's Plantation across the James River. By late March the regiment was back at the front. Ironically, the Reb counterpart facing the Eleventh Maine across no man's land was the Eleventh Mississippi.

On April Fool's Day, Pettingill could hear distant firing to the left; it was the battle of Five Forks. About midnight Union artillery started a barrage that continued for hours like a "continuous roar." All that sleepless night the Eleventh Maine, like every other Union regiment, awaited orders to attack. Heavy fog obscured the dawn. After VI Corps went in, XXIV Corps followed. Taking the initial Rebel breastworks, Pettingill recalled covering about two miles before coming upon a line of forts defending Petersburg's south flank. There was no cover from their fire.

The fort's artillery switched from shells to canister as the blue lines closed in. The men let loose a yell and ran for a wide ditch surrounding Fort Gregg. The ditch, about six feet deep and eight feet across, had about a foot of water within.

"The first to arrive jumped into the ditch and made steps with the bayonets in their guns so that the boys following could run up the other side," Pettingill wrote. "They stuck the bayonets into the side of the ditch, one above the other and a little to the front. Then they held the muskets by the breech and the boys ran up the steps to the breastworks. Some were shot and fell back into the water. At last enough of them got into the fort to capture it."

Few of the Rebs who surrendered inside Fort Gregg were without wounds. Plenty were dead. "The inside of that fort was the bloodiest mess I have ever seen," Pettingill recalled. "The water in the ditches was the color of blood. It was blood."

# Joshua Chamberlain

## *"My intensity may have seemed like excitement."*

Joshua Chamberlain would call it "The Week of Flying Fights." After Federal forces flanked Lee's army and smashed through his Petersburg defenses, the Rebels retreated westward. Petersburg fell without a fight on April 3. Richmond was evacuated and occupied. But Grant was not interested in cities; he meant to catch the Army of Northern Virginia and destroy it as a fighting force. That would not only end the war in Virginia, but guarantee the end of the Rebellion. Thus, for a week in April, the great chase was on.

The much-maligned V Corps, victorious at Five Forks, was in the van. And Chamberlain's First Brigade was in the forefront. II and VI Corps were close behind, with other Union forces following. "Our privilege was to push things," Chamberlain wrote, "and there was no default of that. Our advanced infantry corps were operating with cavalry; which means doing cavalry work marching and infantry work fighting."

They marched through the refuse of their retreating quarry: abandoned caissons and cannon, often with mules still hitched in harness. Tired, hungry horses wandered loose still saddled or packed. Small arms and assorted cast-off equipage of war littered the muddy roads. Captured wagon trains were burned. And everywhere they could, the Union cavalry and infantry punished the ragged rear guard of the Confederacy's last hope. "There was blood at every bridge and ford," Chamberlain remembered.

There was human flotsam as well. At one point the Maine general encountered a bunch of "wild-looking men in homespun gray declaring they are not white, but colored." That was conceivable, he thought, as the gray zone of Southern race. Other times the dusty, sweating boys in faded blue uniforms came upon black waifs surrounded by ebony progeny, poor, ignorant, yet cheerful.

It was hard business, the nearly incessant marching and fighting. Some men were a bit "dainty," wanting to take valuable time to dry wet clothes or dispense with them. Chamberlain admitted it was difficult "to march in gurgling shoes after wading 'neck deep.' But 'dandyism' could not be indulged. Time is an essential element of this contract."

Repeatedly the Yanks tried to force a battle, but the Armageddon they sought eluded them. Chamberlain expected a struggle at Jetersville. The Federal advance units were strung out, and lacking reinforcements, were vulnerable to a counterstroke by Lee. *Jetersville?* "A sonorous name is not necessary for a famous field," Chamberlain observed. But Lee let the opportunity pass.

On April 6 Gordon's corps, Lee's rear guard, was pummeled badly. At nearby Sailor's Creek II and VI Corps converged on Confederates under Ewell and Anderson, cornered by Union cavalry. Lee lost a third of his army that day.

V Corps pushed onward to High Bridge as the cavalry bagged wagon trains carrying food for Confederates living on handfuls of parched corn. Chamberlain believed the infantry should close directly on the faltering Army of Northern Virginia, ending the chase at High Bridge. But Grant thought there had been enough bloodshed and ordered a leftward sweep by V Corps and Sheridan's cavalry to get ahead of Lee and cut off his escape. The other corps would pursue him directly.

On the evening of April 7 Grant wrote a note to Lee demanding surrender to avoid further needless bloodshed, initiating a series of notes over the next two days.

Chamberlain's "Charlemagne," usually so sure-footed, tripped crossing the Buffalo River, dunking the general. Several men had to fish out muddy horse and rider. "What they had to do for us both afterwards, official dignity prevents explaining," Chamberlain wrote much later, with heavy-handed humor.

At one point V Corps, swinging left, got tied up by the plodding mules and men of XXIV Corps. Tempers flared at the head of Chamberlain's column. An attempt to drown out the profane noise by having the bands play "The Girl I Left Behind Me" backfired. It "seemed to make them want to 'get there' all the more," Chamberlain recorded.

Having marched through much of the night, the general tried to catch a nap about six miles from Appomattox Station. Chamberlain was roused by a cavalryman with orders for infantry commanders: Immediately bring up support for Sheridan, who had cut across enemy lines. The final act had opened!

The bugle notes of "The General" called men out of their sleep for another march. They set out before rations arrived. Joshua Chamberlain remembered an image of blackness before dawn as "almost with one foot in the stirrup, you take from the hands of the black boy a tin plate of nondescript food and a dipper of miscalled coffee;—all equally black, like the night around." Officers not only got something to eat; they usually had black servants, and Chamberlain (from the town where Harriet Beecher Stowe wrote *Uncle Tom's Cabin*) was apparently no exception.

By sunrise his hard-marching men had reached Appomattox Station. The air crackled with the noise of Sheridan's dismounted cavalry, the First Maine Cavalry playing a conspicuous part, holding back Lee's army. It was, Chamberlain realized, the supreme hour.

Another black shadow penetrated Chamberlain's consciousness: "One striking feature I can never forget,—Birney's black men abreast with us, pressing forward to save the white man's country."

Chamberlain's brigade was about in the middle of the V Corps column heading toward the sound of the guns when the Maine general was approached by a cavalry staffer.

"General, you command this column?"

"Two brigades of it, sir; about half the First Division, Fifth Corps."

"Sir, General Sheridan wishes you to break off from this column and come to his support. The rebel infantry is pressing him hard. Our men are falling back. Don't wait for orders through the regular channels, but act on this at once."

Chamberlain immediately followed the staff officer, his brigade and Gregory's close behind. He found cavalry fighting to prevent a breakout by Gordon near the courthouse. He rode right up to Sheridan. "A dark smile and impetuous gesture are my only orders."

The V Corps soldiers moved into position in double lines; Gordon's graybacks were "astonished" to find that they faced their old blue infantry antagonists as well as cavalry.

*Like old times in Dixie.*

The Confederates recoiled and the Union infantry followed. Chamberlain was so intent on preparing to attack some Rebs who seemed to be making a stand on a hillside that Griffin rode up to calm his brigadier. "My intensity may have seemed like excitement," Chamberlain confessed. In his usual blunt manner, the V Corps commander accused him of confusing a peach tree with a Rebel flag.

But Chamberlain was no more excitable than Griffin. A few minutes later, Griffin urged him to go back, find Crawford, and bring up his division. "He is acting in the same old fashion that got Warren into trouble at Five Forks," Griffin fumed. "He deserves to be relieved of his command."

Griffin wanted to put Chamberlain in command of Crawford's division. This would give him the divisional authority he had sought. But Chamberlain refused, warning Griffin there would be problems from Crawford's political friends. That was a valid concern, but Chamberlain did not want to leave the front. *That* probably was the compelling reason for his refusal.

Chamberlain was mesmerized by a nearby crest. He wanted to take it. General Ord, of the Army of the James, cautioned Chamberlain: If he charged the hill, he would be exposed to raking fire by the enemy beyond. But Chamberlain thought he detected a "qualifying look" in Ord's expression as he turned and rode off. Certainly he interpreted his position as allowing discretion to "push things" as Grant and Sheridan would. Youth, he would write, struggled with prudence. Unsurprisingly, youth won.

Taking the beckoning crest, Chamberlain was exposed, all right. He was exposed to the panoramic view of the broken remnants of Lee's army swarming about in a bowl-like valley. It resembled a great amphitheater. On the slopes below a tragedy was coming to an end. The whole scene, as blue infantry and cavalry massed about the trapped army, seemed dreamlike to Chamberlain.

The Union host moved down into the valley bisected by the meandering Appomattox, pushing the Rebs back toward the small town bearing the same musical name. A proper name for the last battle. "There is wild work, that looks like fighting; but not much killing, nor even hurting. The disheartened enemy take it easy; our men take them easier. It is a wild, mild fusing,—earnest, but not deadly earnest."

Yet Chamberlain experienced a pang of anxiety. He was advancing with his right "in the air." Some Confederates were visible in the distance, capable of making a flank attack. He saw, closer, a line of Union cavalry forming.

Then he saw something else—the solitary figure of a horseman riding between the lines. Eventually, the rider was joined by another. About a mile away, they headed inexorably forward, across the front of cavalry. The broken ground momentarily obscured Chamberlain's view. Then, suddenly, the horsemen loomed close, apparently Confederate staff officers. One carried a white flag.

"He comes steadily on, the mysterious form in gray, my mood so whimsically sensitive that I could even smile at the material of the flag,—wondering where in either army was found a towel, and one so white."

# Thomas Hyde

*"My own mistaken emotions*
*must have vent for a moment."*

Tom Hyde's brigade did not stop to see Petersburg after it fell, but moved westward in the great chase after the Gray Fox. Day blurred into succeeding day as they marched through, over and around every obstacle toward the distant booming of the guns.

On the sixth day of April they emerged from the woods to see the battle of Sailor's Creek in progress. The horizon was sooty with the smoke of burning Confederate trains. Sheridan and his staff were visibly upset, fuming that the cavalry could not do it all, yet happy to know that Little Phil's favorite corps of infantry was up. It was like old days in the Valley, smoke and fire purging the land.

The Third Division went in ahead. Hyde was thrilled to form his brigade in line under Sheridan's eye. But "before we crossed the creek, which was choked with bodies and black with blood, the enemy, attacked from all directions, disintegrated."

*Damn!*

The brigade hurtled on. There was still the enticing sound of guns beckoning. The final battle. One more chance for glory and promotion.

Then, toward noon on April 9, the guns no longer boomed. A stillness came on, suddenly, strangely. "It seemed," Hyde thought, "as if we were marching in a vacuum."

He rode ahead about a mile to ascertain what was happening, and saw General Getty. He was sitting under a tree, his face hidden in his hands.

"What is it, general?"

"Lee has surrendered."

"I joined him on the ground, and bitter tears fell for a career untimely nipped," Hyde would admit when he was an old man. "Wicked, ill-timed, and selfish as it may have been, grief, that the glorious career of army life was cut short, was filling my boyish heart." He lacked the maturity to appreciate what the news meant for civilization, freedom and coming generations.

Like a boy, this man thought only of himself and mourned the loss of the war that had become part of him. Perhaps all of him.

He explained his behavior: "My own mistaken emotions must have vent for a moment. It was only a moment, however. I must tell the boys."

Hyde raced back down the road as fast as his Virginia stallion could carry him. Two thousand expectant faces greeted him. "The war is over! Lee has surrendered!" Tommy Hyde yelled.

*His boys carried him about on their shoulders. Cheers ended the silence of the hour. All discipline was gone. Batteries thundered.*

Hyde recalled that "we are only patriotic American citizens for the rest of the day [and] the most crazy joy seizes all alike." The following day, Hyde and his brigade were briefly disgusted to learn that they would not get to see the defeated Army of Northern Virginia. "How mad we were, and how unjustly!" They did not want to gloat over a beaten foe, these boy-men. They were curious to see other boy-men

---

who, in an odd way understandable only to soldiers, had become their brothers.

They did catch sight of one, solitary Confederate officer. It was Lieutenant General John B. Gordon, "riding down the road by us like a knight of old." In two days, Gordon had one last act of glory to perform with a general from Maine named Chamberlain.

# Sewall Pettingill

*"Suddenly, everything was confusion."*

April 9th started out a confusing day for the Eleventh Maine. After a week of endless marching through the wet morass of Virginia, the brigade awoke to another sunrise. They were soon confronted by blue cavalry retreating with gray horsemen in pursuit. "We kept going," Sewall Pettingill recalled, "and, as the Johnnies struck us, they seemed to give up and fall back."

They came under artillery fire, jumped a fence, and ran to silence the Reb battery. "Suddenly, everything was confusion," as the soldier from Wayne, Maine, put it. Cavalry was hitting their rear. They scattered, running for the safety of a fence at the edge of some woods. Tensely, they waited to see what would happen next.

What came next was an attack and a flurry of hand-to-hand combat. They heard yelling in their rear. Pettingill could not figure out what *that* meant.

A Federal horseman rode up to them. "Lee has surrendered. The war is over," he told the dazed men.

They did not regret the news.

*Major General Joshua Chamberlain, ca. 1865—Pejepscot Historical Society*

# The Last Salute

On the evening of Palm Sunday, Chamberlain was informed by General Griffin that he had been chosen to command the Union parade at the formal surrender ceremony for the Army of Northern Virginia. He was junior among the Union generals in the field, just brevetted Major General, and did not consider himself to be on equal social terms with the "high boys" at headquarters. Yet Grant, who had left for City Point, had bestowed upon Chamberlain this honor—why?

Chamberlain had not complained when he had been assigned a new brigade and then, later, the Union Army's smallest brigade. "I suppose they thought they were making things equal for me for bearing some things in silence," he surmised. He was sure Griffin had played a role in the selection. And Chamberlain had been in the advance in the campaign just completed.

Griffin told Chamberlain "in a significant tone" that it was Grant's desire that the surrender ceremony "be as simple as possible, and that nothing should be done to humiliate the manhood of the Southern soldiers."

Chamberlain had a request: He wanted to have with him his old Third Brigade. He had been through many battles with its veterans, which included the Twentieth Maine. The request was granted and Chamberlain was transferred back to the Third.

*Soldiers of the Army of Northern Virginia prepare to march in the surrender ceremony at Appomattox (reenactment)—author photo*

So it came to this. Joshua Lawrence Chamberlain would command the war's "final scene." There were Rebel forces in the field elsewhere, but everyone knew the surrender of Lee's army meant the war's end.

"The momentous meaning of this occasion impressed me deeply. I resolved to mark it by some token of recognition, which could be no other than a salute of arms," wrote Chamberlain. He knew such an action would be criticized. It could be explained that it was not a salute to the Confederate cause, but to the Rebel flag going down before the Union's flag. But Chamberlain admitted that his primary reason "was one for which I sought no authority nor asked forgiveness."

He respected the defeated veterans in gray as worthy foes in many battles. He empathized with their emotions, as on the gray dawn of April 12, 1865, he saw them break camp less than a mile away, fold their tents, and start marching toward his men formed in line of battle on Appomattox Court House's main street. "I pitied them from the bottom of my heart," Chamberlain wrote his sister.

As the gray column approached, Chamberlain, astride his great chestnut horse, gave his instructions. "I sent down an order to come up successively to the 'Carry arms!' not to 'Present'—that would be too much."

It was the marching salute.

Lieutenant General John B. Gordon led the defeated army. Gordon—who, shot six times at Antietam's Bloody Lane, joked to his horrified new bride that he had attended an Irish wedding. Gordon—who wanted to push matters on the evening of July 1, 1863, at Gettysburg, but was overruled. Gordon—whose attack in the Wilderness threatened the Union right, who attempted the last Confederate offensive at Petersburg, and who led the last sortie at Appomattox. If any Confederate commander was Chamberlain's counterpart as a dashing, hard-driving, fearless soldier, it was John Brown Gordon.

As Gordon came up opposite Chamberlain, the remnant of Stonewall Jackson's corps immediately behind him, he was dejected, his chin against his gray tunic.

The Union bugle sounded the signal. At once there was the rattle of men coming to the carry, moving from right to left, regiment after regiment.

Instantly understanding the meaning, Gordon straightened up and wheeled his horse to face Chamberlain. In a fluid motion, the Rebel general gently spurred the animal, making the horse rear high in the air as Gordon dropped his sword to his boot toe with a bow.

Then the Confederate commander faced his own last command and ordered them to return the salutation as best they could.

It was, Chamberlain wrote, "honor answering honor."

The man who never read a novel until he was in college had, with the spontaneous *élan* of this former adversary, choreographed a scene worthy of Sir Walter Scott.

"All day it takes—not a sound of trumpet, nor roar of drum, nor even a cheer or whisper of vain glory escapes the lips of a single man of our army," Chamberlain recalled. "We would not look in those brave, bronzed faces, thinking of the battles we had been through and think of such a thing as hatred or mean revenge. Oh no, that was not our part!"

Throughout the drizzly day the Rebel divisions stacked their arms and cartridge boxes, furled their tattered, bloody flags, and laid them down. Many cried.

Chamberlain engaged in conversation with various Confederate officers. The prevalent tone was friendly. But there was a discordant note.

Noting the bearing of the common soldiers on both sides, Chamberlain said to Confederate general Henry Wise,

"This promises well for our coming good-will; brave men may become good friends."

"You're mistaken, sir," Wise replied. "You may forgive us but we won't be forgiven. There is a rancor in our hearts which you little dream of. We hate you, sir."

"Oh, we don't mind much about dreams, nor about hates either," Chamberlain coolly retorted. "Those two lines of business are closed." More words were exchanged. Finally, Chamberlain started to turn away.

Wise cried, "You go home, you take these fellows home. That's what will end the war."

"Don't worry about the end of the war. We are going home pretty soon, but not till we see you home."

"Home! We haven't any. You have destroyed them. You have invaded Virginia and ruined her. Her curse is on you."

Chamberlain, who would later remark he was not of Virginia's blood but she was of *his*, gave what he considered "the obvious reply":

"You shouldn't have invited us down here, then. We expected somebody was going to get hurt when we took up your challenge. Didn't you? People who don't want to get hurt, General, had better not force a fight on unwilling Yankees."

It was Wise who twenty-seven years earlier, as a Congressman, had helped instigate a duel in which Maine Congressman Jonathan Cilley was shot dead. Now even his own staff and men laughed at him.

Chamberlain could not be baited or upset on such a triumphant conclusion for him. His decision, so opposed by family and friends, seemed vindicated. As he wrote his sister on April 13, "I am glad I was not tempted to leave the Army this spring. I would not for a fortune have missed the experiences of the last two weeks. It seems like two years, so many, and such important events have taken place. Father said in his last letter to me that 'the glory of battles was over.' But if he had seen some of these we have had of late he would think differently."

On the last day of the last campaign of the Army of the Potomac, Chamberlain thought of honor, glory and other-worldly exaltation. He rode "Charlemagne" like a knight of old, his staff carrying the V Corps flag, red Maltese cross on a white field bordered with blue, and believed, "it was our glory that the victory we had won was for others, for those very men before us, as well as for ourselves and ours. We seemed to be in the presence of some mighty angel appointed for human destinies, perhaps with the power of correcting errors and even of forgiving sins."

A few days after the surrender ceremony, Sewall Pettingill of the Eleventh Maine joined his friend Payson Sanborn of the Eighth Maine to watch some of the remaining Confederates get their parole papers. The two Mainers were standing on the Appomattox Court House steps when one of Fitzhugh Lee's cavalrymen stopped to chat, and asked: "Now that the war is over, what are you-all going to do with the niggers?"

"We told him that as far as we were concerned we were not going to do anything with them," Pettingill recalled. "We were willing to let them work out their own fortunes."

\* \* \* \*

Chaplain Samuel Merrill of the First Maine Cavalry knew that the business of war was destruction. The impact of armies in and around Petersburg that spring was an ugly scar on the land. Groves, forests, orchards, gardens, fields—all were obliterated. Stinking corpses of dead men, horses, and mules befouled the air. It was impossible even to distinguish roads travelled. "No stranger could find a given place by following a given road, for all the country was all road and no road." The clergyman wondered, "Will life ever bloom on this theater of death?"

Revisiting the same area of Virginia before his departure for Maine, Merrill got his answer.

He found locust and honeysuckle climbing the wheels of a broken gun carriage. Daisies grew in a shattered caisson. Wild roses blossomed above "Fort Hell's" embrasures. The stumps of mutilated forests were lost among shoots of oak, ash, hickory and chestnut. Creeping ivy covered graves. "Broad fields of corn and oats had sprung from seed casually dropped by contending armies, and now owed their life and beauty to the very rottenness so offensive before."

*The land was healing.*

* * * *

Sewall Pettingill got back to Wayne, Maine, that June of '65. "The sun should have been shining, but it wasn't. It was raining, raining quite hard—another thunder shower."

Drying off from the rain, Sewall headed in a wagon to his father's farm. Reunited with some friends and family, the soldier boy was eating supper, when "Father came walking across the hill. I got up from the table and went to meet him at the sitting-room door. We shook hands. This was surely a fine reunion, a happy ending to my soldier's life."

* * * *

Major General Joshua Chamberlain returned to Brunswick that summer. He looked "fit" and "brown" to observers. Grant came to Bowdoin to receive an honorary degree. He stayed at Chamberlain's house. Republican politicians urged Chamberlain, the hero of Little Round Top, to run for Governor of Maine. That August his lastborn child died, aged seven months. So much for glory and fame.

# Drum Roll

In the years that followed Appomattox, the pride of lions Maine sent south remained active.

JOSHUA LAWRENCE CHAMBERLAIN returned, a broken man physically, to a broken home. Fannie wanted him to become a professor again at Bowdoin, but Chamberlain, who would have preferred to remain in the Army, was determined to do something else. He ran for Governor of Maine and was elected by the greatest electoral majority in the Pine Tree State's history. Fannie did not accompany him to Augusta. He was three more times elected by massive victories at the polls. Fannie sought a divorce, saying to friends that the General had raised his hand against her. Chamberlain convinced her not to pursue divorce; they remained married yet separate. Fannie's eyes deteriorated further and she went blind. Joshua read poetry to her. In 1905 she died.

Daughter Daisy married a wealthy Bostonian, and was badly injured by an automobile in the early twentieth century. Her daughters remembered pleasant visits with the "Gennie." Son Wyllys never married, remaining always in his father's shadow. He wanted to be an inventor, was fascinated by electrical gadgets, but never produced the Great Invention. Brother Tom married John's wife after his brother's death, became an alcoholic, and had few good memories of the war.

Joshua was a good governor, but angered party bosses by taking independent positions. Although leaders like

Hannibal Hamlin favored abolition of the death penalty, Chamberlain became the first governor in years to enforce it. He succeeded in enforcing the death sentence of a black rapist. It was very controversial, but Chamberlain was adamant. He also alienated Prohibitionists by opposing the establishment of a constabulary to enforce Maine's anti-liquor law. He felt a state police constituted an intrusion on people's rights.

Chamberlain returned to Bowdoin and became its president. He promised a new renaissance of learning, pushed numerous reforms—but he pushed too hard, too fast. Academia is not the Army; when he tried to institute military drill, students rebelled. When they walked out, he threatened expulsion. They returned, but the trustees, upset by the turmoil, eliminated the drill requirement and chastised Chamberlain for his less than collegial approach.

In 1880 the state was on the verge of its own civil war over a hotly disputed election between Republicans and Democrats aligned with the radical Greenbacker Party. As Commander of the State Militia, Chamberlain left Bowdoin's shaded groves to set up headquarters at the state capitol in Augusta. When a mob broke into the building, he faced it down, unarmed. The election controversy was resolved without the use of force due to Joshua Chamberlain's actions. He called it "another Little Round Top."

But party leaders were angered by his even-handed actions. They made sure he never got a coveted nomination to the U. S. Senate. Chamberlain returned to Bowdoin. Resigning as president, he went back to being a professor, teaching ultimately nearly every course in the curriculum. He literally moved his Potter Street house nearer the College, to across the street from the First Parish Congregational Church. Near the Atlantic, he had another house, sailed a

---

small yacht on Casco Bay, and, for many years, went for long, solitary rides on his beloved "Charlemagne."

Like an aging Galahad, he involved himself in Gouverneur Warren's long campaign to undo the wrong done to Warren on April Fool's Day, 1865. Finally, a military inquiry was opened. Despite Sheridan's testimony, the court exonerated Warren. Chamberlain was pleased, but by this time Warren was dead.

The ex-soldier and scholar dabbled in business ventures in New York and Florida, but never became wealthy. He volunteered for service in the Spanish-American war but was refused. He was finally awarded the Medal of Honor.

Joshua Chamberlain was a frequent speaker at military reunions. Finally, political friends secured him a job as surveyor of the Port of Portland. Longshoremen and lawyers were familiar with the erect old man, invariably in black, who walked the waterfront. He died in 1914, on the eve of World War I, in which the trenches and bloody carnage of Petersburg were recreated on a massive scale. Chamberlain busied himself to the end writing *The Passing of the Armies*, published after his death, a book full of honor and glory as well as horror.

In 1993 a portrait of Chamberlain, locked in a State House anteroom where politicos smoked furtively, was removed after a campaign to free the general by the author of this book. Today it hangs in Maine's Hall of Flags.

OLIVER OTIS HOWARD rode with Sherman at the head of the Western Army during the second day of the Grand Review in Washington in 1865. Against Sherman's advice, he accepted leadership of the controversial Freedman's Bureau. He did his best, but the Bureau ultimately failed due to a lack of political will in Washington and a lessening commitment to freed blacks. Howard *was* committed, and founded Howard College. He was also the prime mover in establishing a college for poor whites in the region he once led Yankee soldiers through. Howard also received the Medal of Honor.

Back in the Army, he made peace with the legendary Apache chief Cochise, after seeking him out, accompanied by only one frontier guide. The great chief of the Southwest, unlike many white officers, was impressed by the courage of "Old Prayerbook" *and* his spirituality. Later Howard pursued Chief Joseph through the mountains of the Northwest. When Joseph surrendered it was to another general, who seized the glory, but his words were addressed to Howard. *"I will fight no more forever."* Perhaps no white military leader of the time truly understood the American Indian, but Howard tried.

Yankee Stepfather to blacks, Great White Father's representative to the Indians, Howard became the father, strong but benevolent, he sought.

ADELBERT AMES went into politics. The Republican carpetbagger Senator from reconstructed Mississippi married the beautiful daughter of the ugly but redoubtable Ben Butler. He always felt Butler was dealt a bad hand in the Fort Fisher affair and himself conducted a feud with Newton Curtis over what really happened in January of 1865. Ultimately, Ames got the credit he was due. He also got the Medal of Honor.

In the meantime, he became the last Republican governor of Mississippi for more than a century. Dedicated to improving the lot of blacks, he instituted a series of reforms. But conservative Democrats won control of the state legislature and, without military support from President Grant, Ames resigned rather than be impeached. He was the last reconstruction governor to be forced out. He believed he had a "Mission to Mississippi." He failed, and is unfairly portrayed in John F. Kennedy's *Profiles in Courage*. His grand-daughter sought a retraction, but did not get it.

Ames himself made out well. He went to the Midwest, where his father had prospered after all, became a successful businessman, and was back in uniform during the war with Spain. He lived on until 1933, played golf with John D. Rockefeller until he was ninety, and was the last general officer of the Civil War to die.

NEAL DOW returned to Maine a hero, and went back to anti-liquor crusading. He was the Prohibition candidate for President. Dow got few votes, but remained active into his nineties. When he had returned to Portland in 1863, doctors worried he would not live another year.

THOMAS HYDE started a shipyard in Bath which ultimately became Bath Iron Works. He made the transition from wood to steel, building ships for the Navy. A dyed-in-the-wool Republican and still aggressive as all hell, he volunteered to lead armed men to assure G.O.P. control during the 1880 election crisis. Chamberlain told him that, while he loved Tom like a son, he must not do it. Hyde listened. He wrote one of the best memoirs of the Civil War, called *Following the Greek Cross*. He died wealthy, very wealthy, although suffering losses from construction of a strange iron ram, the *Katahdin*.

SELDEN CONNOR always required crutches, but he was not a recluse. Also entering politics, he followed Chamberlain as governor of Maine. Later, Connor became a pension agent in Washington. Like Chamberlain, he was a popular public speaker on the G.A.R. circuit. Handsome as a "Boy of '61," he remained a striking figure in old age.

HANNIBAL HAMLIN, passed over for renomination as Vice President in 1864, saw successor Andrew Johnson (so drunk at Lincoln's second inauguration that Hamlin had to yank him back in his seat) become President. Opposed to radical reconstruction and lacking political astuteness, Johnson narrowly avoided impeachment. A radical but not a mean man, Hamlin would have been a better President. He put in a stint as U. S. Ambassador to Madrid, disliked being away from Maine, and was sent back to the U. S. Senate. Still looking like a farmer, the old pol became a venerated figure in the Maine G.O.P. He died believing, wanting desperately to believe, that Abraham Lincoln had nothing to do with his 1864 humiliation.

Other boys of the 1860s lived varied lives after the big war. Many attended encampments and shared the old comradeship. When "ole Lijah" Walker came back to Knox county for a clambake, the graying boys in blue were tickled pink. Holman Melcher became a respected and successful grocer in Portland, pushing goods with the same ability he once led soldiers, and ultimately was honored as Portland's mayor.

Not every soldier boy became a productive citizen. Predictably, the officer of the Twentieth Maine who bullied and shamed Sergeant Buck turned to a life of crime. He robbed Rockland's Limestone Bank, was caught, and ended up in the State Penitentiary.

The great majority returned to their small farms, lumberyards, fishing vessels, and the like. But they too were lions when the Union was in its hour of need.

# Epilogue
## *Old Lions Still Roar*


Joshua Chamberlain had buried his wife and, recently, suffered more pain from his war wound of 1864. But, when he rose to give the keynote address in Camden at the ceremonies honoring William Conway, he was still every inch the general.

"We come here to commemorate not a deed done in the body, but an act of soul," were his first words to the assembled crowd.

He recounted what the sailor from Camden had done in Pensacola on a warm January day in 1861.

"It is a simple story. The actor did not dream he was a hero; did not imagine he was to be noticed, except for punishment for disobedience of orders. He was not acting for the eyes of men."

When William Conway refused to pull down the American flag, he acted out of "lofty loyalty" and displayed "heroic courage," the 78-year-old orator said.

"Think you can confer honor on him? He it is who has done us honor, and we tell to the world, tell to the mountains and sea and skies that he is ours," Chamberlain said in his musical, resonate voice. *No stuttering now.* "That is our glory; all rest is his."

As the applause died for the living general in Camden, a few miles distant in Rockland's Achorn cemetery stood a statue. It had been sculpted many years earlier by a Maine sculptor, Frank Simmons, who would go on to international fame in his field. Everybody agreed it looked just like Major

General Hiram Berry. Today, as every day, framed by the Camden hills, Berry looked out upon the broad horizon of the sea.

*Beyond lay infinity.*

There was a time when Maine produced lions like Ames, Berry, Chamberlain and the rest. It also produced quiet men like Conway whose simple acts of courage spoke for them. That is Maine's glory. America's glory.

If you listen closely to waves crashing against Maine's rocky coast, you can still hear the lions roar. You have to listen closer, standing in the quiet by old gravestones in shaded cemetery plots decorated by little flags on the Fourth of July—but you can still hear the old lions roar.

# Explanatory Note

While manuscript collections at Bowdoin College, the Maine Historical Society, and elsewhere, as well as contemporary newspaper accounts like those in the Portland *Eastern Argus*, were useful as background material, the main sources are the primary and secondary ones listed below.

A very useful source was the four-volume *War Papers Read Before the Commandery of the State of Maine Order of the Loyal Legion of the United States*, abbreviated herein to *War Papers ME MOLLUS*.

Descriptions of Civil War combat are often contradictory. This is hardly surprising, since battles and campaigns never were as well-planned or orchestrated as later (or self-serving) accounts made them appear. Conflict by its very nature is often confused, chaotic, noisy and incredibly violent. Perspectives can vary according to location, role and politics. Key participants vary their depiction of events over time, continuing to refight battles in print long after the guns are silent.

I have, after consulting the sources, reconstructed "what happened" to the best of my ability. In the final analysis, responsibility for any errors of fact or interpretation is mine.

# Bibliography

Abbott, John S. C., *The History of Maine* (Augusta, ME: Brown Thurston Co., 1892).

Adams, Silas, "The Nineteenth Maine at Gettysburg," *War Papers, ME MOLLUS*, Vol. IV (Portland, ME: LeFavor-Tower Co., 1915), 250–263. [Read December 1, 1909.]

Agassiz, George R., Ed., *Meade's Headquarters, 1863–1865: Letters of Colonel Theodore Lyman* (Boston: Atlantic Monthly Press, 1922).

Alexander, E. P., edited by Gary Gallagher, "Why We Lost at Gettysburg," *Civil War Times*, September/October 1989, 46–58.

Alexander, Ted, "Gettysburg Calvary Operations, June 27–July 3, 1863," *Blue & Gray*, October 1988, 8–18, 21–28, 30–32, 36–41.

Ames, Adelbert, "The Capture of Fort Fisher, North Carolina," *The Maine Bugle*, April 1897, 167–187. [Reprint of address to *NY MOLLUS* February 3, 1897.]

Ames, Blanche Ames, *Adelbert Ames, 1835–1933: General, Senator, Governor* (New York: Argosy-Antiquarian Ltd., 1964).

Bangs, I. S., "The Ullman Brigade," *War Papers, ME MOLLUS*, Vol. II (Portland, ME: LeFavor-Tower Co., 1902), 290–310.

Baker, William A., *A Maritime History of Bath, Maine*, 2 Vols. (Portland, ME: Anthoensen Press, 1973).

Barrett, John G., *Sherman's March Through the Carolinas* (Univ. N. Carolina Press, 1956).

_____ , *The Civil War in North Carolina* (Univ. N. Carolina Press, 1963).

Beattie, Donald W., Rodney M. Cole, and Charles G. Waugh, eds., *A Distant War Comes Home: Maine in the Civil War Era* (Camden, ME: Down East Books, 1996).

Beronius, George, "Joe Johnston's Last Charge," *Civil War Times,* May 1996, 44–53.

Bicknell, George W., *History of the Fifth Regiment Maine Volunteers* (Portland, ME: Hall L. Davis, 1871).

Billings, John D., *Hardtack and Coffee* (Boston: George M. Smith, 1887).

Bisbee, George D., "Three Years a Volunteer in the Civil War, Antietam to Appomattox," *War Papers, ME MOLLUS,* Vol. IV (Portland, ME: LeFavor-Tower Co., 1915), 114–149. [Read Sept. 2, 1908.]

Boritt, Gabor S., Ed., *Lincoln's Generals* (New York: Oxford University Press, 1994).

Brooks, Noah, *Washington in Lincoln's Time* (New York: Century, 1895).

Butler, Benj. F., *Butler's Book* (Boston: A. M. Thayer & Co., 1892).

Byrne, Frank L., *Prophet of Prohibition: Neal Dow and His Crusade* (Madison: State Historical Society of Wisconsin, 1961).

Calhoun, Charles C., *A Small College in Maine: Two Hundred Years of Bowdoin* (Brunswick, ME: Bowdoin College, 1993).

Calkins, Chris, "The Battle of Five Forks: Final Push for the South Side," *Blue & Gray,* April 1992, 8–15, 17–22, 41–52.

Cameron, Alexander W., "The Saviors of Little Round Top," *Gettysburg,* January 1993, 31–42.

Carpenter, John A., *Sword and Olive Branch: Oliver O. Howard* (Univ. Pittsburgh Press, 1964).

Carter, Robert G., "The Campaign and Battle of Gettysburg," *War Papers, ME MOLLUS,* Vol. II (Portland, ME: LeFavor-Tower Co., 1902), 150–183. [Read Sept. 13, 1899.]

Cashman, Diane Cobb, *Headstrong: The Biography of Amy Morris Bradley* (Wilmington, NC: Broadfoot Publ. Co., 1990).

---

Castel, Albert, "The Film That Made Me," *Civil War Times*, Summer 1989, 6, 66.

_____, *Decision in the West: The Atlanta Campaign of 1864* (Univ. Kansas Press, 1992).

Chamberlain, Joshua Lawrence, "*Bayonet! Forward*": *My Civil War Reminiscences* (Gettysburg, PA: Stan Clark Military Books, 1994). [A compilation of addresses and articles by Chamberlain.]

_____, " 'Do It! That's How': Four words that Joshua L. Chamberlain learned to live by," *Bowdoin* (Spring/Summer 1991), 3–12. [Uncompleted Chamberlain autobiography.]

_____, "Abraham Lincoln," *War Papers, ME MOLLUS,* Vol. IV (Portland, ME: LeFavor-Tower Co., 1915), 53–62. [Read March 3, 1909.]

_____, "Honor Answering Honor." (Brunswick, ME: Bowdoin College, 1965).

_____, *Not a Sound of Trumpet* (Brunswick, ME: Bowdoin College, 1982). [Remarks at May 3, 1901, meeting of Bowdoin Club of Boston.]

_____, "Reminiscences of Petersburg and Appomattox: October, 1903. *War Papers, ME MOLLUS,* Vol. III (Portland, ME: LeFavor-Tower Co., 1908), 161–182. [Read March 2, 1904.]

_____, *The Passing of the Armies* (New York: G. P. Putnam's Sons, 1915).

Chittenden, Elizabeth F., "Neal Dow: Father of Prohibition," *Downeast*, May 1974, 58–60, 71.

Cilley, Jonathan P., "General Adelbert Ames," *The Maine Bugle,* April 1897, 187–188.

_____, "The Dawn of the Morning at Appomattox" *War Papers, ME MOLLUS,* Vol. III (Portland, ME: LeFavor-Tower Co., 1908), 263–278.

_____, *Memoirs and Services of Three Generations* (Rockland, ME: Courier Gazette, 1909).

*Civil War*, June, 1995. Issue devoted to the Peninsula Campaign and the Seven Days.

Clark, Charles, *Maine: A Bicentennial History* (New York: W. W. Norton, 1977).

Cleaves, Freeman, *Meade of Gettysburg* (Univ. Oklahoma Press, 1960).

Coburn, Jeff L., "A Visit to the Battlefield of Dinwiddie Court House: Incidents and Anecdotes Relating to that Battle," *The Maine Bugle*, January 1895, 52–75.

Cochran, Hamilton, *Blockade Runners of the Confederacy* (New York: Bobbs-Merrill, 1958).

Coffin, Howard, *Full Duty: Vermonters in the Civil War* (Woodstock, VT: Countryman Press, 1993).

Connor, Selden, "In the Wilderness," *War Papers, ME MOLLUS*, Vol. IV (Portland, ME: LeFavor-Tower Co, 1915), 200–229. [Read May 6, 1908.]

Connor, Selden, "Oration at Dedication of Monuments of Gettysburg," *Maine at Gettysburg: Report of the ME Commission* (Portland, ME: Lakeside Press, 1898), 564–580; also "Seventh Regiment Historical Sketch," 438–465.

_____ , "The Boys of 1861," *War Papers, ME MOLLUS*, Vol. 1 (Portland, ME: Thurston Press, 1898) 323–343.

_____ , "The Colored Troops," *War Papers, ME MOLLUS,*, Vol. III (Portland, ME: LeFavor-Tower Co., 1908), 61–82. [Read May 7, 1902.]

Cox, Jacob D., *Atlanta* (New York: Charles Scribner's Sons, 1882).

_____ , *The March to the Sea, Franklin and Nashville* (New York: Charles Scribner's Sons, 1882).

Current, Richard N., *Those Terrible Carpetbaggers* (New York: Oxford Univ. Press, 1988).

Curtis, Newton M., "The Capture of Fort Fisher," *Personal Recollections of the Rebellion, NY MOLLUS*, 3rd Series, 1907.

Dalton, Pete, and Cyndi, *Into the Valley of Death: The Story of the 4th Maine Volunteer Infantry at the Battle of Gettysburg, July 2, 1863* (Union, ME: Union Publishing Company, 1994).

Davis, Burke, *To Appomattox: Nine April Days, 1865* (New York: Rinehart & Co., 1959).

_____, *Sherman's March* (New York: Random House, 1980).

Davis, William C., *Battle of Bull Run* (New York: Doubleday, 1977).

_____, *Death in the Trenches: Grant at Petersburg* (Alexandria, VA: Time-Life Books, 1986).

Deans, Sis, *His Proper Post: A Biography of Gen. Joshua Lawrence Chamberlain* (Kearny, NJ: Belle Grove Publishing Co., 1996).

Desjardin, Thomas A., *Stand Firm Ye Boys From Maine: The 20th Maine and the Gettysburg Campaign* (Gettysburg, PA: Thomas Publications, 1995).

Dibble, Ernest F., *Ante-Bellum Pensacola and the Military Presence* (Pensacola [FL] News-Journal, 1974).

Dow, Neal, *The Reminiscences of Neal Dow: Recollections of Eighty Years* (Portland, ME: Evening Express Co., 1898).

Dowdy, Clifford, *Lee's Last Campaign* (New York: Barnes & Noble, 1988 reprint).

Eaton, Cyrus, *History of Thomaston, Rockland, and South Thomaston* (Hallowell, ME: Masters, Smith & Co., 1865).

Earle, Charles W., "Libby Prison Life and Escape," *The Maine Bugle*, April 1896, 128–153.

Engert, Roderick M., Ed., *Maine to the Wilderness: The Civil War Letters of Private William Lamson, 20th Maine Infantry* (Orange VA: Publisher's Press, 1993).

Fellman, Michael, *Citizen Sherman* (New York: Random House, 1995).

Fernald, Granville, "A General at Twenty-One," *The Maine Bugle*, April 1898, 161–167.

*First Maine Calvary Reunions 1872–1883*, n.p., n.d.

Floca, Samuel W., Jr., "The Valley of Death," *America's Combat History*, Spring 1993, 40–47.

---

Fonvielle, Chris E., Jr., "The Last Rays of Departing Hope: The Fall of Wilmington, Including the Campaigns Against Fort Fisher," *Blue & Gray*, December 1994, 10–16, 18–21, 48–50, 52–62.

Ford, Charles W., "Charge of the First Maine Cavalry at Brandy Station," *War Papers, ME MOLLUS*, Vol. 1 (Portland, ME: Le-Favor-Tower Co., 1902), 268–289. [Read Sept. 5, 1900.]

Forster, Greg, "Sherman's Feuding Generals," *Civil War Times*, April 1995, 40–45, 70–73, 75.

Furguson, Ernest B., *Chancellorsville 1863: The Souls of the Brave* (New York: Knopf, 1992).

Gallagher, Gary W., "Brandy Station: The Civil War's Bloodiest Arena of Mounted Combat," *Blue & Gray*, October 1990, 8–20, 22, 44–53.

Gallagher, Gary W., Ed., *The First Day at Gettysburg: Essays on Confederate and Union Leadership* (Kent State Univ. Press, 1992).

_____ , *The Second Day at Gettysburg: Essays on Confederate and Union Leadership* (Kent State Univ. Press, 1993).

Gardner, Ira B., "Personal Experiences With the Fourteenth Maine Volunteers from 1861–1865," *War Papers, ME MOLLUS*, Vol. IV (Portland, ME: LeFavor-Tower Co., 1915), 90–113. [Read Sept. 2, 1908.]

"General Newton M. Curtis's Address Before the Loyal Legion of New York, on Fort Fisher," *The Maine Bugle*, July, 1897.

Gerrish, Theodore, *Reminiscences of the War* (Portland, ME: Hoyt, Fogg & Donham, 1882).

_____ , and John S. Hutchinson, *The Blue and the Gray: A Graphic History* (Portland, ME: Hoyt, Fogg & Donham, 1883).

Golay, Michael, *To Gettysburg and Beyond: The Parallel Lives of Joshua Lawrence Chamberlain and Edward Porter Alexander* (New York: Crown Publishers, 1994).

Gold, David, "Frustrated Glory: John Francis Appleton and Black Soldiers in the Civil War," *Maine Historical Society Quarterly*, Summer 1991, 174–204.

Gordon, John B., *Reminiscences of the Civil War* (New York: Charles Scribner's Sons, 1903).

Gordon, S. C., "Reminiscences of the Civil War From a Surgeon's Point of View," *War Papers, ME MOLLUS*, Vol. 1 (Portland, ME: Thurston Press, 1898), 73–84. [Read March 4, 1891.]

Gould, Edward K., *Major General Hiram G. Berry* (Rockland, ME: Courier Gazette, 1899).

Gould, John M., *History of the First- Tenth- Twenty–ninth Maine Regiment* (Portland, ME: Stephen Berry, 1871).

Hadden, R. Lee, "The Granite Glory: The 19th Maine at Gettysburg," *Gettysburg*, July 1995, 50–63.

Hall, Clark B., "The Battle of Brandy Station," *Civil War Times*, May/June 1990, 32–42, 45.

Hamlin, Charles E., *The Life and Times of Hannibal Hamlin* (Cambridge, MA: Riverside Press, 1899).

Harkness, Edson J., "The Expeditions Against Fort Fisher and Wilmington," *Military Essays, IL MOLLUS*, Vol. II (Chicago: A.C. McClurg & Co., 1894).

Harrison, Kathleen R. G., " 'Our Principal Loss Was in this Place': Action at the Slaughter Pen and at the South End of Houck's Ridge," *Gettysburg*, July 1989, 45–69.

Hart, B. H. Liddell, *Sherman: Soldier, Realist, American* (New York: Dodd, Mead & Co., 1929).

Haskew, Michael E., "Civil War's Longest Siege," *Military History*, April 1995, 46–52, 87–88.

Hebert, Walter H., *Fighting Joe Hooker* (New York: Bobbs-Merrill Co., 1944).

Hemingway, Al, "Day One at Chancellorsville," *America's Civil War*, March 1996, 42–49, 82.

Hill, J. A., *The Story of One Regiment: The 11th Maine Infantry Volunteers in the War of the Rebellion* (New York: J. J. Little, 1896).

Holloway, Laura, *Howard: The Christian Hero* (New York: Funk & Wagnalls, 1885).

---

Holzer, Harold, "Forgotten Hero of Gettysburg," *American History Illustrated*, December 1993, 48–49.

Hood, J. B., *Advance and Retreat* (New Orleans: G. T. Beauregard, 1880).

Howard, Charles, "First Day of Gettysburg," *Military Essays and Recollections, IL MOLLUS*, Vol. IV (Chicago: Cozzens & Beaton Co., 1907), 238–264. [Read October 1, 1903.]

_____ , "Incidents and Operations Connected with the Capture of Savannah," *Military Essays and Recollections, IL MOLLUS*, Vol. IV (Chicago: Cozzens & Beaton Co., 1907), 430–450. [Read December 14, 1893.]

Howard, Oliver O., "O. O. Howard's Commencement Address to Syracuse University," *Gettysburg*, July 1994, 71–79. [Delivered June 10, 1903.]

_____ , "Sketch of the Life of George M. Thomas," *Personal Recollections of the War of the Rebellion, NY MOLLUS*, 3rd series (New York: G. P. Putnam's Sons, 1907), 329–346. [Read May 4, 1904.]

_____ , *Autobiography*, 2 Vols. (New York: Baker and Taylor Co., 1907).

_____ , *My Life and Experiences Among Our Hostile Indians* (Hartford, CT: A. D. Worthington & Co., 1907).

Howe, M. A. DeWolfe, Ed., *Marching With Sherman: Passages from the Letters and Campaign Diaries of Henry Hitchcock* (Yale University Press, 1927).

Hughes, Nathaniel C., *Bentonville: The Final Battle Between Sherman and Johnston* (Univ. N. Carolina Press, 1996).

Hunt, H. Draper, *Hannibal Hamlin of Maine* (Syracuse NY: Syracuse University Press, 1969).

Hyde, Thomas W., *Following the Greek Cross* (Boston: Houghton Mifflin, 1894).

_____ , "Recollections of the Battle of Gettysburg," *War Papers, Maine MOLLUS*, Vol. I (Portland, ME: Thurston Press, 1898), 191–206. [Read Sept. 7, 1892.]

Johnson, John O., "William Conway: A Forgotten Camden Hero," *War Papers, ME MOLLUS,* Vol. IV (Portland, ME: LeFavor-Tower Co., 1915), 307–320. [Read Sept. 2, 1914.]

Johnson, Robert V., and Clarence C. Buel, eds., *Battles and Leaders of the Civil War* (New York: Century, 1884).

Jones, Katherine M., Ed., *When Sherman Came: Southern Women and the Great March* (New York: Bobbs–Merrill, 1964).

Jones, Michael Dan, "William C. Oates: On Little Round Top, Unsung, In Postwar Politics, Unreconstructed," *Civil War,* December 1994, 26–32.

Jones, Riley I., "With the First Maine," *The Maine Bugle,* October 1893, 46–50.

Jones, Terry L., "Going Back Into the Union at Last: A Louisiana Tiger's Account of the Gettysburg Campaign," *Civil War Times,* January/February 1991, 12, 55–58, 60.

Jordan, William Barnes, Jr., "Gettysburg and the Seventeenth Maine," *Gettysburg,* January 1993, 43–52.

_____ , *Red Diamond Regiment: the 17th Maine Infantry, 1862–1865* (Shippensburg, PA: White Mane Publishing Co., 1996).

Kearny, Thomas, *General Philip Kearny* (New York: G. P. Putnam's Sons, 1937).

Kennedy, Francis H., Ed., *The Civil War Battlefield Guide* (Boston: Houghton Mifflin Co., 1990).

Kennett, Lee, *Marching Through Georgia: The Story of Soldiers and Civilians During Sherman's Campaign* (New York: HarperCollins, 1995).

Kilmer, George L., "Heroes of the Saddle," *The Maine Bugle,* July 1892, 68–74.

Kirck, Robert E. L., Andrus, Michael, and Ruth, David, "Grant and Lee, 1864: From the North Anna to the Crossing of the James," *Blue & Gray,* April 1994, 10–14, 16–22, 44, 46, 50, 52–54, 56–58.

Krolick, Marshall D., "Gettysburg, The First Day, July 1, 1863: The Union Command, Decisions That Shaped a Battle," *Blue & Gray,* November 1987, 10–20.

Kross, Gary, "The Confederate Approach to Little Round Top: A March of Attrition," *Blue & Gray*, Winter 1996, 7–15, 17–20, 22–24.

_____ , "The Alabamians' Attack on Little Round Top: 'A Cheeky Piece of Work on Both Sides,' " *Blue & Gray*, Winter 1996, 54–61.

LaFantasie, Glenn, "The Antagonists of Little Round Top: The Other Man," *MHQ: The Quarterly Journal of Military History*, Summer 1994, 43–49.

Lockwood, Henry C., "A Man From Maine: A True History of the Army at Fort Fisher," *The Maine Bugle*, January 1894, 29–71.

Long, David E., "Cover–up at Cold Harbor," *Civil War Times*, June 1997, 50–56, 58–59.

Longacre, Edward C., *The Cavalry at Gettysburg: A Tactical Study* (Fairleigh Dickinson Univ. Press, 1986).

Longstreet, James, *From Manassas to Appomattox* (New York: Konecky & Konecky, 1992 reprint).

Lord, Stuart B., "Adelbert Ames, Soldier & Politician: A Reevaluation," *Maine Historical Society Quarterly* (Fall 1973), 81–92.

*Maine at Gettysburg: Report of the Maine Commissioners* (Portland, ME: Lakeside Press, 1898).

Manning, William C., "Yorktown and Williamsburg Reviewed in 1897," *War Papers, ME MOLLUS*, Vol. III (Portland, ME: LeFavor-Tower Co., 1908), 139–160. [Read Sept. 2, 1903.]

Marszalek, John, *Sherman: A Soldier's Passion for Order* (New York: Free Press, 1993).

Martin, Samuel J., "Did 'Baldy' Ewell Lose Gettysburg?" *America's Civil War*, July 1997, 34–40.

McFeely, William S., *Yankee Stepfather: General O. O. Howard and the Freedmen* (New York: W. W. Norton & Co., 1994).

Meade, George, Ed., *The Life and Letters of George Gordon Meade*, 2 Vols. (New York: Charles Scribner's Sons, 1913).

Merrill, Samuel, *The Campaigns of the First Maine Cavalry* (Portland, ME: Bailey & Noyes, 1866).

Mertz, Gregory A., "No Turning Back: The Battle of the Wilderness—The Fighting on May 5, 1864," *Blue & Gray*, April 1995, 8–12, 14–15, 19–23, 47–53.

_____ , "No Turning Back: The Battle of the Wilderness—The Fighting on May 6, 1864," *Blue & Gray*, June 1995, 8–15, 18–20, 48–50.

Miles, Jim, *To The Sea: A History and Tour Guide of Sherman's March* (Nashville, TN: Rutledge Hill Press, 1989).

Miller, Algernon S., "Civil War Yesterdays," *Downeast* (April 1861), 18–21, 48–50, Esther F. Wood, Ed.

Mundy, James, *No Rich Man's Sons: The 6th Maine Volunteers* (Cape Elizabeth, ME: Harp Publications, 1994).

_____ , *Second to None: The Story of the 2nd Maine Volunteer Infantry* (Scarborough, ME: Harp Publications, 1992).

Musicant, Ivan, *Divided Waters: The Naval History of the Civil War* (New York: HarperCollins, 1995).

Nesbitt, Mark, *Through Blood and Fire: Selected Civil War Papers of Major General Joshua Chamberlain* (Mechanicsburg, PA: Stackpole Books, 1996).

Newcomb, Jonathan, "A Soldier's Story of Personal Experience at the Battle of Gettysburg," *The Maine Bugle*, January, 1896, 100–102.

Norton, Oliver W., *The Attack and Defense of Little Round Top, Gettysburg, July 2, 1863* (New York: Neale, 1913).

O'Connor, Richard, *Sheridan the Inevitable* (New York: Bobbs-Merrill Co., 1953).

_____ , *Hood: Cavalier General* (New York: Prentice-Hall, 1949).

O'Neill, Robert, Jr., "The Fight for the Loudoun Valley—Aldie, Middlebury and Upperville, Va., Opening Battles of the Gettysburg Campaign," *Blue & Gray*, October 1993, 12–16, 18–21, 46–48, 50, 52–57, 60.

Osborn, Hartwell, "On the Right at Chancellorsville," *Military Essays and Recollections, IL MOLLUS*, Vol. IV (Chicago: Cozzens & Beaton Co., 1907).

---

Patterson, Gerard, "Gustave," *Civil War Times,* July/August 1992, 28–35, 52–54.

Pettingill, Sewall, *Memoirs of the Civil War,* Wayne Library Association, n.d.

Pfanz, Harry W., *Gettysburg—Culps Hill and Cemetery Hill* (Univ. N. Carolina Press, 1993).

_____ , *Gettysburg—The Second Day* (Univ. N. Carolina Press, 1987).

Pindell, Richard, "The True High-Water Mark of the Confederacy," *Blue & Gray,* December-January 1983, 6–15.

_____ , "Phil Kearny: The One-Armed Devil," *Civil War Times,* May 1988, 16–21, 44–46.

Priest, John M., *Antietam: The Soldier's Battle* (New York: Oxford University Press, 1993).

Pullen, John J., *The Twentieth Maine: A Volunteer Regiment in the Civil War* (Philadelphia: J. B. Lippincott Co., 1957).

Racine, Philip N., Ed. *"Unspoiled Heart": The Journal of Charles Mattocks of the 17th Maine* (Knoxville: Univ. Tennessee Press, 1994).

Reed, Rowena, *Combined Operations in the Civil War* (Annapolis, MD: Naval Institute Press, 1978).

*Report of the Adjutant General of the State of Maine 1864 and 1865* (Augusta, ME: Stevens & Sayward, 1866).

Reston, James, Jr., *Sherman's March and Vietnam* (New York: Macmillan, 1984).

*Reunions of the 19th Maine Regiment Association* (Augusta, ME: Sprague, Owen & Nash, 1878).

Roberts, Charles W., "At Gettysburg in 1863 and 1888," *War Papers, ME MOLLUS,* Vol. I (Portland, ME: Thurston Press, 1898), 139–160. [Read Sept. 2, 1903.]

Robinson, Revel, *History of Camden and Rockport* (Camden [ME] Publishing Co., 1907).

Rose, Gideon, "The Antagonists of Little Round Top: The Victor," *MHQ: The Quarterly Journal of Military History,* Summer 1994, 36–42.

Royster, Charles, *The Destructive War* (New York: Knopf, 1991).

Sabine, David, "Selden Connor, Maine Governor 1876–79, Soldier, Statesman, Banker," *Maine History News,* October 1981, 4–5.

Sauers, Richard A., "The 16th Maine Volunteer Infantry at Gettysburg," *Gettysburg,* July 1995, 33–42.

Scott, James G. and Edward A. Wyatt IV, *Petersburg's Story: A History* (Richmond, VA: Whitlet & Shepperson, 1960).

Sears, Stephen, *Landscape Turned Red* (New York: Ticknor & Fields, 1983).

_____ , *To The Gates of Richmond: The Peninsula Campaign* (New York: Ticknor & Fields, 1992).

Selcer, Richard, "Pickett: Another Look," *Civil War Times,* August 1994, 44–49, 60–73.

Shain, Charles and Samuella, eds., *The Maine Reader* (Boston: Houghton Mifflin Co., 1991).

Shannon, James H., "A Few Incidents and Reminiscences of the Civil War," *War Papers, ME MOLLUS,* Vol. IV (Portland, ME: LeFavor-Tower Co., 1915), 321–339 [Read March 1, 1911.]

Sherman, William T., *Memoirs* 2 Vols. (New York: Charles Webster & Co., 1891).

Shurz, Carl, *The Reminiscences,* Vol. II 1852–1863 (New York: McClure Co., 1907).

Silliker, Ruth L., Ed., *The Rebel Yell & the Yankee Hurrah: The Civil War Journal of a Maine Volunteer* [Journal of John Haley, 17th Maine] (Camden, ME: Down East Books, 1985).

Skillings, Charles W., "Sunshine and Shades of Army Life," *The Maine Bugle,* July 1893, 47–53.

Skoch, George, "The Last Ditch," *Civil War Times,* January 1989, 12–18.

Small, Abner R., *The Sixteenth Maine Regiment in the War of the Rebellion* (Portland, ME: Thurston Press, 1886).

Small, Harold Adams, Ed., *The Road to Richmond: The Civil War Memoirs of Major Abner R. Small of the Sixteenth Maine Volunteers* (Univ. California Press, 1939).

Smith, John Day, *The History of the 19th Regiment of Maine Volunteer Infantry 1862–1865* (Minneapolis, MN: Great West Printing Co., 1909).

Spaulding, Joseph W., "Nineteenth Maine at High Bridge," *War Papers, ME MOLLUS,* Vol. IV (Portland, ME: LeFavor-Tower Co., 1915), 294–306. [Read Sept. 2, 1914.]

Staples, Horatio, "Reminiscences of Bull Run," *War Papers, ME MOLLUS,* Vol. III (Portland: LeFavor-Tower Co., 1908), 126–138. [Read May 6, 1903]

Starr, Stephen Z., *The Union Cavalry in the Civil War,* 2 vols. (Louisiana State University Press, 1979–1985).

Staudenraus, P.J., Ed., *Mr. Lincoln's Washington: Selections from the Writings of Noah Brooks, War Correspondent* (New York: Yoseloff, 1967).

Stine, James H., *History of the Army of the Potomac* (Washington, DC: Gibson Books, 1893).

Stratton, Albion W., "What Became of the Flag: How the Sixteenth Maine Saved Their Flag from the Disgrace of Capture," *The Maine Bugle,* April, 1896, 95–97.

Styple, William B., Ed., *With a Flash of His Sword: The Writings of Major Holman S. Melcher, 20th Maine Infantry* (Kearny, NJ: Belle Grove Publishing Co., 1994).

Swanberg, W. A., *Sickles the Incredible* (New York: Charles Scribner's Sons, 1956).

Swinton, William, *The Twelve Decisive Battles of the War* (New York: Dick & Fitzgerald Publishers, 1873).

_____ , *Army of the Potomac* (New York: Smithmark, 1995 reprint).

Taylor, Emerson G., *Gouverneur Kemble Warren* (Boston: Houghton Mifflin, 1932).

"The Conway Celebration, Camden, August 30, 1906," *War Papers, ME MOLLUS,* Vol. IV (Portland, ME: LeFavor-Tower Co., 1915), 15–42.

Thomas, Benjamin P., Ed., *Sylvanus Cadwallader: Three Years With Grant* (New York: Knopf, 1955).

Thomas, Gary, and Richard Andrew, "Houses of Misery and Hope," *Civil War*, December 1996, 10–24, 30–32.

Thorndike, Rachel Sherman, Ed., *The Sherman Letters; Correspondence Between General and Senator Sherman from 1837 to 1891* (New York: Charles Scribner's Sons, 1894).

Tobie, Edward P., *History of the First Maine Cavalry 1861–1865* (Boston: Emery & Hughes, 1887).

Trefousse, Hans L., *Ben Butler: The South Called Him BEAST!* (New York: Twayne Publishers, 1957).

_____ , *Carl Shurz: A Biography* (Univ. Tennessee Press, 1982).

Trobriand, Regis De, *Four Years With the Army of the Potomac* (Boston: Ticknor & Co., 1889).

Trudeau, Noah Andre, *Out of the Storm: The End of the Civil War, April–June 1865* (Boston: Little, Brown and Co., 1994).

Trulock, Alice Rains, *In the Hands of Providence: Joshua L. Chamberlain and the American Civil War* (Univ. North Carolina Press, 1992).

Tucker, Glenn, *Hancock the Superb* (New York: Bobbs-Merrill, 1960).

_____ , *Lee and Longstreet at Gettysburg* (New York: Bobbs-Merrill, 1968).

Turner, Rev. Henry M., "Rocked in the Cradle of Consternation," *American Heritage Civil War Chronicles*, Spring 1993, 24–32, 34–35. Edwin S. Redkey, Ed.

U.S. War Department, *The War of the Rebellion: A Compilation of the Official Records of the Union and Confederate Armies* (Washington, DC: 1891–1895).

Van Doren, Philip, *An End to Valor: The Last Days of the Civil War* (Boston: Houghton Mifflin, 1958).

Verrill, George W., "The Seventeenth Maine at Gettysburg and in the Wilderness," *War Papers, ME MOLLUS*, Vol. I (Portland, ME: Thurston Press, 1898), 260–282.

Vocke, William, "Our German Soldiers," *Military Essays and Recollections, IL MOLLUS,* Vol. III (Chicago: Dial Press, 1899), 341–372.

Walker, Elijah, *The Old Soldier,* n.d., Maine State Archives (from the Rockland, ME *Courier Gazette*).

Warner, Ezra J., *Generals in Blue: Lives of the Union Commanders* (Louisiana State University Press, 1964).

Welch, Richard F., "Gettysburg Finale," *America's Civil War,* July 1993, 50–57.

Wensyel, James W., "Return to Gettysburg," *American History Illustrated,* July/August 1993, 40–51.

_____ , "Tales of a Gettysburg Guide," *American Heritage,* April 1994, 104–113.

West, Richard S., Jr., *Lincoln's Scapegoat General: A Life of Benjamin F. Butler* (Boston: Houghton Mifflin, 1966).

Whitman, William E. S., and Charles H. True, *Maine in the War for the Union: A History of the Part Borne by Maine Troops in the Suppression of the American Rebellion* (Lewiston, ME: Dingley & Co., 1865).

Wiggin, Francis, "Sixteenth Maine Regiment at Gettysburg," *War Papers, ME MOLLUS,* Vol. IV (Portland, ME: LeFavor-Tower Co., 1915), 150–170. [Read Dec. 7, 1910.]

Winther, Oscar O., Ed., *With Sherman to the Sea: The Civil War Letters, Diaries & Reminiscences of Theodore F. Upson* (Louisiana State University Press, 1943).

Wise, W.C., "Fort Fisher-City Point-Richmond 1864–65," *War Papers, ME MOLLUS,* Vol IV (Portland, ME: LeFavor-Tower Co., 1915), 307–320. [Read Sept. 2, 1914.]

Woodworth, Steven E., "Baptism by Fire: John B. Gordon and the 6th Alabama at Seven Pines," *Civil War,* June 1997, 14–23.

Yandoh, Judith, "Mutiny at the Front," *Civil War Times,* June 1995, 32–36, 68–70.